THE TEMPLE IN
TIME AND ETERNITY

TEMPLES THROUGH THE AGES

NUMBER 2

PREVIOUSLY PUBLISHED VOLUMES

TEMPLES OF THE ANCIENT WORLD

THE TEMPLE IN
TIME AND ETERNITY

EDITED BY

DONALD W. PARRY AND STEPHEN D. RICKS

Provo, Utah
The Foundation for Ancient Research and Mormon Studies
at Brigham Young University

Cover design by Rebecca Sterrett

The Foundation for Ancient Research and Mormon Studies (FARMS)
at Brigham Young University
P. O. Box 7113
University Station
Provo, Utah 84602

Printed in the United States of America
07 06 05 04 03 02 01 00 99   6 5 4 3 2

Library of Congress Cataloging-in-Publication Data

The temple in time and eternity / edited by Donald W. Parry and
Stephen D. Ricks.
    p. cm. — (Temples through the ages, ISSN 1527-0386 ; no. 2)
Includes bibliographical references and index.
ISBN 0-934893-46-2 (hbk. : alk. paper)
    1. Temples—History. 2. Mormon Church—Doctrines—History. I.
Parry, Donald W. II. Ricks, Stephen David. III. Series.

BX8643.T4 T45 1999
246'.95893—dc21

                                                        99-049445

CONTENTS

ILLUSTRATIONS

INTRODUCTION

The culture of the ancient Near East and Mediterranean world can be better understood through examining one of its primary religious symbols—the temple—which played a prominent role in the religious as well as in the historic, cultural, economic, political, social, and artistic arenas of society.

The importance of the temple to the religious community can scarcely be exaggerated; its significance to the modern reader may be seen by reviewing several statements regarding the Temple of Herod made by those who lived near the time of its destruction around A.D. 70. The historian Josephus wrote much about his own high regard for Herod's Temple. In a polemic against Apion, Josephus endeavored to legitimize the business of the temple by writing that it was a "temple of world-wide fame and commanding sanctity."[1] On another occasion, and for another purpose, Josephus explained that the temple was "the most marvellous edifice which we have ever seen or heard of, whether we consider its structure, its magnitude, the richness of its every detail, or the reputation of its Holy Places."[2] He also wrote, "as for the various buildings which we have erected in our country and in the cities of our land," the Temple of Herod "is the most pious and beautiful."[3]

The Jewish sages shared the sentiments of Josephus with respect to the primacy of the temple in the community. In a host of expressions, the rabbis demonstrated their feelings toward the temple. To cite only a few examples, a midrash concerning Abraham explains that God offered the entire world to Abraham, but the patriarch responded by saying, "Unless you give to me a temple . . . , you have given me nothing" (*Exodus Rabbah* 15:8). Three separate witnesses, although perhaps derived from a common source, gave authority to the concept of the temple by recording the relative urgency with which God commanded the house of Israel to build a temple soon after the tribes conquered Canaan under the direction of Joshua (see *Sifre on Deuteronomy Pisqa* 67, TB *Pesaḥim* 5a, TB *Sanhedrin* 20b).[4]

The rabbis bestowed extraordinary praise on the temple, itself an expression of the singular regard in which it was held. One well-known statement tells of the temple's extreme beauty: "He who has not seen the Temple of Herod has never seen a beautiful building" (TB *Baba Bathra* 4a), while another warns humanity not to pattern the family residence, courtyard, or porch on the temple complex to maintain the temple's unique quality (see TB ʿ*Avoda Zara* 43a; compare TB *Menaḥot* 28b). A statement attributed to Rabbi Joshua ben Levi declares that if the nations of the world had known that the temple was a blessing to them, they would have built fortifications around it for protection against destruction. Why? Because the temple was a boon for all nations and not intended for Israel alone (see *Numbers Rabbah* 1:3).

One ancient source maintains that the temple's windows were not constructed to let the light of the sun into the building but to permit the divine light within the temple to go out into the world (see *Pesikta de-Rav Kahana Pisqa* 21:5; *Exodus Rabbah* 36:1). This accords with an old Jewish belief that during the creation, light was created from the place of the temple (see *Genesis Rabbah* 3:4). Another source explains that the Jewish sages strengthened their oaths by swearing "by the temple," meaning that the temple with its authority and sanctity would add legitimacy to one's oath (TB *Yevamot* 32b).

The Jewish community's regard for the Temple of Herod may serve as a parallel to the veneration shown by other religious groups of the ancient Near East and Mediterranean world for the temple.

The Latter-day Saints have likewise held their temples in great esteem. It may be significant that the first church buildings constructed in our era, subsequent to the restoration of the gospel, were not ward chapels or stake centers, but temples. In connection with this, Joseph Smith taught that "the Church is not fully organized, in its proper order, and cannot be, until the Temple is completed, where places will be provided for the administration of the ordinances of the Priesthood."[5] It is still evident more than a century and a half after the first temple was built in this dispensation that church leaders and lay members alike continue to revere their temples—church leaders continue to build temples and church members continue to worship within these sacred edifices. And in recent years the church has developed a temple-building program that blesses and reaches out to more of the earth's inhabitants than ever before.

In 1994, Deseret Book and FARMS published a volume

entitled *Temples of the Ancient World* (edited by Donald W. Parry) that contained twenty-four essays on temples past and present. Interest in the volume by many—including nonspecialists, students, and scholars alike—exceeded expectations. The success of this first volume prompted FARMS to begin a series of volumes on ancient temples entitled Temples through the Ages. This volume, *The Temple in Time and Eternity,* represents the second in this series. It is comprised of eleven articles that are divided topically into three sections—Temples and Ritual, Temples in the Israelite Tradition, and Temples in the Non-Israelite Tradition.

As editors of this volume, we have profited greatly from many individuals who have assisted in its preparation. We are greatful to Josi J. Brewer, Rebecca S. Call, Wendy H. Christian, Alison V. P. Coutts, Melissa E. Garcia, and Robyn Patterson for source checking and proofreading the volume in its various stages; we extend special thanks to Shirley S. Ricks and Jessica Taylor for seeing the volume through to completion. Michael P. Lyon has assisted in the preparation of the illustrations for the volume.

Notes

1. Josephus, *Against Apion* 2.79. All Josephus's citations are taken from H. St. J. Thackeray et al., *Josephus* (Cambridge: Harvard University Press, 1926–65).

2. Josephus, *Wars* 6.267.

3. Josephus, *Antiquities* 15.384.

4. See the *Hebrew-English Edition of the Babylonian Talmud,* trans. H. Freedman, ed. I. Epstein (London: Soncino, 1967) for references in the Babylonian Talmud.

5. *History of the Church,* 4:603.

CHAPTER 1

ABRAHAM'S TEMPLE DRAMA

Hugh W. Nibley

The Pearl of Great Price is rightly named. It contains enormous value in a very small scope. Also, it has long been lying with "purest ray serene" in the dark caves of the ocean, or in a shabby back lot where the merchant discovered it (see Matthew 13:45–46). Like no other book, it contains in its sixty-five pages the answers to the ultimate questions of philosophy, religion, and science. Even more wonderful, it fills those enormous gaps in our records of the past for which science must give an accounting. What was going on during all those lost millennia that the Egyptologist Jan Assmann calls "the great forgetting"?[1] We should know, and this book is good enough to tell us.

The Pearl of Great Price is a book of dispensations. Both Joseph Smith and Brigham Young said we do not know how many dispensations there have been, but the classic number in most ancient records is seven. A dispensation is a time when the heavens are open and truth is dispensed or handed out to men. It happened with Adam, Enoch, and Noah "before Abraham was," and after Abraham with

Moses, Christ, and Joseph Smith. Each one of these contributed his own story to this small handbook. Abraham's
story is the only apocryphon written in the first person—
an oddity not overlooked in the Pearl of Great Price. The
key passages to all of these books appear at length in our
wonderful Pearl of Great Price. Notice that Abraham is
squarely in the middle; all things seem to zero in on him.
He has been called the most pivotal and strategic man in
the course of world history. In his position he binds all
things together and gives meaning and purpose to everything that happened. The whole world was rent by strife
and rancor, and Abraham was like a man who sews together a badly rent garment. It was said that "charity . . .
was asleep [in the world], and [Abraham] roused it."[2] He
joined man to God when he and his wife won souls to God.
"Were it not for men like Abraham," said the Lord, "I
would not have bothered to create heaven and earth, sun
and moon."[3] Converting them was as if he had created
them anew. He was the perfect one who brought man
nearer to God. He entered into the covenant the world is
based on, as if the world were firmly established for his
sake, as if he were the Messiah come to establish the kingdom of God on earth. "My name was not known among
My creatures, and thou hast made it known among them,"
said God to Abraham. "I will regard thee as if thou wast
associated with Me in the creation of the world."[4] "As
many as receive this Gospel," said the Lord, "shall be called
after thy name, and shall be accounted thy seed" (Abraham 2:10). "God said to Abraham: As I put Adam and then
Noah in charge of all my creatures, I now put you in charge
of them, and order you to give my blessing to them."[5]

Before we get any further we must see the rest of the
picture, for this superman is simply Everyman. What office
did he hold? We know of none. What miracles did he per-

form? What dazzling appearances? He lived in the heroic age, a time of great migrations, of epic literature, but we read of no mighty combats, blow-by-blow, or challenges boasting heroic genealogy. His ten trials were Everyman's trials. He was in trouble in business. The grass, water, and grazing rights on which he depended were often withheld from him. He never drove a hard bargain (the first rule of success according to Mr. Marriott), not even with the king of Sodom, or the generous Ephron the Hittite, who would have given him the burial cave for nothing. He yielded to Lot's greedy cattlemen and gracefully withdrew. We never hear of him punishing anyone, though when the time came to get back his nephew's property, he struck the marauding chieftains with brilliant strategy and knockout force. He forbade his children to marry into alien races, but they promptly went ahead and did so.

He seemed to be generous to the point of lacking common sense. He first sent out his servant Eliezer to look for lost wanderers, but he found none. Then Abraham on his one hundredth birthday, old and very sick, went out alone on the hottest day of the year because he thought he might find some wanderer lost in the desert. He found no one, but when he got home three men dropped in to visit him;[6] "Lord of the Universe," he cried, recognizing one of them, "is it the order of the Cosmos that I sit while you remain standing?"[7] The scene, as the archaeologist André Parrot, the discoverer of Mari, a city of Abraham, remarks, "is as magnificent as it is strange."[8]

Abraham was the essential Everyman, but never was there a less-ordinary individual. A recent issue of *Time Magazine* (29 March 1999) is devoted entirely to the study of this century's twenty most influential scientists, thinkers, and inventors. The short biographies that accompany the accomplishments of each of these people point up the particular and peculiar idiosyncrasies of their creative genius. Interestingly, Albert Einstein and Philo Farnsworth are both on that list. But in a list of the twenty greatest minds of the last *forty* centuries, Abraham must surely make a strong bid for number one. Brief sketches given in the magazine describe the special traits and qualifications of the hundred geniuses of this century;[9] those traits give an almost perfect character profile of Abraham. The first quality of all is precocious curiosity, which means a hunger for knowledge; as children these people were always disturbing their elders with searching questions about everything. To this weakness Abraham frankly confessed in that revealing second verse that lays out his goals in life: "desiring also to be one who possessed great knowledge, . . . and to possess a *greater* knowledge" (Abraham 1:2). A goodly portion of Abraham's legendary biographical record tells how his question-asking as a child got him and his family into no end of trouble. From infancy he was asking searching questions about God, the cosmos, and the ways of men—embarrassing questions.[10] When he emerged from the cave (at the age of ten days, or according to some reports, ten years, or according to others, thirteen years)[11] in which his parents had been hiding him from the jealous king, he saw the sun and decided it was God; then the sun set and the moon and stars came up, and he thought that must be God and his attendants. When they set, he started asking questions.[12] In one version he decided that the clouds must be the creative power because they darkened the sun; when the wind blew the clouds away, it was the wind. Then he asked whether the king, Pharaoh Nimrod, was God, and his parents got very nervous. When he refused to believe that Nimrod was God and started pointing out logical inconsistencies in such a claim, his parents saw trouble. But he went on asking questions. He was especially good at making fun of the worship of idols, a practice in which his own family indulged.[13]

As he grew older the questions grew more dangerous—he debunked the idols by clever arguments which, worst of all, he applied to the king. This threatened the high social position of the family at court, and they finally volunteered him for sacrifice. If you think this sounds fantastic, you should read the Instructions of Pharoah Amenemhēt I (1991–1962 B.C.), who tells how a conspiracy of ambitious courtiers and members of his own family attempted to murder him as he was napping after supper one night—Abraham's story is thoroughly typical of real conditions at the perilous court of Egypt.[14] The title of Abraham's biography in the great Midrash is *lech lecha,* "keep moving!"[15] Perpetual migration was one of the ten trials of Abraham, for the famine "wax[ed] sore in the land" (Abraham 2:1; see Genesis 12:10). In his suffering he knew how to feel for others.

The extreme independence of thought and action of our geniuses makes them all appear eccentric and willful to the rest of us, but that originality fostered their great inventiveness. At age fifteen Abraham had a job frightening the birds away from the fields at sowing time because they ate up all the seed in a time of great food shortage; he invented a sowing machine that covered the seeds with soil as it dropped them, thus protecting them from the birds—to whom, however, he apologized handsomely for cutting their rations—but gaining renown for his public service. This great zeal for the common good led him to plant trees and dig wells wherever his wanderings in the drought-ridden land led him—with no expectation of personal benefit—for the enjoyment of those who would come after.

At Hebron he ran a school for outcasts where he received all comers. He always played fair: "Charity was dead and Abraham revived it" was a proverb. In our obsession with crime and Western scenarios, the *Hauptthema* (central theme) is always the pleasure of revenge, watching the bad guys suffer, afflicting exquisite tortures, if possible far surpassing those administered by the villain. Such vengeance was not for Abraham; Josephus tells us that Abraham stubbornly pleaded with God to spare the wickedest people in the world because he felt sorry for them, "because they were his friends and neighbors."[16] That is almost inconceivable to us in our modern Sodom and Gomorrah. "It is compassion and forgiveness *alone* that are the unfailing traits of the true descendants of Abraham."[17]

He was eager to exchange ideas with the greatest thinkers of his time and in his continual travels he visited the courts and schools of Egypt and the Near East, where he made an enormous impression on the wisest and most learned men of the time. One of the best-known stories about him is how, when he was studying the stars on his own, the Lord himself came down and instructed him personally in astronomy. In receiving such blessings, Abraham always made the first move: "Thy servant has sought thee earnestly; now I have found thee" (Abraham 2:12).

We are told that that is the only case in which God appeared to man and talked with him person to person.[18] Today we can add another one; the youth of Joseph Smith shows astonishing parallels to that of Abraham. Both were curious about everything, especially the stars, and asked searching questions that got their families into trouble and made them seek "another place of residence" (Abraham 1:1).

Still delving deeply into popular science, we turn to the current *Astronomy Magazine* (April 1999), where we learn that the questions that absorb the most advanced branches of science today are the same ones that have always done so, namely: Where did we come from? How does it all begin? Is this all there is? Where are we going? As Karl Popper tells us, all the answers to the questions of science remain forever tentative ones.[19] And so it is that Abraham scores again. He, and if we look around, he *alone* has given us the answers to those very questions—in the temple.

Abraham and the Temple

The altar where Abraham and Isaac met the supreme test was on Mount Zion, the cosmic rock uniting heaven and earth, "whereon Adam had brought the first sacrifice"; it was the altar of Cain and Abel and Noah; "Abraham . . . knew that it was the place appointed for the Temple."[20] Maimonides says that Abraham chose Mount Moriah and dedicated it as the place of the future temple.[21] As the great intercessor, Abraham joined Michael and Abel in a project of work for the dead, established in the temple.[22] It was he who introduced prayers for the dead.[23] Another link between God and man—every follower of Abraham must receive certain signs and tokens relating to sacrifice; Abraham and Isaac were both tested as offerings on the altar, and both arose unharmed in similitude of the Only Begotten and the resurrection.[24]

Today Jews are claiming Abraham rather than Moses as the founder of their religion, arguing that the covenant with Moses on Sinai was "but the fulfillment of the covenant made with Abraham." All the great sacrifices of the past, "lost at the time of the Tower," were restored by Abraham. God summoned Abraham to the site of the altar where Adam and Noah "offered the first sacrifice to me," with the commandment, "It is now your duty, Abraham, to build it up again!"[25] Again, according to Maimonides, God showed the future temple to Adam, who had received all of its ordinances. Everything Abraham does Adam did before him: Abraham restored what Adam had lost.[26]

It was Abraham who restored the temple after locating the site of Adam's altar, which he rebuilt, renewing the covenants and ordinances.[27] When the world turned to idolatry, Abraham alone was faithful, and so we get such sayings of the Lord: "If it were not for Abraham, I would not have created the world."[28] He carries on the work of Adam, Seth, and Noah at the altar, uniting heaven and earth in the ordinances and covenants between God and man.[29] With Michael and Abel he inaugurated and still supervises the work for the dead with special permission, so now the righteous go to "Abraham's bosom" (Luke 16:22). God gave Abraham the law—the ordinances and covenants—and declared to him the complete plan of salvation.[30] Indeed, we are told that Abraham was associated with God in the creation of the world.[31] We are even told that the marks on the garment which Joseph brought to Jacob showed it to be the original garment of Abraham which he received from Adam.[32] He and Sarah were the greatest of missionaries, preaching wherever they went, their converts receiving the signs and tokens of the covenant and becoming the true seed of Abraham. This made him "the father of many nations" (Abraham 1:2) in whom "all the nations of the earth shall be blessed" (Genesis 18:18).

In ancient times the world was covered with temples. What was done in them? Surprisingly, all followed the same general pattern. Over sixty years ago I wrote a paper on the subject, comparing a score of temple rites at the great ceremonial centers throughout the world from the remotest times to the present.[33] They were astonishingly alike; many scholars had to check over the lists of their common traits again and again to realize that we may be dealing with one single worldwide institution. Thus Samuel Hooke listed five main elements that "constitute the underlying skeleton . . . not only of such seasonal rituals as the great New Year Festivals, but also of coronation rituals, [and] initiation ceremonies."[34] "In extremely diverse cultural contexts we always find the same cosmological pattern and the same ritual scenario," writes Eliade, and as "man progressively occupies increasingly vast areas of the planet, . . . all he seems to do is to repeat indefinitely the same archetypal gesture."[35] He pointedly observes that "man would not know these tales if they were not revealed to him. Consequently, a myth is the story of what happened . . . at the beginning of time."[36]

Carl Jung accounted for these resemblances by what he called the *primal images,* though he confesses that he hasn't the vaguest idea how they began and that we don't even know where to begin to research the subject.[37] On the other hand, Lord Raglan and the diffusionists[38] say it all went forth from a single planting on the earth by aliens from somewhere.

The Temple Drama

The ancient state or nation was hierocentric, focused on one sacred place of power and authority; such places were sometimes referred to as "places of emergence," that is, of contact between the Upper and the Lower Worlds, where at the New Year all the people met to rehearse the creation. Regarding this practice, Mircea Eliade writes, "It was the . . . sacred place, . . . the celestial prototype, . . . the act of creation which . . . brought the ordered cosmos out of chaos, . . . the sacred marriage, . . . the ritual confrontation with evil as the dragon and the victory of the King, whose triumphant coronation inaugurates the new age of the world and the cosmos." There is an "atoning sacrifice" to "restore the primal unity between God and man and enable the latter to regain the Divine presence." In this, "Reality is conferred through participation in the 'symbolism of the Center': cities, temples, houses become real by the fact of being assimilated to the 'center of the world.' . . . The temple in particular—preeminently the sacred place—had a celestial prototype,"[39] the holy mountain, "the mountain of the Lord's house" (Isaiah 2:2).

Donald Redford begins the most recent comprehensive history of Egypt by noting that that nation first "bounced overnight, as it were, out of the Stone Age and into urban culture " and also that for "this quantum leap . . . no satisfying answer has been given."[40] Yet he unconsciously provides the explanation when he tells us about the great popular assembly going back in Egypt to prehistoric times: "All the community, high and low, the ancestral 'souls' and town gods and local numina, all convened to lend their approbation to the incarnate god-king."[41] There is no need to ask why they went to all that trouble, for they realized that the only hope of continuing life indefinitely was to be born again from time to time, following the example of the sun, which, of course, represented the king, himself having to overcome the powers of darkness in a ritual contest, celebrate a brilliant new coronation and marriage, and get on with the usual affairs.

Since World War II, Egyptologists have displayed a sudden and lively interest in that vast Egyptian funerary literature which the older generation of scholars despised and deplored, and they have come to the agreement that the abiding goal of the people was nothing less than resurrection and eternal life. It was that which made Egyptian civilization what it was. And in a hundred other places in the world people went through the same routine at the same time. Every year in a hundred ancient capitals the creation was dramatized with joyful celebration at the prospect of a new life; singing, dancing, feasting, and drinking were the order of the day, as the angel chorus sings at the beginning of Goethe's *Faust:* Everything was *herrlich wie am ersten Tag,* as glorious as on the day of creation.[42]

But does all this singing, dancing, dramatizing, and preaching really make it happen? The performance at the temple was a preparation, a training, a school, and a theater, teaching by precept and example. They knew it was not the real thing. Shakespeare apologizes repeatedly in his great superspectacular *Henry V,* begging the pardon of the audience, "Can this cockpit hold / The vasty fields of France? Or may we cram / Within this wooden O the very casques / That did affright the air at Agincourt? / O, pardon!"[43] He excuses himself for the sheer gall of daring to stage a great battle with "four or five most vile and ragged foils / (Right ill dispos'd, in brawl ridiculous)."[44] Still, he is performing a service as he concludes, "Yet sit and see, / Minding *true* things by what their mock'ries be."[45] The whole thing is just a mockup, as a stage is, a make-believe, frankly, a mockery. But still it will give you an idea of the "*true* things" it is supposed to represent.

So it is with the temple. Anyone who has ever taken a guided tour through an LDS temple before its dedication or seen the extensive guide to temples published by the *Improvement Era*[46] may recognize the situation. Outside, the temple is boxed to the compass, oriented to the whole universe; we are often told today that the ancient temple was nothing but a scale model of the universe, a place where we take our bearings in eternity. But what about the Provo Temple? While it was being built, I was shocked to notice that it was not so oriented. I was upset, since Brigham Young laid such stress on that arrangement, and I wrote to the Brethren about it. Then it occurred to me that Brigham Young also reminded the Saints that they should not be scandalized if one temple had two towers and another only one.[47] In Provo, the architect, while displaying the building itself as an arresting spectacle seen from the valley, took advantage of the phenomenal view of the lake and the valley from the temple—strictly following the directions of the compass would have spoiled all that (see fig. 1). I readily accepted the margin allowed by taste and practicality. While temples are still in the planning stage to suit various climes and settings throughout the world, we need not be alarmed at sundry shifts and alterations. For this is not the final real temple, the ideal future temple of the *Temple Scroll.* This is a training center, a school for precepts and a showplace for examples (see D&C 109). Here we do not receive crowns of glory but only the promise that if we are true and faithful the day will come when we shall be eligible for such.

To resume the temple tour, the first room is the creation room, where we are introduced to the reality with which we have only recently become accustomed of a world waiting to be born, "empty and desolate, because they had not formed anything but the earth" (Abraham 4:2). And then cloud-covered darkness, from which we escape into the infinite expanse of the starry heavens to learn that this earth is made of the same materials and on the same pattern and following the same physical laws as other worlds that have

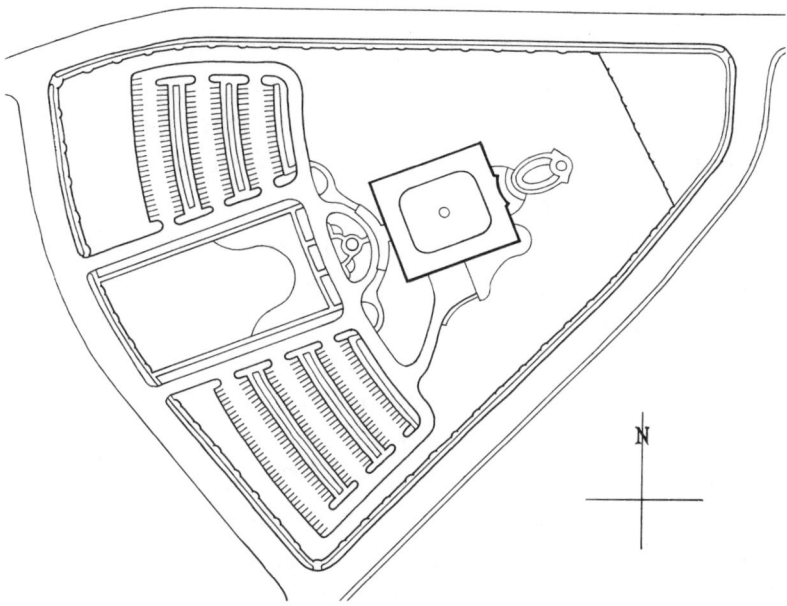

Figure 1. The Provo Temple was oriented 21 degrees south of due east in order to fit the site more perfectly. The inscription "Holiness to the Lord" follows tradition by being placed on the east and surrounded by a quiet garden, while the entrance faces west, like the Nauvoo Temple.

already been formed. This teaches us a basic principle of Mormonism, that we are living in the physical universe. Though medieval and modern theologians vigorously condemn "cosmism," that is, the inclusion of the visible universe in the plan of eternal life,[48] there is, to quote the Egyptologist G. van der Leeuw, "a human inclination (in general as well as in Christianity) . . . to base trust on one's salvation in the cosmos. . . . [O]nly when the human passion of a divine Savior has a cosmic background does salvation seem sufficiently assured."[49] Hence, Arthur Lovejoy can conclude that in religious writings of any period "the language of acosmism . . . is never to be taken too liter-ally."[50] So Origen, first and best informed of all theolo-gians, declares triumphantly, "When finally, by the grace of God, the Saints shall reach the celestial place, then they shall comprehend all the secrets of the stars. God will re-veal to them the nature of the universe."[51] This is the teach-ing of the early brethren of which Origen is an authority, but his own Alexandrian training breaks through at the end of the passage when he appeals for "perfect knowl-edge, purged of all that is physical and corporeal." And since the scriptures tell us nothing about the heavens, he recommends consulting another Alexandrian, Philo the great allegorizer, on the subject.[52]

The next room is the Garden of Eden, the scene of the greatest primal drama of them all. Now it becomes even plainer that the whole thing is a stage set; everything has been properly set up and we are ready for the play to be-gin. Where is the stage? The room itself is the stage; it is an auditorium filled with seats for everybody, but the audi-ence is part of the play. They are all actors, each in the ima-ginary role of Adam or Eve. Each individual, in fact, who is not visiting the temple for the first time, has taken the name and is playing the part of another person; he speaks for him, thinks for him (it is all by proxy), and that makes us all actors, role-playing. But this is no "insubstantial pag-eant faded," which "leave[s] not a rack behind."[53] The Lord left his peace and blessing when he departed after the drama of the last supper. For it was a drama too: He ex-plained to the apostles that they were to think thereafter of the wine and the bread as something far more than wine and bread, and to think of him as if he were present. He was teaching them as Jeremiah taught the people when he went around armed with a lamp like Diogenes, staging a

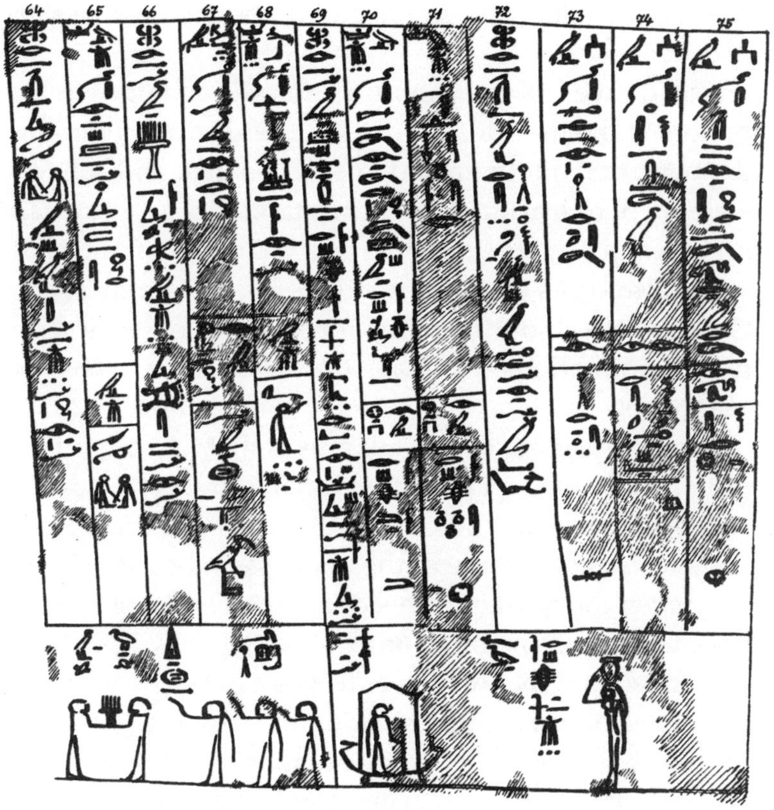

Figure 2. This New Kingdom copy of a much older script has directions and small drawings telling the priests how to perform rituals in honor of Senwsret I, whose statue appears in a boat (C), while his daughters (D) bring in jars of wine. Embalmers (A) carry in offerings, and ritual dancers (B) perform. Line 75 describes the red carnelian stones.

like "mystery," for the Bible calls it a mystery. The "mysteries of the kingdom of heaven" are things understood only by those who have been initiated and taught (Matthew 13:11). One of the oldest Egyptian ritual plays, the so-called Ramesseum Drama (see fig. 2), is careful to explain to the audience that each of the properties represents something else—the carnelian stones are blood, the green stones are bread, etc.

Why do we call the temple a school? The initiatory ordinances make that clear. We begin there with the first requirement, that our brain and intellect be clear and active—we are there to learn and to understand. Bring your brain with you and prepare to stay awake, to be alert and pay attention; also come often for frequent reviews repeating the lessons to refresh our memory, for you cannot leave without an examination—you have to show you have learned some things.

A famous saying of Aesculapius is that "All Egypt is a temple." Indeed, everywhere you look in Egypt, you are faced with teaching devices boldly displayed on the outside as well as the inside of the many sacred edifices. That is why even the most hard-headed Egyptologist of the Old School felt he was being haunted, "bugged" by somebody trying to tell him that wherever he went in Egypt, the place had a sense of uneasiness and "ennui"—one seems to be living in two worlds at once. The temple, like the medieval cathedral, presents us on every hand with symbols to remind and instruct the worshiper.

Leaving the garden room, we go into the dismal world in which we are now living to take care of certain matters that have to be expedited in this world. Then we pass on to a better world. Thus we progress by going higher and higher for each new chamber. It was exactly so in the Egyptian temples. The final ascent takes us to the place of transition, where we take the step into the next world. In the wonderful temple at Denderah, the devotee makes his departure from the roof into the world above. The recently discovered *Temple Scroll* calls the large assembly room at the top of the temple at Jerusalem (the model temple of the future) the room of the golden veil because the veil was hung from one side to the other. One reaches it in Manti by a spiral ascent, a freestanding stairway that defies gravity, supported only by its own weight—the neat expression of an idea.

Today the various steps of creation are made vivid to us by superb cinematographic and sound recordings, showing the astral, geological, and biological wonders described by the actors and the vast reaches of time that the gods called days before time was measured unto man. Along with that, we are regaled by haunting background music that touches the feelings without intruding on the attention of the audience. Yes, the temple is a theater, and no one directs it so well as Abraham. He gives us the creation story and the plan of salvation in a privileged personal showing. He did not have the visual and sound effects that we do, but he had the common resources of all the ancients—the song, dance, and recitation. It was long debated among Egyptologists whether the Pyramid Texts were recited by a priest or acted out, following instructions held in the hand or written on the walls.

The Sacred Dance

The Greeks called the great yearly celebration the *panegyris,* meaning everyone gathered. Singing and dancing are the natural modes of expression among archaic peoples throughout the world, and the ring dance is universal.

Philo, in his work on the creation, says the true initiate during the rites moves "in the circuit of heaven, and is borne around in a circle with the dance of the planets and stars in accordance with the laws of perfect music"[54]— the music of the spheres. Lehi in vision "thought he saw God sitting upon his throne, surrounded with numberless concourses of angels in the attitude of singing and praising their God" (1 Nephi 1:8). From that meeting he saw twelve appointed agents descending to earth ("their brightness did exceed that of the stars in the firmament," 1 Nephi 1:10), transferring the glories of heaven to earth with the preaching of the gospel.

Lucian, a clever Syrian who wrote in Greek and spoke for the whole Near East, reports that "You cannot have a single ancient *teleten* (high religious celebration, a mystery) without an *orchesis* or pantomime dance."[55] Plato says dancing is mandatory at every public offering,[56] and Athenaeus says no respectable dinner party could be without song and dance.[57] The Old Testament is rich in dancing situations. Israel came out of Egypt dancing, and the victory dances that followed were by choruses of maidens (see Exodus 15:20; 1 Samuel 18:6). We read of a company of prophets carrying instruments (see Psalm 149:3); they danced as they prophesied. There was a daily procession, with song and dance around the altar in the temple; David and Solomon both participated in it. In the dance of the water drawers, "Pious men and men of affairs danced with torches in their hands, singing songs of joy and praise, with a full orchestra of Levites."[58] Rabbi Simeon ben Gamal juggled eight torches in the dance. The Song of Solomon was an antiphonal between two choirs of maidens. Rival maiden choruses got David into big trouble when one sang "Saul hath slain his thousands," while the others topped with "But David his ten thousands" (1 Samuel 18:6–7). Just such competitions took place in Greece, preserved in the "Maiden Songs" of Alcman.

So we should not be shocked when we find Abraham composing a ballet on the creation. The Greek name for it was *chorus*. Aeschylus, the first and greatest writer of sacred

Figure 3. In William Blake's magnificent engraving, God answers Job, his wife, and three comforters by demanding to know where he was at the creation of the sun and the moon, shown under his outstretched arms, while the morning stars lift their arms in rejoicing.

plays, choreographed his own dramas. In fact, the chorus *was* the play; it was the chorus that was awarded the prize; the author's first step in celebrating the sacred rites was to "ask for a chorus." Plato says in the *Laws* that "The chorus was nothing more nor less than the *educating (paideia)* of the people."[59] It was the chorus that sang and danced the creation song. We all know the challenge to Job when he was moping and wailing: "Where wast thou when I laid the foundations of the earth? . . . When the morning stars sang together, and all the sons of God shouted for joy?" (Job 38:4, 7; see fig. 3). We consistently ignore the words: "Answer thou me" (Job 38:3) and "declare if thou knowest it all" (Job 38:18). Job was there, and the Lord is reminding him that his sufferings and the defects of this world are for a purpose. In the *War Scroll* of the Dead Sea Scrolls, the same speech is addressed to the army of Israel when they are downcast after a defeat, saying in effect, "Remember how glad we were to come down here? Bad times were to be part of the picture."[60]

I have shown elsewhere that the round dance of the creation drama takes the form of the prayer circle in the temple.[61] The *Testament of Job* brings it vividly to mind. Job himself is not committed to any tribe or nation; like Abraham he was just one of the "men of the East." Job's story is indeterminate in time and place but is still full of ancient reminiscences and familiar undertones. The valuable apocryphal *Testament of Job*, discovered at the beginning of the century, lays special emphasis on temple ordinances. It has long been generally accepted that the book of Job is authentic theater. The texts go back to the fifth century.[62]

In the opening lines of his *Testament*, Job tells his three virgin daughters and seven sons (see Job 1:2) to form a circle around him (the second son's name is Choros):

Figure 4. Blake shows Job encircled by his three fair daughters as he recounts his trials by pointing to their depictions on either side. In the center above him God answers him out of the whirlwind.

"Make a circle around me, and I will demonstrate to you the things which the Lord expounded to me, for I am your father Job who is faithful in all things."[63] Job next tells the circle how the Lord, after healing him of his awful ailments, said, "Arise, gird up thy loins like a man!"[64] "And the Lord spoke to me in power, showing me things past and future."[65] He tells his daughters that they will have nothing to fear in this life from the adversary (see fig. 4) because the garments they wear are "a power and a protection from the Lord."[66] Then he tells them to arise and gird themselves to prepare for heavenly visitors.[67] "Thus it was that when one of the three daughters . . . arose and clothed herself . . . she began to utter words of wisdom in the angelic language, and sent a hymn up to God, using the manner of praising of the angels. And as she recited the hymns, she let the Spirit make marks [*charagmata*, cuts or rents] on her garment."[68]

The next daughter girded herself likewise and recited "The Hymn of the Creation of the Heavens," speaking "in the dialect of the archons [cf. the council in heaven]."[69] The third daughter "chanted verses in the dialect of those on high . . . and she spoke in the tongue of the cherubim," her words being preserved as "the prayers of Amaltheias-Keras."[70] Amaltheias-Keras as Amitla was the mother of the infant Abraham when she concealed him from the murderous Nimrod and fed him from her milk in a cave: she was also the horned Amaltheia, the she-goat whose milk fed the infant Zeus when his mother was hiding him in the Dyktaeian Cave from the bloodthirsty Saturn, even as the infant Horus was concealed in the marshes of Chemmis from Seth by his mother Isis. What can all this be leading to, all these strange parallels? This is the most striking aspect of the histories of Abraham, including the longest biography in the Bible (see Genesis 11–25). It would seem that parallel instances cling to Abraham as to few other figures, including his rivals Nimrod and Alexander the Great.

After this artistic treat—and no one will deny that the temple makes no apologies for appealing to our gentler senses and our delight in the Good, the True, and the Beautiful—we now turn to another medium. Just as it is impossible to present the vast panorama of the creation in its enormous stretches of time without the aid of Steven Spielberg and our modern techniques, we find ourselves obliged to fall back on the age-old procedures of voices offstage, describing the scene and the situation by solo voices or various combinations. We still do this in the temple teachings. In the Book of Abraham we also have both the descriptive recitation and the spectacular choral dance themes.

The Terrible Questions

Of the former, the factual recitation, Abraham gives us the most marvelous text of all, the miraculous third chapter of the book that answers with astonishing economy the most fundamental and baffling questions of our existence. Various individuals have struggled with those questions. For example, I like to recall the case of Clement of Rome, the precocious boy in the first century who tells us the story of how in his school days he started asking himself the baffling questions of existence, which almost drove him out of his mind. The young Clement's main problem was to find someone who could answer his questions—he tried every famous teacher in Rome and found no satisfaction; a friend advised him to go to Egypt, the only place where they had answers to such questions. Instead of going to Egypt, Clement had a chance meeting with the missionary Barnabas that sent him to Caesarea, where he met Peter at a general conference. At last his questions were answered.[71]

And here is an interesting coincidence: I know of two other boys who had exactly the same problems with exactly the same questions and received exactly the same answers. They were Abraham and Joseph Smith. We do not need to attribute their inspiration to the schools of Alexandria or Athens.

So the Prophet Joseph recalled:

At about the age of twelve years my mind became seriously imprest with regard to the all important concerns for the wellfare of my immortal Soul. . . . [T]hus from the age of twelve years to fifteen I pondered many things in my heart concerning the sittuation of the world of mankind the contentions and divi[si]ons the wickedness and abominations and the darkness which pervaded the minds of mankind my mind become excedingly distressed . . . for I looked upon the sun the glorious luminary of the earth and also the moon rolling in their magesty through the heavens and also the stars shining in their courses and the earth also upon which I stood and the beast of the field and the fowls of heaven and the fish of the waters and also man walking forth upon the face of the earth in magesty and in the strength of beauty . . . even in the likeness of him who created them and when I considered upon these things my heart exclaimed . . . all these bear testimony and bespeak an omnipotent and omnipreasant power a being who makith Laws and de-creeeth [*sic*] and bindeth all things in their bounds who filleth Eternity who was and is and will be from all Eternity to Eternity and when I considered all these things . . . I cried unto the Lord for mercy for there was none else to whom I could go.[72]

And how about Abraham? An important part of his biography, mentioned in all the principle sources, is his precocity as a boy. It began with his asking the usual questions, the same elementary questions that Clement and Joseph asked at the same age and, like the other two, Abraham was answered only by the highest source: Clement by Peter, Joseph by the Lord himself, and Abraham likewise: "Thy servant has sought thee earnestly; now I have found thee" (Abraham 2:12). That was when the Lord appeared to him in the nighttime as he was studying the stars, giving him lessons on the nature and structure of the universe, which Abraham has handed on to us in convenient notation of Facsimile 2.

The knowledge is handed on to us in chapter 3 of the Book of Abraham, a statement of principles and doctrines that answer the ultimate mysteries of our existence. I consider this a miraculous chapter because of its brevity and the astonishing expanse of knowledge it covers. Here are some of the "Terrible Questions" and their answers:

1. *The inevitable Where do I come from?* The spirits "have no beginning; they existed before, they shall have no end . . . for they are gnolaum, or eternal" (Abraham 3:18). "And God saw these souls that they were good, and he stood in the midst of them. . . . Abraham, thou art one of them; thou wast chosen before thou wast born" (Abraham 3:23). It is strange that the doctrine of premortal existence should be so hard for the world to accept. The *Sefer Yetzirah,* the oldest Hebrew book, usually attributed by the rabbis to Abraham, ends with a resounding declaration of his greatness in the premortal existence. If it is possible for us to be here now, it is just as possible for us to have been there then. Neither proposition, as Roger Penrose has shown, can be proved by algorithm or allegory, yet we have to accept their reality.[73]

2. *Why am I here?* "We will make an earth whereon these may dwell; And we will prove them herewith, to see if they will do all things whatsoever the Lord their God shall command them; And they who keep their first estate shall be added upon; . . . and they who keep their second estate shall have glory added upon their heads for ever and ever" (Abraham 3:24, 26). The oldest Egyptian creation drama, portrayed on the Shabako Stone, says that when the earth was adorned and ready to receive its inhabitants, a law was given by which every action of every creature would be judged: "To him who does what is agreeable (lovable, *mr.wt*) shall be given a life of eternal rest or happiness (*ꜥnḫ n ḫr-ḥtp,* rest, peace, happiness), while to him who does what is hateful (detestable, *msḏi*) shall be given death and condemnation (disfavor, *mtnḫr ḥbn.t*)."[74] Note that it is not necessary to categorize what is good and bad: everyone knows it; it is the Golden Rule. There is no need for centuries of probabilistic head-splitting to define and assign precise numerical values to degrees of good and evil.

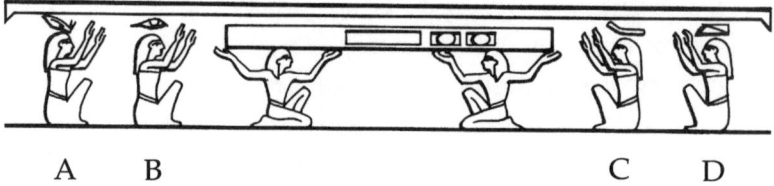

A   B   C   D

Figure 5. From the temple-library of Edfu, the two central figures support a scribal palette venerated by four figures, representing all that is heard (A), seen (B), uttered by Hu (C), or understood by Sia (D).

3. How did it all begin? It is the Egyptian *sia*, "intelligence," awareness, that comes first. But it is lost without *hu*, "authoritative utterance,"[75] "communication" (see fig. 5). As the Lord made clear to Moses, "there is no end to my *works*, neither to my *words*" (Moses 1:38). The one is incomplete without the other, and this is made very clear in the oldest Egyptian creation drama, where God "conceives in his mind" and then "utters with his mouth," communicating his intention to the council of the gods at each step of the creation. This is the very modern doctrine of anthropism. Without *sia*—intelligence, awareness—what would exist? And if it were confined to one mind only, what would be accomplished? The Creator must communicate that others may share his "most glorious and beautiful" works of creation, to bring about "the immortality and eternal life of man."

4. How does the real universe figure in the gospel? Ever since Alexandria all the clergy have condemned "cosmism." But Abraham puts us into the real universe forever: "He said unto me: My son, my son. . . . And he put his hand upon mine eyes, and I saw those things which his hands had made . . . and I could not see the end thereof" (Abraham 3:12). It was all real and visible; this is the latest definition of universe—everything.

5. The question of the Big Bang: How did it all begin and how will it all end? Intelligent beings "existed before, they shall have no end, they shall exist after, for they are gnolaum, or eternal" (Abraham 3:18). It is the Hebrew *en sof* ("without end") principle of the rabbis and Penrose—an idea beyond definition but not beyond our conception.

This brings up a theological question to which only the Book of Abraham offers a clear solution, namely the problem of hierarchy. This was the secret of Egypt's strength and stability, a strict hierarchical order of everything, which everyone respected. If it was hard for Satan to subject himself to any other being, it is still hard for the individual human to recognize his inferiority to another. Again and again we are reminded of the strangely obvious principle that one thing can be above another. According to Miriam Lichtheim, who supplies us with over seven hundred gems of Egyptian wisdom, every man's ego is constantly threatened by other egos, and none is secure—the weakest can damage the strongest.[76] Again and again Abraham takes the trouble to remind us of what should be obvious: "Now, Abraham, these two facts exist, behold thine eyes see it. . . . And where these two facts exist, there shall be another fact above them" (Abraham 3:6, 8). "If two things exist, and there be one above another, there shall be greater things above them" (Abraham 3:16). Why is he so insistent on anything so obvious? And so society throughout history has been locked in a paralyzing round of Thorstein Veblen's "invidious comparison." We have to live with it; why can't we admit it cheerfully? I have children who can run circles around me brainwise—should that depress me?

In our competitive society every ego aspires to assert itself, and it does that by comparison. Thus the deadly Christological controversy in which the Athanasians accused the

Arians of belittling the Son of God by making him inferior to the Father, while the Arians accused the Athanasians of insulting God by making the Son equal to him. Does the Son envy the Father, or is the Father jealous of him? Christians were willing to shed blood over the issue. Joseph Smith gives us four follies that must be avoided at any cost. One should *never,* he says, (1) aspire, for that is what Satan did to bring about his fall; (2) accuse—Satan is the devil, and *diabolos* means "accuser of his brethren"—never mind that the brethren are as guilty as he is; (3) contend—the first rule the Lord gave to the Nephites was, "For verily, verily I say unto you, he that hath the spirit of contention is not of me, but is of the devil, who is the father of contention, and he stirreth up the hearts of men to contend with anger, one with another" (3 Nephi 11:29); and (4) coerce, or use force to persuade.

Abraham removes the mean, invidious element and makes the order of things accessible to all: "If there be two spirits, and one shall be more intelligent than the other, yet these two spirits, *notwithstanding* one is more intelligent than the other, have no beginning; they existed before, . . . they shall exist after. . . . And the Lord said unto me: These two facts do exist, that there are two spirits, one being more intelligent than the other; there shall be another more intelligent than they; I am the Lord thy God, I am more intelligent than they all" (Abraham 3:18–19). One cannot plead that he is a latecomer, that others came early and got the jump on him: "*Ye were also* in the beginning with the Father; that which is Spirit, even the Spirit of truth" (D&C 93:23). Opportunity is not a matter of early arrival, for "Man was *also* in the beginning with God. Intelligence, or the light of truth, was not created or made, neither indeed can be" (D&C 93:29). This nullifies the whining excuse of Omar

Khayyam that God created us that way, and there is nothing that we can do about it: "He who did man of baser metal make."[77] Who is responsible then? It is all in my own hands. Intelligence was not created—it unfolds; no matter how backward I may be I can rejoice in my ignorance, knowing that wonderful things are awaiting my discovery. When I am honest, that is, intelligent enough to search out and dwell upon the things I do not know or in which I have been mistaken, rather than preening myself on the little I do know, surveying such latent discoveries is like a child waiting to open packages on Christmas morning.

6. *What is man's position relative to the universe?* Five times in our remarkable third chapter we are reminded that everything that he sees is to be understood only as viewed from the place "upon which thou standest" (Abraham 3:5, 6, 7, 9; see Abraham 3:4). Like Einstein's man on the boat who thinks that the dock is moving away from him, so Abraham must remember his real position relative to the universe. In all that the Lord showed him, Abraham has still only a limited view. When Moses asked to see more than the scope and range of mission assigned him, he was sharply rebuked: "Worlds without number have I created; and I also created them for mine own purpose" (Moses 1:33). "But only an account of this earth, and the inhabitants thereof, give I unto you" (Moses 1:35). In the next verse Moses apologizes: "Be merciful unto thy servant, O God, and tell me concerning this earth . . . and then thy servant will be content" (Moses 1:36).

Our temple drama began like the book of Job, the Gospel of John, and Goethe's *Faust*, with the "Prologue in Heaven." In the temple today the prologue is spoken offstage, that is, in another world far removed from our present one. We hear the council in heaven discussing the plan to organize a world like other worlds that have been formed. They will "take of these materials, and . . . will make an earth whereon *these* may dwell" (Abraham 3:24). The definite pronoun *these* plainly points to or indicates something, showing that the drama is in progress. Then they appoint two others from among those who stood "among those that were spirits" (Abraham 3:23). Again the definite pronoun that calls our attention to parties who are not mentioned but are obviously indicated by gesture—these are stage directions.

Things being thus decided, the Lord said "Whom should I send?" Here we should note that thirty-three of the forty-two verses in Moses 1 begin with the word *and*. This in our narrative is the so-called *wāw*-conversive in Hebrew, which converts the past to a future tense, giving it the sense of stage direction: "The Lord *shall* say." To his question, "one answered [or one shall answer] like unto the Son of Man," obviously stepping forward: "Here I am, send me" (Abraham 3:27). The action is clearly indicated, but why "one *like unto* the Son of Man?" Why not simply the Son of Man? Because plainly this is not the real character but an impersonation of him, one taking his part: *"like* the Son of Man."

"And another answered and said: Here am I, send me. And the Lord said: I will send the first. And the second was angry, and kept not his first estate; and, at that day, many followed after him" (Abraham 3:27–28). Here we have a drama that was played out at the new year in the temples of Egypt. Dozens of texts still exist, recounting the rivalry of the two leaders, sometimes taking the form of a litigation before the court of the council in heaven, sometimes the form of a knock-down-and-drag-out duel. But it always ends with the expulsion of the aspiring party. (These dramas include that on the Shabako Stone, the Ramesseum Drama, the Celestial Cow, the Contendings of Horus and

Seth, etc.) At this point the chorus divides into two, the usual half-choruses that engage in an antiphonal contest. The losers follow the leader off the stage. End of first act.

The Second Act

We now get to the ballets. They start with all useful vegetation, the first step in making the earth—formed, divided, and beautified—habitable for man. The Gods said: "Let us prepare the earth to bring forth grass; the herb yielding seed; the fruit tree yielding fruit, after his kind . . . and it was so, even as they ordered" (Abraham 4:11). This script was made to order for a ballet. The oldest dances in the world have to do with planting and harvesting (in Egypt the *haker* dance); their significance as fertility rites was the subject of much study in the 1920s and 1930s. This episode of the plants ends a period: from "morning until the evening they called day; and it was the third time" (Abraham 4:13). End of ballet.

Now a quite different dance. "And the Gods organized the lights in the expanse of the heaven" (Abraham 4:14). We have already mentioned the torch dances in Israel, and many of us fondly recall the lively fire dances at the LDS Polynesian Cultural Center. The key word is "organized." That means everything arranged from subatomic particles to molecules, to organizing the family, an army, a church, or a galaxy. Here we see the mazy motion of the dancers' chorus and semichorus, as they divide the day from the night and organize themselves into groups to take position, "To be for signs and for seasons, and for days and for years" (Abraham 4:14). Again it says not "to be signs," but to be *for* signs, and for days, and for seasons and for years; they are taking their places for the benefit of man. "And the Gods organized the two great lights, the greater light to rule the day, and the lesser light to rule the night; with the lesser light they set the stars also; And the Gods set them in the expanse of the heavens, to give light upon the earth, and to rule over the day and over the night, and to cause to divide the light from the darkness" (Abraham 4:16–17). Is all that repetition necessary? This is not a laborious tale for the simpleminded, but the unfolding of a splendid pageant, the Dance of Life, the ever-popular torch dance. Not long ago we used to laugh our heads off at the idea that God created the stars and their motions for the benefit of puny man. Today the shoe is on the other foot. Now we are asked to believe how the unimaginable raging forces of the universe, completely uncontrolled and undirected, should zero in on this little planet with nothing but the most benevolent results, adjusting a score of fine-tuned constants to each other with unerring accuracy in defiance of entropy. Not long ago it was believed that such a coincidence was so rare that it could have happened only once in the universe, that is, that this could be the only possible habitable world. But today it seems that the main concern of astronomers is life on other worlds. Carl Sagan resented the suggestion of any mind equal to his own elsewhere in the universe, and yet he designed a missive to be sent into outer space with a message directed to whom it may concern.[78]

It was all for an appreciative audience, for "the Gods watched [these] things which they had ordered until they [were] obeyed" (Abraham 4:18). The thing was done properly, and then the lights go down: "It was from evening until morning that it was night; and . . . from morning until evening that it was day; and it was the fourth time" (Abraham 4:19).

Next the Dance of the Waters, always a favorite. In the oldest Greek play the chorus is made up of water maidens, the Oceanids; they sail above the stage weeping for poor Prometheus and shedding their tears over the Caucasus.[79] The episode is reflected in the Enoch drama of the Pearl of Great Price, where the hero asks, "How is it that the heavens weep, and shed forth their tears as rain upon the mountains?" (Moses 7:28). It is an equally poetic and dramatic passage from the same antediluvian milieu—for both tales are an immediate preparation for the flood. There is a stunning bas-relief from the Theban tomb of Kheruef depicting the water maidens imitating the waves of the Nile, though quite unaware of the parallel with the Rhine Daughters.

This prepares us for the waters to "bring forth great whales, and every living creature that moveth, which the waters were to bring forth abundantly after their kind; and every winged fowl after their kind" (Abraham 4:21). The impression is that all life began in the waters and that there was an element of the experimental in the undertaking, with the Creators watching the developments until they "saw that they would be obeyed, and that their plan was good" (Abraham 4:21).

Next comes the great animal show. Everyone's favorite. It is the circus-parade, of course, splendidly displayed on the walls of Paleolithic caves of Lascaux, etc.; it meets us on the prehistoric standards and palettes of Egypt and Mesopotamia from the First Dynasty right through the cosmic chorus of Aristophanes, the bestiaries and mummings of the Middle Ages, and the fancy-dress *Fasching* celebrations along the Rhine. It takes us back to the earliest drama of Adam and the animals. He lives with them on intimate terms. He must have because he called them all by name, and they were all around him in overwhelming force. He was living in another world then, and we don't know how long it lasted since "as yet the Gods had not appointed unto Adam his reckoning" (Abraham 5:13). This was before he entered with Eve into the garden and the covenant of marriage. It was the earth's turn to bring forth new types of "beasts after their kind, and cattle after their kind, and every thing that creepeth upon the earth after its kind; and the Gods saw they would obey" (Abraham 4:25). Again the moment of testing; it is as if new ideas were being tried out in the new world.

Before the wonderful photographic images of today, the creation drama was conveyed by dialogue offstage. After Satan's dismissal, "the Lord said: Let us go down. And they went down at the beginning . . . and formed the heavens and the earth. And the earth, after it was formed, was empty and desolate, because they had not formed anything but earth; and darkness reigned upon the face of the deep" (Abraham 4:1–2). These are the two pictures we get of lifeless worlds, painted on the walls of the creation room: "the earth . . . empty and desolate, because they had not formed anything but the earth." This we see in Mercury and Venus. This corresponds to dense cloud coverings on other planets, soon to explode into torrential rains. Both conditions are clearly displayed in our older creation rooms. Then "darkness reigned upon the face of the deep, and the Spirit of the Gods was brooding upon the face of the waters" (Abraham 4:2). "Brooding" implies a long time of preparation for life as we know it. In the fifth chapter we learn that no plants were growing on the earth because it had not yet rained (see Abraham 5:5). Up to this point we are still in the council and planning stage. This raises an interesting question which at present is the object of debate among quantum-mechanics scientists, namely, which world is the real world? According to one school of thought, we cannot say a thing exists until we are aware of it. Recently the eminent French Egyptologist Philippe Derchain has noted that the Egyptians were convinced that if they ever stopped thinking about the universe it would cease to exist.[80] This is the Copenhagen doctrine, also called "the anthropic principle," that light does not exist until we see it.[81]

The Significance of Temples

There are two parts to the temple ceremony, the dramatic and the pragmatic. So far we have only mentioned the first. The play is ended by the appearance of heavenly messengers who now bid farewell to the artifice of the antique theater and engage us in a new type of learning. Everything up to this point has been by way of explaining our position in *this* world. The dramatic motifs of the temple and its ordinances are found throughout the world from the very earliest times. President Joseph F. Smith pointed this out when he noted that we find everywhere broken remnants of teachings familiar to Latter-day Saints, going back to a time before world apostasy.[82] Where does the gospel differ from all the rest? There is no difference at all where their teachings are true. An old maxim of Mormonism states that all religions have some truth that we share with them. The first part of the endowment, the drama, is found throughout the world. Shakespeare sees the point when he says, "*All* the world's a stage / And *all* the men and women merely players."[83] We are all actors in this world, "merely players," and nothing else. This was also Abraham's predicament; according to Martin Buber his life was "an ever-new separation for him and his progeny"; his "entire history . . . is a consequence of choices and partings."[84] He no sooner settled down to living in a place than he had to leave *(lech lecha)*. If all the men and women "have their exits and their entrances, / And one man in his time plays many parts, / His acts being seven ages," and if each part is completely different—the baby, the schoolboy, the lover, the soldier, the magistrate, the senior citizen, and then, "last scene of all, . . . / Is second childishness and mere oblivion, / Sans eyes, sans teeth, sans taste, sans everything"—if all that is so, which is the real you?[85] Shakespeare got this from Solon, the wisest of the Greeks, who wrote on the seven ages of man and concluded that "all are miserable upon whom the sun shines down."[86]

But now comes the serious business of our temple. The antique temple drama ends in nothing. The stage lights go out and the house lights go up. Now *we* must be introduced to the rites and principles that will carry us far beyond this world. We are introduced to special messengers, teachers, and guides and told to pay heed to their counsel, which will continue to lead us on the path of life and salvation. Significantly, those instructions are all in the nature of restrictions and limitations to be set on what could be the exercise of unlimited power through unlimited time. Satan wanted power all for himself: "because that Satan . . . sought . . . that I should give unto him mine own power; by the power of mine Only Begotten, I caused that he should be cast down" (Moses 4:3). And so like the Ten Commandments the promises and covenants of the temple seem strangely negative to the vanity and arrogance of men. The first is obedience, the restraint on the individual's power. The second is restraint on possession of things; the eternal spirit cannot be attached to them—one must be willing to sacrifice. The third puts restraints on personal behavior, it mandates deportment, self-control to make oneself agreeable to all. The fourth is restraint on uncontrolled appetites, desires, and passions, for what could be more crippling on the path of eternal progression than those carnal obsessions which completely take over the mind and body? Finally, the fifth covenant is a limitation on the innate selfishness of the other four—everything you have must be set apart to the everlasting benefit of all.

But we cannot leave it here. Everything about the temple calls for conclusion and a decision; we cannot remain in limbo suspended between the two worlds. Whether we catch a glimpse of the inside of the temple as we approach it from without, or of the outside world once we are inside, they are worlds apart. Latter-day Saint temples have always provided a soothing transition to soften the culture shock, the passing from one existence to another. Gardens of almost unearthly beauty offer an easy and credible passage by sharing the essential qualities of both worlds, "most glorious and beautiful."

But the wonder is that everything about this experience is real. For seventy-two years I have gone to the temple and listened carefully to everything, and at no time could I say, "There is something wrong here; this is not the way it is!" On the contrary, the lesson is brought home with irresistible force that we do not know everything. There is wonder upon wonder awaiting. What the temple teaches is as real as the temple itself.

Notes

This chapter is based on a presentation given on 6 April 1999 as part of the Book of Abraham Lecture Series sponsored by the Foundation for Ancient Research and Mormon Studies at Brigham Young University.

1. See Jan Assmann, *Ma'at* (Munich: Beck, 1990), 24–25, 42.

2. *Midrash on Psalm* 110:1, in *The Midrash on Psalms*, trans. William G. Braude (New Haven: Yale University Press, 1959), 2:205.

3. Micha J. bin Gorion, *Die Sagen der Juden* (Frankfurt am Main: Rütten & Loening, 1914), 2:203.

4. *Midrash Rabbah Genesis* 43:7.

5. Bin Gorion, *Die Sagen der Juden*, 2:137.

6. This tradition is discussed by J. Perlès, "Ahron ben Gerson Aboulrabi," *Revue des études juives* 21 (1890): 247.

7. The stories, based on Genesis 18, are told with the sources in bin Gorion, *Sagen der Juden*, 2:201–3, and Bernhard Beer, *Leben Abraham's nach Auffassung der jüdischen Sage* (Leipzig: Leiner, 1859), 37.

8. Compare André Parrot, *Abraham et son temps* (Neuchâtel, Switzerland: Delachaux and Niestlé, 1962), 42.

9. Other issues of *Time Magazine* covered leaders and revolutionaries, artists and entertainers, builders and Titans, and heroes and icons; see *Time Magazine*, 13 April 1998, 8 June 1998, 7 December 1998, and 14 June 1999, respectively.

10. See Louis Ginzberg, *The Legends of the Jews*, trans. Henrietta Szold (Philadelphia: Jewish Publication Society of America, 1909), 1:210–11.

11. See Geza Vermes, *Scripture and Tradition in Judaism* (Leiden: Brill, 1973), 78; and Beer, *Leben Abraham's*, 3.

12. See Vermes, *Scripture and Tradition in Judaism*, 70–71.

13. See ibid., 70–72; Beer, *Leben Abraham's*, 9–14.

14. See Adolf Erman, *The Ancient Egyptians: A Sourcebook of Their Writings*, trans. Aylward M. Blackman (New York: Harper and Row, 1966), 72–73. Some scholars think the plot succeeded and the account was delivered by the king's ghost!

15. See *Midrash Rabbah Genesis* 39:7–9.

16. See Josephus, *Antiquities* 1.176.

17. Josef S. Bloch, *Israel und die Völker* (Berlin: Harz, 1922), 513, emphasis added.

18. See Harry Torcszyner, "The Riddle in the Bible," *Hebrew Union College Annual* 1 (1924): 140.

19. See Karl R. Popper, "Science: Problems, Aims, Responsibilities," *Federation Proceedings of the American Societies for Experimental Biology* 22 (1963): 964, 970.

20. Ginzberg, *Legends of the Jews*, 1:285.

21. See Maimonides, *Dalalat* 3.45.

22. See K. Kohler, "The Pre-Talmudic Haggada," *Jewish Quarterly Review* 7 (July 1895): 587.

23. See J. G. Wiess, "The Kavvanoth of Prayer in Early Hasidism," *Journal of Jewish Studies* 9/3–4 (1958): 170–71.

24. See Hugh W. Nibley, "The Sacrifice of Isaac," *Improvement Era*, March 1970, 88–89.

25. *Pseudo Jonathan*, cited in Beer, *Leben Abraham's*, 66.

26. See Sofia Cavalletti, "Abramo come messia e 'ricapitolatore' del suo popolo," *Studi e Materiali* 35 (1964): 251–52.

27. See Hugh W. Nibley, "Setting the Stage: The World of Abraham," *Improvement Era*, January 1970, 63.

28. Bin Gorion, *Die Sagen der Juden*, 2:203.

29. See Nibley, "World of Abraham," 61–62.

30. See M. H. Segal, "The Religion of Israel before Sinai," *Jewish Quarterly Review* 52 (1961–62): 41.

31. See *Midrash Rabbah Genesis* 43:7.

32. See Nibley, "World of Abraham," 64.

33. See Hugh W. Nibley, "The Roman Games" (Ph.D. diss., University of California at Berkeley, 1938), introduction; "The Expanding Gospel," *BYU Studies* 7/1 (1965): 3–27, given as the Second Annual BYU Faculty Lecture on 17 March 1965; compare "The Hierocentric State," in *The Ancient State* (Salt Lake City: Deseret Book and FARMS, 1991), 99–147.

34. Samuel H. Hooke, ed., *Myth and Ritual* (London: Oxford University Press, 1933), 8.

35. Mircea Eliade, "The Prestige of the Cosmogonic Myth," *Diogenes* 23 (1958): 9.

36. Ibid., 1.

37. Carl Jung, *Man and His Symbols* (New York: Doubleday, 1979), 21, 73.

38. See Lord Raglan, *The Origins of Religion* (London: Watts, 1949), 35–38. Lord Raglan makes several statements about the diffusionist theory on pp. 51, 55, and 58.

39. Mircea Eliade, *Cosmos and History: The Myth of the Eternal*

Return, trans. Willard R. Trask (New York: Harper and Brothers, 1959) 5, 7.

40. Donald B. Redford, *Egypt, Canaan, and Israel in Ancient Times* (Princeton: Princeton University Press, 1992), 3.

41. Ibid., 25.

42. On new year's celebrations, see Nibley, "The Hierocentric State," 99–147.

43. William Shakespeare, *Henry V*, act 4, prologue, lines 11–15.

44. Ibid., lines 50–51.

45. Ibid., lines 52–53, emphasis added.

46. See, for example, *Temples and the Latter-day Saints,* Improvement Era Temple Issue (Salt Lake City: The Church of Jesus Christ of Latter-day Saints, 1967); see also a section on temples in the *Improvement Era,* November 1963, 941–84, and *Temples of The Church of Jesus Christ of Latter-day Saints* (Salt Lake City: Ensign, 1988).

47. See Brigham Young, in *Journal of Discourses,* 1:133: "[The Salt Lake Temple] will have six towers, to begin with, instead of one. Now do not any of you apostatize because it will have six towers, and Joseph only built one. It is easier for us to build sixteen, than it was for him to build one."

48. See Hugh W. Nibley, "The Terrible Questions," in *Temple and Cosmos* (Salt Lake City: Deseret Book and FARMS, 1992), 356–78.

49. G. van der Leeuw, "Zum Mythus und zur Gestalt des Osiris," *Archiv für Orientforschung* 3 (1926): 11.

50. Arthur O. Lovejoy, *The Great Chain of Being: A Study of the History of an Idea* (Cambridge, Mass.: Harvard University Press, 1964), 92–93.

51. Origen, *Liber Secundus,* 2.11.7, in *Patrologiae Cursus Completus . . . Series Graeca* (hereafter *PG*), ed. Jacque-Paul Migne (Paris: Garnier, 1857–66), 11:246.

52. Origen, *Contra Celsum,* 6.21, in *PG,* 11:1321–25.

53. William Shakespeare, *The Tempest,* act 4, scene 1, lines 154–55.

54. Philo, *De Opificio Mundi* 70.

55. Lucian, *De Saltatione (On the Dance)* 15.

56. Plato, *Laws* 7.

57. See Athenaeus, *Deipnosophistae* 14.627–68.

58. TB *Sukkah* 51a–51b.

59. Plato, *Laws* 2.672e, emphasis added.

60. *War Scroll*, frg. 11, lines 11–16.

61. See Hugh Nibley, "The Early Christian Prayer Circle," in *Mormonism and Early Christianity* (Salt Lake City: Deseret Book and FARMS, 1987), 45–99.

62. See Robert A. Kraft, ed., *The Testament of Job according to the SV Text* (Missoula, Mont.: Scholars Press, 1974), on the various texts. For the Greek versions, see F. C. Conybeare, "The Testament of Job and the Testaments of the XII Patriarchs," *Jewish Quarterly Review* 13 (October 1900): 111–13.

63. *Testament of Job* 1:2.

64. Ibid., 47:5.

65. Ibid., 47:10.

66. Ibid., 47:11–12.

67. See ibid., 47:12.

68. Ibid., 48:1–4.

69. Ibid., 49:1–3.

70. Ibid., 50:1–3.

71. See Clement of Rome, *Recognitions* 1.106, in *PG,* 1:1207–10.

72. An 1831–32 account of the first vision, dictated to Frederick G. Williams, reproduced in *BYU Studies* 9/3 (1969): 279–82, spelling retained.

73. See Roger Penrose, *The Emperor's New Mind: Concerning Computers, Minds, and the Law of Physics* (New York: Oxford University Press, 1989).

74. Author's translation. See also Kurt Sethe, *Das "Denkmal Memphitischer Theologie" der Schabakostein des Britischen Museums* (London: Egypt Exploration Society, 1930), 1:64–65.

75. Alan H. Gardiner, *Egyptian Grammar*, 3rd ed. (1927; reprint, London: Oxford University Press, 1966), 588, 580.

76. See Miriam Lichtheim, *Late Egyptian Wisdom Literature in*

the International Context (Göttingen: Vandenhoeck & Ruprecht, 1983), 16–18.

77. Compare the translation in *The Rubáiyat of Omar Khayyám,* trans. Edward Fitzgerald (Roslyn, N.Y.: Black, 1942), 38.

78. This message was a 6x9-inch gold-anodized aluminum plate that was sent to outer space in Pioneer 10; see Carl Sagan, *The Cosmic Connection: An Extraterrestrial Perspective* (New York: Dell, 1973), 16–20.

79. See Aeschylus, *Prometheus Bound,* lines 140–49, 161–71.

80. See Philippe Derchain, *Le Papyrus Salt 825 (British Museum 10051), rituel pour la conservation de la vie en Égypte* (Brussels: Academy Royale, 1965), 10–11, 14, 82.

81. See Penrose, *The Emperor's New Mind,* 354, 433–34.

82. See *Journal of Discourses,* 15:325–26.

83. William Shakespeare, *As You Like It,* act 2, scene 7, lines 139–40, emphasis added.

84. Martin Buber, "Abraham the Seer," *Judaism* 5/4 (1956): 295, 296.

85. Shakespeare, *As You Like It,* act 2, scene 7, lines 141–43, 163–66.

86. Solon, *Elegiacs* 13.

CHAPTER 2

OATHS AND OATH TAKING
IN THE OLD TESTAMENT

Stephen D. Ricks

The well-being and security of a community depend on its members speaking the truth in matters of crucial importance. Oaths provide a means of impressing on those party to such a matter their obligation to truthfulness and dependability, while at the same time increasing the oath takers' seriousness and credibility in the eyes of others. Oaths and oath taking are well documented among the peoples of the world throughout history and are abundantly attested in the Old Testament. This essay will consider the structure and significance of oaths in the Old Testament.

In his treatise *On Christian Doctrine*, John Milton describes the oath as "that whereby we call God to witness the truth of what we say, with a curse upon ourselves . . . should it prove false."[1] This succinct definition suggests the three major elements of the oath in the Old Testament: (1) the *oath statement*, in which the swearer asserts that he has or has not done something or in which he promises that he will or will not do something,[2] (2) the *witness invocation*, in which God or some other person, being, or object is called on to witness the words of the oath and, by implication, to act as an accuser if the oath is not fulfilled,[3] and (3) the *curse formula*, which is either explicitly stated or implied by some bodily gesture.

The Oath Statement

A look at oaths recorded in *direct speech* (usually, though not exclusively, in the first person) and in *first-person narrative* passages[4] reveals that only the oath statement is an indispensable element of the oath. Further analysis discloses that the oath statement will invariably be accompanied either by a witness invocation or a curse formula, but rarely by both.[5] This fact suggests that both the witness and the curse formulas are viewed as being potent (perhaps equally so) and that either, of itself, is deemed sufficiently powerful to validate the oath. This viewpoint stands in contrast to the widely held opinion that the words of the curse are imbued with supernatural power and are frequently omitted in superstitious recognition of their independent power of self-fulfillment: *"The curse was automatic or self-fulfilling,* having the nature of a 'spell,' the very words of which were thought to possess reality and the power to effect the desired results."[6] If our view is correct, then the curse formula is omitted, not necessarily because of any concern for its power to harm an individual's well-being, but because it represents only one of several possible means of validating an oath, each of which has equal potency. The strength of the oath does not reside in the supernatural power of the words of the curse but in the sovereign response of God, who is viewed as the ultimate witness to and executor of all oaths.[7]

In addition to oral oaths, bodily gestures not specifically connected with the curse formula (such as raising the hand) also occasionally accompany oath taking. These constituent elements of oaths will be discussed later.

The Witness Formulas

Deuteronomic injunctions expressly command that oaths be taken in the name of God (and, by implication, not in the name of other gods): "Thou shalt fear the Lord thy God, and serve him, and shalt swear by his name. Ye shall not go after other gods, of the gods of the people which are round about you" (Deuteronomy 6:13–14; see Deuteronomy 10:20). Indeed, God himself swears by himself or his life[8] (see Genesis 22:16; Exodus 32:13; Numbers 14:21; Jeremiah 22:24; 46:18; Ezekiel 5:11; 14:16, 18, 20; 16:48; 17:19; 18:3; 20:3, 31, 33; 33:11, 27; 34:8; 35:6; Amos 6:8; and Zephaniah 2:9), his great name (see Jeremiah 44:26), or his holiness (see Amos 4:2).

In Jeremiah the Lord protests against a backsliding Israel: "How shall I pardon thee for this? thy children have forsaken me, and sworn by them that are no gods" (Jeremiah 5:7; see Amos 8:14 and Zephaniah 1:5). In a more conciliatory passage, the Lord promises: "And it shall come to pass, if they will diligently learn the ways of my people, to swear by my name, The Lord liveth; as they taught my people to swear by Baal; then shall they be built in the midst of my people" (Jeremiah 12:16). In addition, oath taking in the name of God to no good intent (Hebrew *laššāw'*, translated "in vain" in the King James Version of the Bible) is expressly forbidden in the third commandment of the Decalogue.[9] Deceptive swearing is prohibited in the Holiness Code in Leviticus (see Leviticus 19:12).

The most common formula in the witness invocation is "as the Lord liveth,"[10] which is frequently found with slight modifications, extensions, and variations: "As the

Lord liveth, and as thy soul liveth" (1 Samuel 20:3; 25:26; 2 Kings 2:2; 4:30), "as surely as you live" (1 Samuel 1:26; 17:55 NIV).

On a few occasions God is explicitly called to witness, as in Jeremiah 42:5: "Then they [the remnant of Judah at Mizpah] said to Jeremiah, The Lord be a true and faithful witness between us, if we do not even according to all things for the which the Lord thy God shall send thee to us." This phrase is, however, more generally to be found in the context of covenant making, which differs from oath taking in its reciprocal character (i.e., covenants are mutual oaths).[11]

The Curse Formulas

The force of an oath may be strengthened by expressly stating the penalties incurred for failure to perform it. The number of explicitly mentioned curses is relatively limited in the Old Testament.[12] An outstanding example of the oath and curse appearing together is in Job 31, where Job, in defense of his actions, calls down a series of terrible curses upon himself if he has failed to live uprightly: "If I have walked with vanity, or if my foot hath hasted to deceit; Let me be weighed in an even balance. . . . Then let me sow, and let another eat; yea, let my offspring be rooted out" (Job 31:5–8; see Psalms 7:3–5; 137:5–6).

A further example of the explicitly stated curse in an oath is the so-called "ordeal oath" in Numbers 5:20–22.[13] Here the priest charges the woman suspected of unfaithfulness to her husband with "an oath of cursing." The priest is to say to the woman, "The Lord make thee a curse and an oath among thy people, when the Lord doth make thy thigh to rot" (Numbers 5:21), in the event that she has sworn falsely concerning her innocence. The woman's guilt or innocence is immediately established by her drinking the "water that causeth the curse." If she is guilty, the water will cause that "her belly shall swell, and her thigh shall rot: and the woman shall be a curse among her people. And if the woman be not defiled, but be clean; then she shall be free, and shall conceive seed" (Numbers 5:27–28).[14]

More frequent than explicit oral curses are curses implied by some bodily gesture. The most common curse of this sort is similar to the one found in Ruth 1:17: "The Lord do so to me, and more also, if ought but death part thee and me" (see 1 Samuel 3:17; 14:44; 20:13; 25:22; 2 Samuel 3:9, 35; 1 Kings 2:23; 19:2; 20:10; 2 Kings 6:31). The Hebrew word *kōh,* translated "so" in the Authorized Version, suggests that some bodily gesture accompanied the statement. In his commentary on the book of Ruth, Edward Campbell observes that the statement in this verse was "presumably accompanied by a symbolic gesture, something like our index finger across the throat."[15] With this curse may be compared Moses 5:29: "And Satan said unto Cain: Swear unto me by thy throat, and if thou tell it thou shalt die," although this is in an oath-taking context of a rather more sinister sort.

In the context of covenant making, the symbolic acts implying curses (as well as imprecations that are expressly stated) are widely attested in the Old Testament, the Book of Mormon, and in the ancient Near East. In Genesis 15, the Lord commanded Abraham to take a heifer, a she-goat, a ram, a turtledove, and a pigeon; slaughter them; and lay each of the halves in two rows opposite each other so that there was a space between them. Thereafter there appeared "a smoking furnace, and a burning lamp that passed between those pieces" (Genesis 15:17), whereupon the Lord renewed his covenantal promises to Abraham.

This unusual sacrificial procedure is clarified by an allusion in which the Lord declared to Jeremiah:

> And I will give the men that have transgressed by covenant, which have not performed the words of the covenant which they had made before me, when they cut the calf in twain, and passed between the parts thereof, the princes of Judah, and the princes of Jerusalem, the eunuchs, and the priests, and all the people of the land, which passed between the parts of the calf; I will even give them into the hand of their enemies, and into the hand of them that seek their life. (Jeremiah 34:18–20)

Though for a different purpose (affecting atonement and not covenant making), a somewhat similar procedure may be seen in the rites described in Leviticus, where the priests were instructed to "cut it [the sacrificial animal] into his pieces . . . [and] lay them in order on the wood that is on the fire which is upon the altar" (Leviticus 1:12). In the sacrifices mentioned in Leviticus as well as in Genesis, the animal is divided and the pieces set in order. Perhaps the pieces were arranged on the altar in the Levitical rite so that the fire on the altar should represent "the smoking fire and fiery torch" mentioned in Genesis.[16]

A similar use of a symbolic act implying a curse in a covenant setting is seen in Alma 46 where Moroni calls on the people to take up arms against Amalickiah, in response to which they rend "their garments in token, or as a covenant, that they would not forsake the Lord their God; or in other words, if they should transgress the commandments of God . . . the Lord should rend them even as they had rent their garments" (Alma 46:21; see Alma 44:12–15; 46:22–23; 3 Nephi 4:28–32).

The notion of covenant making among the peoples of the ancient Near East between God and man seems unique to the Israelites; nevertheless, symbolic curses similar to those recorded concerning the Israelites may be seen in ancient Near Eastern suzerain and vassal treaties. A characteristic example of these symbolic curses is found in the treaty between Ashurnirari V of Assyria and Mati'ilu of Arpad, in which the suzerain Ashurnirari directs that "if Mati'ilu sins against (this) treaty made under oath by the gods, then, . . . so may, just as the head of this spring lamb is torn off, . . . the head of Mati'ilu be torn off." [17]

Examples of this sort could be multiplied.[18] One of particular relevance to the passage in Ruth is the cutting of a sheep's throat in a treaty made between Abban and Iarimlim,[19] particularly in light of Edward Campbell's observation that "deep behind this [symbolic gesture implied by the Hebrew word *kōh,* "so, thus," in Ruth 1:17] lay, in all probability, a ritual act involving the slaughter of animals, to whom the one swearing the oath equated himself."[20]

Other Symbolic Acts Accompanying Oath Taking

The raising of the hand or hands, a symbolic act not specifically associated with the curse formula, also occasionally accompanies oath taking, though not with the regularity of the witness and curse elements. It is recorded as a concomitant of swearing in Genesis 14 where Abram tells the king of Sodom, "I have lift up mine hand unto the Lord, the most high God, the possessor of heaven and earth" (Genesis 14:22). In Exodus 6:8 the Hebrew *nāśāʾtî ʾet-yādî* (literally, "I raised my hand") is rendered "I did swear," where the Lord recounts to Moses his promises made to the patriarchs: "And I will bring you in unto the land, concerning the which I did swear to give it to Abraham, to Isaac, and to Jacob" (Exodus 6:8). In Daniel 12:7 the angel of the Lord raises both hands while swearing, perhaps as a means of stressing the importance of the prophecy he utters. In other instances not associated with oath taking, a single hand is raised as a token of blessing (see Leviticus 9:22) or both hands are raised in praise and supplication (see Psalms 28:2; 63:4; 134:2; 143:6).[21]

The Order of Elements in the Oath

The order of the constituent elements in Old Testament oaths displays a considerable degree of consistency. The witness formula generally precedes the oath statement, as in Saul's pledge to Jonathan concerning David's life: "As the Lord liveth, he shall not be slain" (1 Samuel 19:6). On the other hand, explicitly stated curses, when they appear, follow the oath statement: "If I have rewarded evil unto him that was at peace with me . . . let the enemy persecute my soul, and take it; yea, let him tread down my life upon the earth, and lay mine honour in the dust" (Psalm 7:4–5). Curses suggested by some gesture may precede the oath, however: "So do God to me, and more also, if I taste bread, or ought else, till the sun be down" (2 Samuel 3:35; Hebrew *kōh*, here translated "so," implies, as we have noted above, some concomitant ritual gesture). The type of oath statement involved, whether assertory or promissory, seems to have no influence on the order of elements in the oath.

Conclusion

Over the lengthy period of Old Testament history during which it is attested, oath taking remained remarkably consistent in its shape and meaning and in the formulas of which it was composed. The oath (as well as the covenant) remained an important institution among the peoples of the Old Testament. Studying this and other traditions and institutions of ancient Israel has significance in providing deepened insights into latter-day Israel.

Notes

1. John Milton, *Christian Doctrine* (n.p.: n.d.), 579, cited in Enoch Lewis, *A Dissertation on Oaths* (Philadelphia: Hunt, 1835), 4.

2. For the distinction between oaths of an assertory and of a promissory nature, common in Anglo-Saxon and European legal theory, see Henry C. Black, *Black's Law Dictionary*, 4th ed., rev. (St. Paul, Minn.: West Publishing, 1968), 1220–21. Such a distinction has also been applied to oaths among the peoples of the Near East; see Johannes Pedersen, *Der Eid bei den Semiten* (Straßburg: Trübner, 1914), 179–89; see also Gene M. Tucker, "Covenant Forms and Contract Forms," *Vetus Testamentum*, 15 (1965): 491; John A. Wilson, "The Oath in Ancient Egypt," *Journal of Near Eastern Studies* 7 (July 1948): 129–56. Assertory oaths occur much less frequently in the Old Testament than do promissory oaths. Examples of assertory oaths are found in 1 Samuel 1:26; 17:55; 20:3; 1 Kings 17:12; 18:10; and Ezekiel 33:11.

3. The witness formula may also be viewed as an invocation of God or some other person to act as a compurgator—that is, a character witness who vouches for the good reputation or upright character of the individual making the oath.

4. Direct speech includes passages that contain quoted speech, such as 1 Samuel 25:32, 34: "And David said to Abigail, . . . For in very deed, as the Lord God of Israel liveth." First-person narrative passages are written in the first person but are, however, not in quoted speech, such as Psalm 137:5–6: "If I forget thee, O Jerusalem, let my right hand forget her cunning. If I do not remember thee, let my tongue cleave to the roof of my mouth; if I prefer not Jerusalem above my chief joy."

5. "As the Lord liveth, if ye had saved them alive, I would not slay you" (Judges 8:19) may be understood as having all

three major constituent elements of the oath if the apodosis ("I would not slay you") is construed as the curse formula.

6. Sheldon H. Blank, "The Curse, Blasphemy, the Spell, and the Oath," *Hebrew Union College Annual* 23/1 (1950–51): 78 .

7. See Anthony C. Thiselton, "The Supposed Power of Words in the Biblical Writings," *Journal of Theological Studies*, n.s. 25 (October 1974): 283–99.

8. For a discussion of this matter, see Hugh W. Nibley, *An Approach to the Book of Mormon* (Salt Lake City: Deseret Book and FARMS, 1988), 129.

9. Herbert C. Brichto suggests that this commandment is directed specifically against "conditional curses" made with frivolous or vain intent of the type: "If A has taken my such-and-such may YHWH do this-and-that to him." *The Problem of "Curse" in the Hebrew Bible* (Philadelphia: Society of Biblical Literature, 1968), 63; in such an instance the individual swearing is fully aware that A has done nothing of the sort. At all events, the original intent of this commandment was almost certainly not as a prohibition against profane or vulgar language, as it is now frequently interpreted.

10. See Judges 8:19; Ruth 3:13; 1 Samuel 14:39, 45; 19:6; 20:21; 25:34; 26:10, 16; 28:10; 29:6; 2 Samuel 2:27; 4:9; 12:5; 14:11; 1 Kings 1:29; 2:24; 17:1, 12; 18:10, 15; 2 Kings 3:14; 5:16, 20; 2 Chronicles 18:13; Jeremiah 38:16. In Genesis 42:15 the witness formula "by the life of Pharaoh" is recorded in the narrative of Joseph in Egypt (on the Egyptian background of and parallels to this statement, see J. Vergote, *Joseph en Égypte* [Louvain: Publications Universitaires, 1959], 162–67).

11. The relationship between treaty and covenant is deep and intimate. As Tucker, in "Covenant Forms and Contract Forms," 494–95, shows, a considerable correspondence exists between the biblical oath and covenant: both may contain stipulations (oath statements), witnesses, and curses. However, the formal covenant also regularly contains other elements, such as the preamble and historical prologue, that are not found in the oath in the Old Testament. For a thoroughgoing study of the biblical covenant,

see Dennis J. McCarthy, *Treaty and Covenant* (Rome: Biblical Institute Press, 1978).

12. The reason for this relatively limited number of explicitly stated curses is probably that cursing is only one of several means of validating the oath. It is not due to a supposition that a curse, once pronounced, has a supernatural power of self-fulfillment.

13. For an excellent brief introduction to the biblical ordeal, see T. S. Frymer, "Judicial Ordeal," in *The Interpreter's Dictionary of the Bible,* ed. Keith Crim, supp. vol. (Nashville: Abingdon, 1976), 638–40.

14. See ibid., 639.

15. Edward F. Campbell Jr., *Ruth: A New Translation with Introduction, Notes, and Commentary* (Garden City, N.Y.: Doubleday, 1980), 74.

16. I owe this perceptive suggestion to Terrence L. Szink.

17. "Treaty between Ashurnirari V of Assyria and Mati'ilu of Arpad," in *Ancient Near Eastern Texts relating to the Old Testament,* ed. James B. Pritchard, 3rd ed. (Princeton: Princeton University Press, 1969), 532.

18. "Just as (these) yearlings and spring lambs, male and female, are cut open and their entrails are rolled around their feet, so may the entrails of your sons and daughters be rolled around your feet," "The Vassal-Treaties of Esarhaddon," in Pritchard, ed., *Ancient Near Eastern Texts,* 539.

19. See Donald J. Wiseman, "Abban and Alalaḫ," *Journal of Cuneiform Studies* 12/4 (1958): 129.

20. Campbell, *Ruth,* 74.

21. See John A. Tvedtnes, "Temple Prayer in Ancient Times," pages 79–98, in this volume.

CHAPTER 3

BAPTISM FOR THE DEAD IN EARLY CHRISTIANITY

John A. Tvedtnes

In a letter written to the twelve apostles in England, dated 19 October 1840, the Prophet Joseph Smith indicated that during a funeral sermon for Seymour Brunson in Nauvoo the previous August, he had introduced the ordinance of baptism for the dead.[1] "The Saints have the privilege of being baptized for those of their relatives who are dead," he wrote, "whom they believe would have embraced the Gospel, if they had been privileged with hearing it, and who have received the Gospel in the spirit, through the instrumentality of those who have been commissioned to preach to them while in prison."[2] Though the practice began soon after that time, it was not until September 1842 that the Prophet issued instructions in the form of two letters, which have become Doctrine and Covenants 127 and 128. In the latter, he cited several scriptures to indicate the efficacy of baptism for the dead, including the only Bible passage to specifically mention the subject, 1 Corinthians 15:29. "You may think this order of things to be very particular," he wrote to the Saints, "but let me tell you that it is only to answer the will of God" (D&C 128:5).

As peculiar as the new practice may have been to the Saints, it was met with incredulity by other Christian groups. The general feeling among Christians then, as now, is that Paul's mention of those who are "baptized for the dead" (1 Corinthians 15:29) was enshrouded in mystery. If such a practice ever existed, they believed, it was certainly not part of the Christian church. Since then, much information has come to light from ancient documents that support the idea that some early Christians indeed baptized others by proxy for those who had died unbaptized.

The Marcionites

Two of the early church fathers, Epiphanius (A.D. 315–403) in *Panarion* 1.28.6 and Tertullian (A.D. 145–220) in *Against Marcion* 5.10, note that the Marcionites, an early Christian group, baptized others in the name of the dead. St. Chrysostom (A.D. 347–407) tells how, when one of their catechumens died without baptism, the Marcionites would place a living person under the dead man's bed and ask whether he desired to be baptized. The living person would respond in the affirmative and was then baptized as a proxy for the deceased (see *Homily 40 on 1 Corinthians 15*). Some dismiss this evidence on the grounds that the Marcionites were heretics. Latter-day Saints, believing that the great apostasy was already well under way by Marcion's time and that no Christian group then possessed the full truth, see the practice as a remnant of an earlier rite dating from the time of the apostles.

The Marcionites gave a literal interpretation to Paul's words, "Else what shall they do which are baptized for the dead, if the dead rise not at all? why are they then baptized for the dead?" (1 Corinthians 15:29). Tertullian, though acknowledging in one place that the Corinthians practiced proxy baptism (see *On the Resurrection of the Flesh* 48), declares elsewhere that Paul was referring to baptism of the body, which is subject to death (see *Against Marcion* 5.10). St. Chrysostom similarly rejected Marcion's interpretation of Paul and concluded that the apostle's real referent was the profession of faith in baptism, part of which was, "I believe in the resurrection of the dead" (*Homily 40 on 1 Corinthians 15*). These words, recited before baptism, indicated to Chrysostom that baptism is performed in hope of this resurrection.[3]

It is true that in other passages (see Romans 6:3–5; Colossians 2:12) Paul spoke of baptism as symbolic of the death, burial, and resurrection of Christ and of those who wish to follow him into a new life. But despite attempts by some of the early church fathers to give a symbolic meaning only to the passage in 1 Corinthians 15:29, the wording of this verse clearly implies proxy baptism.[4]

Work for the Dead

That baptism for the dead was indeed practiced in some orthodox Christian circles is indicated by the decisions of two late fourth-century councils. The fourth canon (fifth in some lists) of the Synod of Hippo, held in 393, declares, "The Eucharist shall not be given to dead bodies, . . . nor baptism conferred upon them." The ruling was confirmed four years later in the sixth canon of the Third Council of Carthage.[5]

Some churches not represented at these minor councils did not feel bound to discontinue the practice. Consequently, the Copts of Egypt continued baptisms for the dead.[6] The vast majority of Christianity, however, rejected proxy baptism. In some cases—as in the Roman Catholic faith—proxy baptism was replaced by prayers and masses for the dead. As early as the second century, prayers of this nature were known.[7] Cyril of Jerusalem wrote, "Many say, what is a soul profited, which departs from this world either with sins, or without sins, if it be commemorated in the prayer? . . . We, when we offer to Him our supplications for those who have fallen asleep, though they be sinners, wear no crown, but offer up Christ sacrificed for our sins, propitiating our merciful God for them as well as for ourselves."[8]

The same philosophy appears to have existed in some Jewish circles. The earliest reference to the idea is from the history of the Hasmonaeans. Following the battle of Marisa in 163 B.C., it was discovered that each of the Jewish soldiers killed in the fight had been guilty of concealing pagan idols beneath his clothing. In order to atone for their wrong, Judas Maccabaeus collected money from the survivors to purchase sacrificial animals for their comrades.

> And when he had made a gathering throughout the company to the sum of two thousand drachmas of silver, he sent it to Jerusalem to offer a sin offering, doing therein very well and honestly, in that he was mindful of the resurrection: for if he had not hoped that they that were slain should have risen again, it had been superfluous and vain to pray for the dead.[9] And also in that he perceived that there was great favour laid up for those that died godly, it was an holy and good thought. Whereupon he made a reconciliation for the dead, that they might be delivered from sin. (2 Maccabees 12:43–45 KJV)

In a sense, sacrifice did in ancient Judaism what baptism does in Christianity: it cleansed from sin. Since Jesus declared that baptism is essential for salvation (see John

3:5–7) and that he later went into the spirit world to bring the message of salvation to those who had not received it in mortality (see 1 Peter 3:18–21; 4:6; compare John 5:25–29), it seems reasonable to expect that the Lord would have provided a means for those who died without hearing the gospel to receive this sacred ordinance.

Christ's Visit to the Spirit World

Latter-day Saints have always understood baptism for the dead to be related to Christ's visit to the spirit world during the three days that his body lay in the tomb. Peter wrote that Christ was "quickened by the Spirit: By which also he went and preached unto the spirits in prison; Which sometime were disobedient, when once the longsuffering of God waited in the days of Noah, while the ark was a preparing, wherein few, that is, eight souls were saved by water" (1 Peter 3:18–20; compare John 5:25–29). He then added, "for this cause was the gospel preached also to them that are dead, that they might be judged according to men in the flesh, but live according to God in the spirit" (1 Peter 4:6).[10] It was Peter's words that President Joseph F. Smith was contemplating when he received a vision explaining how Christ organized the righteous spirits to teach those who had not heard and accepted the gospel on earth (see D&C 138:10).

In the *Shepherd of Hermas,* a mid-second-century composition widely read in the early Christian church,[11] Hermas's angelic guide tells him that the apostles and teachers who fall asleep (die) faithful in Christ preach to others who have died, then go down into the water with them to give them the seal, a term usually referring to baptism (see *Similitude* 9:16). The passage is cited by Clement of Alexandria in *Stromata* 2.9 and again in *Stromata* 6.6, where he notes that not only Jesus, but his apostles, too, taught the dead in Hades. This is a point made in Doctrine and Covenants 138:29–32.

A number of early Christian documents speak of Christ's "descent" into hell, the realm of the dead.[12] That it was a matter of faith is indicated by its inclusion as the fifth article in the *Apostles' Creed.* Two second-century writers, speaking of Christ's preaching to the dead, attributed to the prophet Jeremiah a prophecy, not found in our current versions of that book, that the Lord would descend to preach salvation to the dead.[13] Ignatius, a late first-century Christian leader, wrote that Christ had visited and taught the prophets in the spirit and raised them from the dead (see *Epistle to the Magnesians* 9). The second-century Christian theologians Hippolytus (see *Treatise on Christ and Anti-Christ*) and Origen (see *Against Celsus* 2.43) also noted that Christ preached to the dead.

Early Christian stories of the descent of Christ into hell are virtually unanimous in noting the joy felt by the righteous dead when they learned of Jesus' baptism. Of this, J. Rendel Harris wrote, "In the earliest times, the Baptism of Christ was the occasion of His triumph over Hades."[14] Harris saw *Ode of Solomon* 24 as connecting baptism (note the mention of the dove over Jesus' head) with anointing and the deliverance of the dead (i.e., resurrection). In *Ode of Solomon* 6:8–18, too, we have a stream that brings water to the temple and brings back from the dead those who are dying. *Ode of Solomon* 42:15–17 depicts the dead running to Christ to plead that he open the door and free them.

The baptism of the souls of the dead or of their resurrected bodies is a frequent theme in the stories of Christ's descent into the spirit world. The *Epistle of the Apostles,* known from a complete Ethiopic version, a fragmentary

fifth-century Latin manuscript (now in Vienna) and a fourth-
or fifth-century mutilated Coptic manuscript in Cairo, is an
example. It places the following words in the mouth of Jesus
as he visits with his apostles after the resurrection:

> For to that end went I down unto the place of
> Lazarus, and preached unto the righteous and the
> prophets, that they might come out of the rest which is
> below and come up into that which is above; and I
> poured out upon them with my right hand the water
> [*baptism*, Ethiopic text] of life and forgiveness and salva-
> tion from all evil, as I have done unto you and unto them
> that believe on me.[15]

In the Ethiopic document known as the *Testament of Our
Lord and Our Savior Jesus Christ* 38–39, Jesus tells his apostles, "For this reason I descended and conversed with
Abraham, Isaac, and Jacob, with your fathers the prophets,
and I announced to them, in Sheol, the rest in the heavens
where they shall come. With my right hand, I gave them
the baptism of life, pardon and remission of all sin, as I did
for you, and (as I shall do) hereafter for those who shall believe in me." He then tells them that he who believes "shall
come out of the prison and will be delivered from chains,
from punishment and from the fire," to which the apostles
respond, "O Lord, you have truly given us joy and rest, for
because of their faith and their confidence, you have announced to our fathers and to the prophets; also for us and
for all (who believe in you)."[16]

The fifth-century *Acts of Pilate* has a later appendage
(Part II, The Descent into Hell) that probably predates the
first sections. It tells how, when Christ descended into hell,
he removed therefrom the spirits of the righteous and of
the repentant. The latter were then baptized in the Jordan River (see *Acts of Pilate* 4:2; 6).[17] A Mandaean text has

Adam, apparently after his death, ascending "to the House of Life; they (the *uthras* [angels]) washed him in the [heavenly] Jordan and protected him. They washed him and protected him in the Jordan; they placed their right hand on him. They baptized him with their baptism."[18] The Irish *Death of Adam* 40–41 also has the angels immersing the soul of Adam in the stream before bringing it to God.[19] The Armenian *Penitence of Adam* 42 has Adam baptized in the Jordan River only after the resurrection.[20]

The Sacred Lake or River

The *Gospel of Bartholomew* informs us that when Siôphanes, son of the apostle Thomas, died, his soul was taken by Michael, who washed him three times in the Acherusian lake.[21] This lake plays a similar role in other pseudepigraphic works.[22] In *Apocalypse of Moses* 37:3–6,[23] we read that when Adam died, a seraph carried him off to the Lake of Acheron and washed him three times in the presence of God and then conducted him to the third heaven.

A similar idea is found in the fifth-century *Apocalypse of Peter*, known from both an Ethiopic text and a fifth-century Greek text in the Bodleian Library. A portion of the Greek version was also found at Akhmim and is now called the Gizeh Manuscript. Though the latter breaks off before the others, the original text reads of the judgment day, when men are brought before God and receive a baptism in the "field of Akrosja."[24]

Apparently deriving directly from the *Apocalypse of Peter* is the *Apocalypse of Paul*, of which Coptic, Syriac, Ethiopic, and Latin versions exist. In the story, Paul is taken by an angel and shown a lake situated before the heavenly city:

> And I said unto the angel: What is this? and he said unto me: This is the lake Acherusa where is the city of Christ: but not every man is suffered to enter into that city: for this is the way that leadeth unto God, and if any be a fornicator or ungodly, and turn and repent and bear fruits meet for repentance, first when he cometh out of the body he is brought and worshippeth God, and then by the commandment of the Lord he is delivered unto Michael the angel, and he washeth him in the lake Acherusa and so bringeth him into the city of Christ with them that have done no sin.[25]

In some pseudepigraphic works, a river of heavenly fire replaces the lake. Thus, in *Chronicles of Jerahmeel* 52:7, Moses saw a river of fire during his heavenly vision. The river of fire issuing from beneath a throne is described in Daniel 7:10 and *1 Enoch* 14:18–20. In Revelation 22:1–2, it is a crystalline river of water that flows from beneath the throne, similar to the fountain of righteousness at the throne in *1 Enoch* 48:1–2. Heavenly rivers of fire are also mentioned in *1 Enoch* 17:4–6; 71:2; and *3 Enoch* 22B:3–4; 33:3–5; 36:1–2; 37:1–2; 42:6–7; 47:1–2. Abraham also saw fire in his heavenly vision (see *Apocalypse of Abraham* 17:1; 18:1–8, 12–13). An encomium on John the Baptist, falsely attributed to St. Chrysostom, cites an apocalypse by James, the brother of Christ, in which the Savior tells the apostles that John the Baptist lives in the third heaven and ferries those who honor him on earth across a river of fire in a golden boat.[26] The mention of John the Baptist would relate the river of fire to the ordinance of baptism.

In *1 Enoch* 14:19–23, we read that streams of fire come out from beneath the throne of God while flaming fire surrounds him, making it impossible for mortals and all but the highest rank of angels to approach. Montague R. James noted that an old Latin homily on the ten virgins says that the river of fire, according to the *Apocalypse of Peter,* keeps the ungodly out of the kingdom of God.[27] Similar ideas are found in various pseudepigraphic works. Enoch saw that sinners who denied the Lord were dragged off, unable to remain in the presence of God "because of the plague which proceeds forth from the Lord of the Spirits" (*1 Enoch* 41:2).[28] Isaac reportedly saw the river of fire which, he noted, allowed the righteous to pass but burned the wicked; he also saw angels of fire who punished the wicked in the depths of the river (see *Testament of Isaac* 5:21–29). The Ethiopic text of *Apocalypse of Peter* similarly notes that, after floods of fire have been let loose on the wicked and destroy the earth, men appear before the judgment throne and enter into a river of fire, where the righteous survive but the wicked are tormented by angels, go into darkness, and are punished eternally in fire.

The story is paralleled by the second book of the *Sibylline Oracles,* in which we read that a river of fire will flow from heaven to destroy the earth (see *Sibylline Oracles* 2:196–213), after which comes the resurrection, when all men will pass through a river of fire where the righteous are saved but the wicked suffer (see *Sibylline Oracles* 2:252–86; in the Greek version of *3 Baruch* 2:1, we read that no one is able to cross the heavenly river). Angels remove the wicked for punishment (see *Sibylline Oracles* 2:286–308) and then remove the righteous from the fiery river and reward them by placing them beside the Acherusian lake (see *Sibylline Oracles* 2:313–18, 330–38). This idea may be behind both the statement in Sirach (Wisdom of Ben Sira) 15:16–17 that the Lord places fire and water, life and death before man, and the declaration in Genesis 14:35 JST that "the sons of God should be tried so as by fire." (In the Book of Mormon, compare 2 Nephi 30:10: "the wicked will he destroy; and he will spare his people, yea, even if it so be that he must destroy the wicked by fire.") In one of the Nag Hammadi texts, angels descend to rescue the righteous from the fire sent to destroy the earth and bring them to heaven (see *Apocalypse of Adam* V, 5, 75.9–76.6).[29] Compare Zechariah 3:2, where the high priest Joshua is termed "a brand plucked out of the fire."

Similar imagery is found in the medieval Jewish text known as *Sepher ha-Razim,* which speaks of troops of angels who "immerse themselves in rivers of purity. And wrap themselves in garments of white fire."[30] Another medieval Jewish text, the *Zohar,* frequently refers to the fiery stream of Daniel 7:10 in similar terms. Thus, *Zohar* Exodus 210a, speaking of "the heavenly dew," says, "it is in that dew that the souls bathe and recuperate after their previous immersion in the *Nehar dinur* (river of fire) for purification."[31] *Zohar* Exodus 210b, speaking of "the soul that quits this dark world," says,

> the souls sit there by that river that flows out of Eden; they find rest there whilst clad in the ethereal garments. Without those garments they would not be able to endure the dazzling light around them; but protected by this covering they are in comfort and drink their fill of that radiance without being overwhelmed by it. It is the river which renders the souls fit and able to feast on and to enjoy that radiance.[32]

Zohar Exodus 211b indicates that

> The souls of men before ascending into Paradise are immersed in that "river of fire," where they are purged without being consumed. . . . Yet let it not be thought from this that the soul undergoes no penance. For, indeed, woe to the soul that has to endure a strange fire, although it thereby be purged and made white; and still

more, woe to the soul which is greatly defiled, for that soul will have to pass twice through the fire in order to come out pure and white. . . . A second ordeal has to be undergone by the soul on its passage from Lower Paradise to Upper Paradise; for whilst in Lower Paradise it is not yet entirely purged of the materialities of this world, so as to be fit to ascend on high. They thus pass it through that "river of fire" from which it emerges completely purified and so comes before the presence of the Sovereign of the universe beatified in every aspect.[33]

A similar statement is found in *Zohar* Numbers 159b: "The spirit has to be cleansed in the 'stream of fire' to receive its punishment, and then it enters the terrestrial Garden of Eden, and it is furnished with a robe of light resembling its appearance in this world."[34]

Zohar Exodus 239b says that the wood used for the fire on the altar represented "the 'fiery stream' *(n'har di-nur)*, the place where the 'unstable' (spirits) have to pass through the burning fire and be deprived of their power."[35] *Zohar* Leviticus 53a declares:

When a man is on the point of leaving this world, his soul suffers many chastisements along with his body before they separate. Nor does the soul actually leave him until the Shekinah shows herself to him, and then the soul goes out in joy and love to meet the Shekinah. If he is righteous, he cleaves and attaches himself to her. But if not, then the Shekinah departs, and the soul is left behind, mourning for its separation from the body, like a cat which is driven away from the fire. Afterwards both are punished by the hand of Dumah. The body is punished in the grave and the soul in the fire of Gehinnom for the appointed period. When this is completed, she rises from Gehinnom purified of her guilt like iron purified in the fire, and she is carried up to the lower Garden of Eden, where she is cleansed in the waters of Paradise and perfumed with its spices, and there she remains till the time comes for her to depart from the abode of the righteous. Then she is carried up stage after stage until she is brought near like a sacrifice to the altar . . . to the angelic Priest above.[36]

That baptism was intended by these passages is evidenced by *Zohar* Numbers 205a, which explains 1 Samuel 2:6 by saying, "As for the words 'He bringeth down to the grave and bringeth up,' this means that He takes that spirit of holiness down to Sheol and there baptizes it to purify it, after which it ascends to its rightful place in the Garden of Eden."[37]

In *Zohar* Numbers 220b, there is even a hint that others can help bring salvation to the dead:

A man who does not labour with his "might" in this world to bring it into "work and device and knowledge and wisdom," will eventually enter into Gehinnom, where there is no work nor device nor knowledge nor wisdom. For all men go down to Sheol, but they come up again at once, save those sinners who never harboured thoughts of repentance, and who go down and do not come up. Even the completely righteous go down there, but they only go down in order to bring up certain sinners from there, to wit, those who thought of repenting in this world, but were not able to do so in time before they departed from it. The righteous go down and bring these up.[38]

Coptic Baptism for the Dead

Among the ancient documents that mention baptism for the dead, a large preponderance were written in Coptic, the latest form of the Egyptian language.[39] Though no longer spoken, Coptic remains the liturgical language of the Coptic Church of Egypt. Though there is abundant textual evidence for this practice among early Christians in Egypt, some of my Coptic friends assure me that it is still practiced in the case of family members who die unbaptized. To date, I have found only one modern story of an Egyptian girl who was baptized by proxy after her death.[40]

It is likely that the Egyptians more readily accepted baptism for the dead because of earlier pagan practices prevalent in that country. Hugh Nibley noted that the Coptic pseudepigrapha is not only related to other early Christian literature but is also highly dependent on earlier Egyptian texts. Concerning baptism for the dead, for example, he gave many references to water purification in ancient Egypt, both for the living and the dead. Indeed, washing in water was essential to the resurrection from the dead in ancient Egypt, just as is baptism in the pseudepigraphic literature.[41]

With this in mind, we can suggest some of the factors that contributed to the ease with which the Christianized Egyptians accepted baptism for the dead:

1. The general Egyptian view of the dead was that they continued to live on in spirit form, hopeful of the resurrection of the body. Great care was therefore taken to preserve the body through embalming and incarcerating in rocky tombs.

2. There was great stress in ancient Egypt on the proper performance of rituals, in both the world of the living and the world of the dead. Even where the deceased had not lived a praiseworthy life, it was typical to ascribe to him righteousness and to deny any wrongdoing on his part. Lest his heart and other facets of his being betray him

to the gods sitting in judgment on his spirit, magic rituals and talismans were employed to ensure his safe passage into the worlds of glory.

3. Initiation, including water purification, was already extant in both earth life and the mortuary rituals preceding burial. This was readily identified with Christian baptism for both living and dead.

4. The great honor and respect shown toward one's ancestors in ancient Egypt was reflected in the building and maintenance of mortuary temples, where food and drink were brought for the spirit of the deceased and where rituals necessary for safe passage through the dangers of the afterlife were performed.[42] With such an attitude toward one's progenitors, it is little wonder that the Christianized Egyptians were happy to carry on the practice of proxy ordinances for those who had gone before.

To these, we could add that gnosticism was common to both the Marcionites and to the early Christians of Egypt. With its heavy dependence on initiatory ceremonies, there was bound to be an attempt on the part of the gnostic movement to impart these blessings to their honored dead.[43]

One of the most important Coptic documents for a study of baptism for the dead is the *Pistis Sophia,* a gnostic document thought to date to the second century A.D. In *Pistis Sophia* 146 we read that certain types of sinners, such as robbers, thieves, and arrogant persons, are saved by being chastised, and are then led to a body of water that becomes a seething fire to purify them. In the following chapter we find that the soul of an unbaptized righteous person is brought by angels to God, chastised, and then brought to the same body of water that becomes a seething, purifying fire, after which the individual inherits the light (*Pistis Sophia* 147).

An even more significant passage is found in *Pistis Sophia* 128, where we read that Mary asked the resurrected Christ,

> If a good man has fulfilled all the mysteries [ordinances], and he has a relative, in a word, he has a man and that man is an impious one who . . . has come forth from the body; and we have known of him . . . what should we do to him so that we save him from the punishments of the dragon of the outer darkness, so that he is returned to a righteous body which will find the mysteries of the Kingdom of the Light, and become good and go to the height, and inherit the Kingdom of the Light?

Jesus responded,

> If you want to return them from the punishments of the outer darkness and all the judgments, and return them to a righteous body which will find the mysteries of the light, and go to the height and inherit the Kingdom of the Light—perform the one mystery of the Ineffable which forgives sins at all times [i.e., baptism]. And when you have finished performing the mystery, say: "The soul of such and such a man on whom I think in my heart, . . . may it be taken to the presence of the Virgin of the Light; and may the Virgin of the Light seal it with the seal of the Ineffable, and cast it in that very month into a righteous body which will find the mysteries of the light in it, and become good, and go to the height and inherit the Kingdom of the Light. And furthermore, when it has completed the cycles of the changes, may that soul be taken to the presence of the seven virgins of the light which are in charge of the baptism. And may they place it (the baptism) upon that soul, and seal it with the sign of the Kingdom of the Ineffable, and may they take it to the ranks of the light."[44]

Christ then explained that if the person has not been completely faithful, the soul is turned over to Yew or Jeu, who proves him and then leads him to the seven virgins of the light for baptism and passage through the veil into the Treasury of the Light (see *Pistis Sophia* 130).

Baptism for the Dead in Ethiopic Documents

Christianity spread from Egypt into Ethiopia, where the Abyssinian church was founded. There has been much Egyptian influence in Ethiopia, including influence from pre-Christian Egyptian practices, especially those associated with rites performed for the dead.[45] It is therefore not surprising to see baptism for the dead mentioned in Ethiopic documents.

In the medieval *Book of the Mysteries of the Heavens and the Earth,* we find God sending the archangel Michael into Sheol (hell) to rescue a man taken there by demons. He searched three times, each time bringing out some of the wicked before finding the man he was seeking.

> And the number of those [souls] who through that man escaped from Sheol was five hundred and forty-six thousand. And some of these were heathen. And the angels said, "this thing is terrifying."
>
> And our Lord saith in the Gospel, "He who believeth and who is baptized shall be saved, but he who believeth not shall be damned" (Mark xvi. 16). How then was it possible for these [souls] to escape? And thee, O son of man, hast thou heard that some of the heathen have been saved? [No doubt thou hast], but they did not enter the Garden (Paradise) without being baptized, for Michael baptized them, and they shone with splendour like the son. And the Holy Abbâ (Father) marvelled, and said, "Amânûʾêl hath the power to do everything."[46]

The same text, after mentioning "the Prophets and the

sons of the Prophets, who have not found completely the baptism of life," speaks of the "two companies of prophets,"[47] evidently referring to those who are dead, in these terms:

> They ascend out of Sheol and they settle themselves to rest in the Tabernacle. Now this taketh place on Sabbath days. Similarly among Christians, there are some who have been (or, who are) sinners, and in whom there is little of the grape; these shall not be repulsed. [Those who have received] a little of the grape are those who have received the Faith, that is to say the seal of baptism. Such shall not be destroyed.[48]

In the first section of the Ethiopic *Lefafa Sedek* ("bandlet of righteousness"), Mary tells Christ she is afraid for her soul and those of her parents, siblings, and her ancestor David and then asks, "And now, tell me, O my Son, clearly and certainly, by what means these are to be saved from this devouring fire." Jesus then goes on to tell her about the magical text that can be written and buried with the dead.[49] In a later section, the text cites the *Prayer of the Virgin Mary on Behalf of the Apostle Matyas in Parthia* regarding a petition, "by means of it those who are fettered in the bonds of Satan, and are in captivity to him, shall be set free."[50]

Conclusions

Though most Christians stopped baptizing for the dead in the early centuries after Christ, documentary evidence makes it clear that the practice was known in various parts of the Mediterranean world and that it found ready acceptance in such areas as Egypt. The ordinance is especially attested in pseudepigraphic texts whose authorship is open to question; nevertheless, from their geographical distribution it seems that these documents were widely circulated among early Christian groups and therefore contain doctrines with which those Christians were familiar.

Notes

1. For earlier studies of baptism for the dead, see Hugh W. Nibley, "Baptism for the Dead in Ancient Times," *Improvement Era,* December 1948–April 1949, reprinted as chapter 4, "Baptism for the Dead in Ancient Times," in *Mormonism and Early Christianity* (Salt Lake City: Deseret Book and FARMS, 1987), 100–167; Hugh Nibley, *The Message of the Joseph Smith Papyri: An Egyptian Endowment* (Salt Lake City: Deseret Book, 1975), 93–96, 277, 282, 285–86; John A. Tvedtnes, "Baptism for the Dead: The Coptic Rationale," Special Papers of the Society for Early Historic Archaeology, no. 2, September 1989; and John A. Tvedtnes, "Proxy Baptism," *Ensign,* February 1977, 86.

2. *History of the Church,* 4:231.

3. In the Coptic Church, which still recognizes baptism for the dead, this is emphasized by the fact that during baptismal ceremonies *for the living,* a prayer is offered for the dead. See Cyrille Salib, trans., *La liturgie des sacrements du baptême et de la confirmation* (Cairo: El Kateb El-Arabi, 1968), 88–90.

4. For a recent study by a non-LDS scholar, see Richard E. Maris, "Corinthian Religion and Baptism for the Dead (1 Corinthians 15:29): Insights from Archaeology and Anthropology," *Journal of Biblical Literature* 114/4 (1995): 661–82.

5. For the canons and details, see J.-P. Migne, ed., *Dictionnaire universel et complet des conciles,* Première encyclopédie théologique, vol. 13 (Paris: Ateliers Catholiques, 1847), 1:477, and Charles J. Hefele, *A History of the Councils of the Church* (Edinburgh: Clark, 1896), 2:397–402.

6. A non-Christian group, the Mandaeans, also practices baptism for the dead. See the following, translated by E. S. Drower: *The Mandaeans of Iraq and Iran: Their Cults, Customs, Magic*

Legends, and Folklore (1937; reprint, Leiden: Brill, 1962), 44, 46, 90, 129–30, 132, 198, 214–22; *Diwan Abatur or Progress through the Purgatories* (Vatican: Biblioteca Apostolica Vaticana, 1950), 22; *The Canonical Prayerbook of the Mandaeans* (Leiden: Brill, 1959), 10; *A Pair of Naṣoraean Commentaries (Two Priestly Documents)* (Leiden: Brill, 1963), 39; *The Thousand and Twelve Questions* (Berlin: Akademie-Verlag, 1960), 13, 143, 150, 223–26, 262–64, 272; and *The Secret Adam: A Study of Naṣoraean Gnosis* (Oxford: Clarendon, 1960), 51, 73–75, 79, 94. The Mandaeans probably continue the practice because of their heavy reliance on repeated baptisms. They also perform other rites for the dead. One Mandaean text even notes that the fallen angels, after judgment has been pronounced on them, "shall be baptized in the Jordan of the powerful, first Life." Robert Haardt, *Gnosis: Character and Testimony,* trans. J. F. Hendry (Leiden: Brill, 1971), 396. A Syriac Orthodox priest recently told me that his church still recognizes baptism for the dead, but I have not yet received the promised documentation to support that claim.

7. Prayers for the dead are mentioned in Arnobius, *Against the Heathen* 4.36; *Apostolic Constitutions* 8.12, 41; and Tertullian, *On Monagamy* 10. For a translation of an Ethiopic prayer for the dead, see E. A. Wallis Budge, *The Bandlet of Righteousness: An Ethiopian Book of the Dead* (London: Luzac, 1929), 12. Budge adds that "in the same Anaphora, which is attributed to Saint Basil, a prayer is made on behalf of those who pray for the dead, and who make offerings to them" (ibid.).

8. *Catechetical Lectures* 23:10, trans. Edward H. Gifford, in *Nicene and Post-Nicene Fathers,* second series, ed. Philip Schaff and Henry Wace (1894; reprint, Peabody, Mass.: Hendrickson, 1995), 7:154–55. With such a philosophy, it is strange that Cyril did not make the transition to performing rites such as baptism for the dead, since, in Christianity, these too make available the atoning sacrifice of Christ.

9. This is precisely the point made by Paul in 1 Corinthians 15:29.

10. Christ's entry into the spirit prison was made possible by

the "keys of hell and of death," which he possessed (Revelation 1:18; compare 3:7).

11. The earliest mention of the *Shepherd of Hermas* (or *Pastor of Hermas*) is from the mid-second century A.D. Some early Christian fathers placed it on a par with other New Testament books.

12. Among these are Melito of Sardis (ca. 160–177), *Homily on the Passion,* and Tertullian (ca. 145–220), *A Treatise on the Soul* 55.1 am indebted to Matthew Roper for bringing some of these to my attention.

13. These were Justin Martyr (ca. 110–165), *Dialogue with Trypho* 72, and Irenaeus (ca. 120–202), *Against Heresies* 3:20; 4:22.

14. J. Rendel Harris, *The Odes and Psalms of Solomon* (Cambridge, England: Cambridge University Press, 1909), 123. Again, I am indebted to Matthew Roper for this reference.

15. *Epistle of the Apostles* 27, cited from Montague R. James, *The Apocryphal New Testament* (1924; reprint, Oxford: Clarendon, 1960), 494.

16. Author's translation from Louis Guerrier and Sylvain Grébaut, trans., *Le Testament en Galilée de Notre-Seigneur Jésus-Christ* (Paris: Firmin-Didot, 1912), *Patrologia Orientalis,* 9:209–10. In another Ethiopic text, Christ descends into Sheol and brings out his chosen ones, sending them to the garden (paradise) under the leadership of Demas, one of the thieves crucified with him. They are stopped at the gates by the seraphim and cherubim, who do not allow them passage until Demas showed them the writing Christ had given him, written in Christ's own blood. See E. A. Wallis Budge, *The Book of the Mysteries of the Heavens and the Earth and Other Works of Bakhayla Mîkâ'êl (Zôsîmâs)* (Oxford: Oxford University Press, 1935), 135–37.

17. In one of the Chenoboskion documents (Coptic gnostic books found in an earthen jar in Egypt in 1945), *The Apocryphon of John,* the "celestial power" (the gnostic Celestial Mother, rather than Jesus) describes her descent into hell, saying that on her third descent, she awoke Adam and sealed him with light and water so death could no longer have power over him (see *The Apocryphon of John* 30:32–31:25).

18. Werner Foerster, *Gnosis: A Selection of Gnostic Texts,* trans. R. McL. Wilson (Oxford: Clarendon, 1974), 2:259.

19. See Máire Herbert and Martin McNamara, eds., *Irish Biblical Apocrypha* (Edinburgh: Clark, 1989), 15.

20. See Michael E. Stone, trans., *The Penitence of Adam* (Louvain: Catholic University, 1981), 11. My thanks to Matthew Roper for bringing the Irish and Armenian texts to my attention.

21. See E. A. Wallis Budge, ed., *Coptic Apocrypha in the Dialect of Upper Egypt,* Coptic Texts, vol. 3 (1913; reprint, New York: AMS, 1977), 207–8.

22. The lake is alluded to in the Ethiopic *Conflict of Adam and Eve* I, 1:2–3, in S. C. Malan, *The Book of Adam and Eve, Also Called the Conflict of Adam and Eve with Satan* (Edinburgh: Williams and Norgate, 1882), 1–2:

And to the north [of the garden] there is a sea of water, clear and pure to the taste, like unto nothing else; so that, through the clearness thereof, one may look into the depths of the earth. And when a man washes himself in it, he becomes clean of the cleanness thereof, and white of its whiteness—even if he were dark. And God created that sea of His own good pleasure, for He knew what would come of the man He should make; so that after he had left the garden, on account of his transgression, men should be born in the earth, from among whom righteous ones should die, whose souls God would raise at the last day; when they should return to their flesh; should bathe in the water of that sea, and all of them repent of [their] sins.

23. Called *The Life of Adam and Eve (Apocalypse)* in *The Old Testament Pseudepigrapha,* ed. James H. Charlesworth (New York: Doubleday, 1987), 2:259.

24. James, *The Apocryphal New Testament,* 518.

25. *Apocalypse of Paul* 22, in ibid., 537–38.

26. See James, *The Apocryphal New Testament,* 37.

27. See ibid., 507.

28. *1 Enoch*, trans. E. Isaac, in *The Old Testament Pseudepigrapha*, 1:32.

29. See James M. Robinson, ed., *The Nag Hammadi Library in English* (San Francisco: HarperCollins, 1990), 282.

30. Michael A. Morgan, trans., *Sepher ha-Razim, The Book of the Mysteries* (Chico, Calif.: Scholars Press, 1983), 83.

31. Maurice Simon and Paul P. Levertoff, trans., *The Zohar* (New York: Bennet, 1958), 4:214.

32. Ibid., 4:216.

33. Ibid., 4:218–20.

34. Maurice Simon and Harry Sperling, *The Zohar* (New York: Bennet, 1958), 5:226.

35. Simon and Levertoff, *The Zohar*, 4:315.

36. Simon and Sperling, *The Zohar*, 5:26.

37. Ibid., 5:304–5.

38. Ibid., 5:328–29.

39. Coptic means "Egyptian." The Coptic language was written using the Greek alphabet with the addition of several symbols from Egyptian demotic to represent sounds not present in Greek.

40. See S. H. Leeder, *Modern Sons of the Pharaohs: A Study of the Manners and Customs of the Copts of Egypt* (London: Hodder and Stoughton, 1918), 101.

41. See Nibley, *Message of the Joseph Smith Papyri*, 93–96. I reiterated the point in my "Baptism for the Dead: The Coptic Rationale."

42. These dangers, known from the Egyptian Book of the Dead literature, are also noted in Coptic texts dealing with the afterlife.

43. It might be worth further noting that proxy rituals are not unique in the worlds of ancient Egypt and early Christianity. Rites performed for one's ancestors are found throughout the world. Even in Islam, it is possible to perform the *hajj* by proxy, provided that the proxy has himself already made the pilgrimage in his own behalf. See Gaye Strathearn and Brian M. Hauglid, "The Great Mosque and Its Kaʿba as an Islamic Temple Complex

in Light of Lundquist's Typology of Ancient Near Eastern Temples," in this volume, page 290.

44. Violet MacDermot, trans., *Pistis Sophia*, ed. Carl Schmidt (Leiden: Brill, 1978), 322–24.

45. For a discussion and a sample text, see Budge, *Bandlet of Righteousness.*

46. Budge, *Book of the Mysteries of the Heavens and the Earth,* 23–24.

47. Ibid., 60, 61.

48. Ibid., 61.

49. Budge, *Bandlet of Righteousness,* 62.

50. Ibid., 99.

CHAPTER 4

TEMPLE PRAYER IN ANCIENT TIMES

John A. Tvedtnes

Ye that stand in the house of the Lord, in the courts
of the house of our God, Praise the Lord; for the Lord is
good: sing praises unto his name; for it is pleasant.
(Psalm 135:2–3)

Among its other functions, the ancient Israelite temple
was a place of prayer.[1] When Solomon dedicated the first
temple in Jerusalem nearly three millennia ago, he devoted
a large portion of his prayer to asking the Lord to hearken
to the prayers of those who would pray in or toward his
holy house (see 1 Kings 8:29–50; 2 Chronicles 6:20–40). For
this reason, Jews throughout the world still pray facing
Jerusalem,[2] while those living in Jerusalem face the Temple
Mount or go to the Western ("wailing") Wall, one of the few
remnants of the temple built by Herod on the site of
Solomon's earlier structure.

In his dedication of the temple, Solomon specified the
manner of devotion, for he spoke of the man who prays
while "spread[ing] forth his hands toward this house"
(1 Kings 8:38; compare 2 Chronicles 6:29). Indeed, Solomon
followed the same practice: "And Solomon stood before

the altar of the Lord in the presence of all the congregation of Israel, and spread forth his hands toward heaven" (1 Kings 8:22; compare 2 Chronicles 6:12). According to 2 Chronicles 6:13, he then "kneeled down upon his knees before all the congregation of Israel, and spread forth his hands toward heaven." "And it was so, that when Solomon had made an end of praying all this prayer and supplication unto the Lord, he arose from before the altar of the Lord, from kneeling on his knees with his hands spread up to heaven" (1 Kings 8:54).

Christianity is virtually unique in requiring that prayers be said in a kneeling position. Standing is the norm in many non-Christian religions.[3] Some religions, such as Islam[4] and Buddhism, require varying positions to be used during prayer, but standing is always included. In the pseudepigraphic *Conflict of Adam and Eve,* we frequently read that our first parents stood up to pray, usually spreading their hands to God.[5] The text sometimes notes that they spread their hands to God but does not always indicate whether they were standing.[6]

Although it is permissible to sit during prayers, standing for prayer is the norm in Judaism and is required during the *Amidah* ("standing") prayer.[7] In the story of the Pharisee and the publican told by Jesus in Luke 18:11–14, both men stand to pray. Standing prayer is also noted in 1 Chronicles 23:30. *Targum Neofiti* and *Targum Pseudo-Jonathan* on Exodus 14:15 and *Targum Pseudo-Jonathan* on Numbers 10:35–36 have Moses standing to pray to the Lord. *Targum Pseudo-Jonathan* on Exodus 38:8 speaks of women who stood praying at the entrance of the tabernacle. *Zohar* Exodus 183a notes that during the "high days" associated with the Feast of Weeks, a man "must pray or sing standing, his thighs taut, his feet firm, his body erect."[8]

Spreading the Hands

The spreading of hands in prayer is common among Muslims, Greek Orthodox, and other eastern Christian groups; such a custom is used by Catholic priests and some Protestant clergy during the prayers at communion. The raising of hands in prayer is mentioned in the Old Testament (see 1 Kings 8:22, 38, 54; Ezra 9:5; Job 11:13; Psalm 68:31; 143:6; Isaiah 1:15; and Lamentations 2:19; 3:41), the New Testament (see 1 Timothy 2:8), and various pseudepigraphic texts,[9] including Christian gnostic texts found at Nag Hammadi in Egypt.[10] The Mandaeans, who claim to be descendants of the disciples of John the Baptist, also spread their hands in prayer. *Mandaean Canonical Prayerbook* 35 contains the words, "I address to thee . . . for this congregation of people who have bent their knees to the ground and stretched forth their hands to the intermediate and upper *(worlds)*."[11]

In the Armenian *History of Abel and Cain the Sons of Adam* 11, we read that when Abel offered his firstborn lamb, it was "with outstretched hands [that] he prayed to the Lord."[12] In one Ethiopic document, Abraham stretches out his hands while offering prayer,[13] while in another Joseph does the same before he dies.[14] In the pseudepigraphic *Gospel of Bartholomew* 2:6–13, Mary stands with the apostles in prayer, spreads out her hands to heaven, and prays. The *History of the Virgin* 156a also has Mary spreading out her hands to pray for the apostles, who were then preaching in various nations.[15] In *Acts of the Holy Apostle and Evangelist John the Theologian*, John "stretched forth his hands, and prayed."[16]

The Bible recounts that when the priest Ezra assembled the Jews who had returned from Babylon to Jerusalem, he "blessed the Lord, the great God. And all the people answered, Amen, Amen, with lifting up their hands: and they bowed their heads, and worshipped the Lord with their faces to the ground" (Nehemiah 8:6). In the Book of Mormon, when Alma and Amulek spoke of "stretch[ing] forth our hands, and exercis[ing] the power of God which is in us," they evidently had reference to an intercessory prayer (see Alma 14:10–11).

Targum Neofiti and *Targum Pseudo-Jonathan* on Exodus 9:28–29 declare that when Moses prayed to God to remove the plague of hail from Egypt, he stretched out his hands before the Lord.[17] *Pirqe de Rabbi Eliezer* 44, speaking of the time of the Exodus, notes that "all the Israelites (were standing) outside (their tents); they had gone forth from their tents, and saw Moses kneeling on his knees, and they were kneeling on their knees. He fell on his face to the ground, and they fell on their faces to the ground. He spread out the palms of his hands towards the heavens, and they spread out their hands to heaven."[18] In *Bahir* 139, we read that "when among Israel there are people who are wise and know the mystery of the Glorious Name, and they lift up their hands, they are immediately answered."[19]

Targum Pseudo-Jonathan and *Targum Neofiti* on Exodus 17:11–12 indicate that when Moses held out his hands during the Israelite-Amalekite conflict, he was praying—a fact also noted in *Zohar* Exodus 66a, which adds, "from which we derive the lesson that, although the priest spreads out his hands at the sacrifice to make his mediation complete, yet Israel must co-operate with him in prayer."[20] Regarding this event, *Bahir* 135 says, "this teaches us that the whole world endures because of the Lifting of Hands."[21]

Prayer with outstretched hands was also known in the Jerusalem temple.[22] In *3 Maccabees* 2:1, 21, we read that the high priest, Simon, knelt before the temple with hands outstretched and prayed to God, his prayer being heard because he offered it according to the prescribed pattern. *Zohar* Leviticus 67a notes that before the high priest entered the holy of holies on the day of atonement, "he bathed himself and washed his hands in preparation for another service, in which he was to enter into a place more holy than all. The other priests, the Levites and the people stood around him in three rows and lifted their hands over him in prayer."[23] *Pirqe de Rabbi Eliezer* 8 ordains that for group prayer, the men should sit "in a circle . . . and (then) they stand and spread out their hands before their Father who is in heaven, and the chief of the assembly proclaims the name (of God)."[24] These actions are reminiscent of a prayer circle.

The Psalms, many of which are prayers, reflect the method of prayer in the temple. In one, the petitioner asks the Lord, "Hear the voice of my supplications, when I cry unto thee, when I lift up my hands toward thy holy oracle" (Psalm 28:2). Another Psalm declares, "I have seen thee in the sanctuary . . . , my lips shall praise thee. Thus will I bless thee while I live: I will lift up my hands in thy name" (Psalm 63:2–4; see Psalm 88:9). In Psalm 141:2, the lifting of hands in prayer is associated with temple sacrifice: "Let my prayer be set forth before thee as incense; and the lifting up of my hands as the evening sacrifice."[25] This lifting of the hands in prayer is reflected in a variant of Psalm 135, cited at the beginning of this article, which immediately precedes it in the psalter: "Behold, bless ye the Lord, all ye servants of the Lord, which by night stand in the house of the Lord. Lift up your hands in the sanctuary, and bless the Lord" (Psalm 134:1–2).

A nonbiblical psalm found in a Dead Sea Scroll psaltery (11QPs[a], also called 11Q5) contains a prayer also known from late Syriac psalteries (e.g., 5ApocSyrPs3) as Psalm 155 and attributed to Hezekiah, king of Judah, during the time of the Assyrian siege of Jerusalem in 701 B.C. It reads, "YHWH [Jehovah], I call to you, listen to me; I extend my hands to your holy dwelling; bend your ear and grant my plea, and my entreaty, do not reject it."[26]

Clean Hands and a Pure Heart

There is symbolism in raising the hands in prayer. The gesture exposes to God both the breast and the palms of the petitioner to show that they are pure (clean). This is reflected in one of the temple hymns found in the Bible, Psalm 24, which Donald W. Parry has suggested may relate to a prayer circle:[27]

> Who shall ascend into the hill of the Lord? or who shall stand in his holy place? He that hath clean hands, and a pure heart; who hath not lifted up his soul unto vanity, nor sworn deceitfully. (Psalm 24:3–4)

The message of the Psalm is clear: In order to enter into the temple (the "hill of the Lord," called "the mountain of the Lord's house" in Isaiah 2:2), one must have clean hands and a pure heart.[28] In other words, both acts (represented by the hands) and thoughts (represented by the heart) must reflect righteousness, along with the lips that utter the prayer.[29] This is probably what the author of Job had in mind when he wrote, "prepare thine heart, and stretch out thine hands toward him" (Job 11:13). Note also Lamentations 3:41, "Let us lift up our heart with our hands unto God in the heavens."

The Crucified Lord

In early Christian lore, the spreading of the hands symbolized Christ. Thus, *Ode of Solomon* 27 reads, "I extended my hands and hallowed my Lord; for the expansion of my hands is his sign. And my extension is the upright cross."[30] Another of the odes declares, "I extended my hands and approached my Lord, because the stretching out of my hands is his sign. And my extension is the common cross, that was lifted up on the way of the Righteous One."[31]

Early Christians apparently saw in the manner of prayer a representation of the cross on which Christ was crucified.[32] The cross is, in early traditions, the tree of life, bringing us back into the presence of God through the Savior's atonement (see *Epistle of Barnabas* 11:1–11). *Epistle of Barnabas* 11:1–6 sees the cross and Christ's crucifixion prefigured by the tree of life, while *Epistle of Barnabas* 12:2–3 says it was represented by Moses raising his hands to provide salvation to Israel during their struggle with the Amalekites (see Exodus 17:8–13) and by Isaiah stretching out his hands to his people to call them to repentance (see Isaiah 65:2, cited in Romans 10:21). Both the sixth-century A.D. Ethiopic document *Kebra Nagast* 98[33] and *Sibylline Oracles* 8:251–53 indicate that Christ's crucifixion was symbolized by Moses stretching out his hands during the Amalekite war. Two of the earliest Christian writers, Justin Martyr (see *Dialogue with Trypho* 111) and Tertullian (see *Against Marcion* 3.18), indicated that Moses' actions were a prayer and that he prefigured the cross.

The Priestly Blessing

We have already noted examples of priests spreading their hands in prayer at the temple in Jerusalem. In Christ's time, when pronouncing the priestly blessing of Numbers 6:24–26 on the people, the priests also lifted their hands.[34] The practice is based on Leviticus 9:22, where we read, "And Aaron lifted up his hand toward the people, and blessed them" (Leviticus 9:22).[35] *Targum Neofiti*, in citing this passage, notes that Aaron lifted his hands (plural) in prayer. The biblical passage is cited in Mishnah *Tamid* 7:2, where it is noted that in the temple the priests raised their hands above the head, while in other places they were allowed to raise the hands only to shoulder height during the blessing.[36]

Today, the priestly blessing is recited in Jewish congregations on the eve of the Day of Atonement. Of the blessing, we read in *Targum Pseudo-Jonathan* on Numbers 6:23, "Thus shall you bless the Israelites while they (the priests) spread their hands upon the pulpit."[37] Ecclesiasticus 50:20 describes the high priest Simon, saying that he "lifted up his hands over the whole congregation of the children of Israel, to give the blessing of the Lord with his lips" (KJV Apocrypha). Philo wrote in *De Abrahamo* 235 that when Melchizedek blessed Abraham (see Genesis 14:18–20), "the great high priest . . . raised his hands to heaven."[38]

Theodor Reik, recalling an experience from his childhood, noted that "the priest pulls the prayer shawl over his head so that his face is concealed; he raises both hands, blessing the community with fingers spread."[39] Of the hand gesture, he wrote, "the third and the fourth fingers of the hand must be held together and be held separately from the other fingers."[40] Known as the Aaronic sign,[41] it can be seen in Jewish cemeteries engraved on the headstones of *kohanim*, "priests," descendants of Aaron. Reik notes that his friend, Karl Abraham, believed that the spread fingers represented the cloven hoof of the clean animals that Israel was permitted to eat, as described in Leviticus 11:3–8.[42]

Reik and Abraham also saw the prayer shawl, or *tallith*, worn by Jews during certain prayers,[43] as a representation of the sacrificial ram. Though often made of silk, the prayer shawl is ideally made of sheep's wool, and some worshipers prefer the wool of lambs raised in the Holy Land. The rectangular shawl has tassels *(zizzith)* attached to each corner,[44] each tassel consisting of four white and four blue threads and bound together by knots formed by the longest thread.[45] Reik suggests that "the tallith, made from the wool of a ritually clean animal, might be the substitute for the fleece of a ram, originally roughly cured and worn by the Hebraic tribes. The zizzith would then allude to the animal's four legs, and the knotting of the many threads would represent the joints,"[46] to which I would add that the blue threads may have originally represented the veins running through the legs.

Reik concludes that wearing the *tallith,* a garment sacred to the Jews, was originally intended to identify the wearer with the God of Israel.[47] To the Christian—and to Latter-day Saints in particular—this would suggest that the wearer "put on Christ" (Galatians 3:27; compare Romans 13:14), thus representing "the Lamb of God, which taketh away the sin of the world" (John 1:29).[48] When, therefore, the priests wore the prayer shawl and raised their arms to bless the people, they unknowingly symbolized the Messiah to come.

The Prayer Circle

One further stipulation regarding the priestly blessing is that the priests were not allowed to raise their hands unless ten adult males were present (see M *Megillah* 4:3).[49] The ten constitute the minimum number required in Jewish law to form a *minyan,* or quorum for group prayers. These prayers are typically offered while the group stands in a circle, which is hence often termed a *minyan.*

The prayer circle is also known from early Christian texts and has been discussed at length elsewhere.[50] One of the most remarkable descriptions is in the fourth book of the Coptic *Pistis Sophia,* where we find Jesus standing at the altar praying, surrounded by his apostles and women disciples clad in linen garments (see *Pistis Sophia* 136). A short while later, Jesus sets out an offering of wine, water, and bread. He then stands before the offering, with the disciples behind him clad in linen garments and making signs with their hands as Christ prays (see *Pistis Sophia* 142). The account of this offering is also found in another Coptic document, *2 Jeu* 45–47. The scene is followed by Jesus' instructions on how the disciples can use the signs and names to pass beyond both gods and angels to enter the presence of the Father (see *2 Jeu* 48–50). In *1 Jeu* 41, Jesus has the twelve surround him while he prays and they repeat after him. In *2 Jeu* 42–43, Jesus asks that the twelve and the women disciples surround him so he can teach them the mysteries of God. What then follows in the text is a discussion of signs, seals, and how to pass by the guardians at the veils to the presence of God. Hugh Nibley noted

> how the bishop leading the prayer circle in the Syriac Testament of Our Lord "stands with upraised hands and offers a prayer at the veil," after which he proceeds "to make the sacrifice, the veil of the gate being drawn aside." St. Augustine's version of the Priscillian prayer circle ends with the apparently incongruous statement, "I am the Gate for whoever knocks on me," which Augustine explains in terms of Psalms 24:7, referring to the veil of the temple [*Letters* 237].[51]

Prayer Opens the Veil

Anciently, a veil or curtain separated the holy of holies from the rest of the tabernacle or temple (see, for example,

Exodus 26:31–33; 2 Chronicles 3:14; and Hebrews 9:3, 5). The Lord instructed Moses that the high priest should not pass through the veil until he had been washed, dressed in priestly clothing, and brought a sacrifice (see Leviticus 16:2–4).

The earthly veil is paralleled by the veil of the heavenly temple mentioned in many early Jewish and Christian texts. When the brother of Jared prayed, "the veil was taken from off the eyes of the brother of Jared, and he saw the finger of the Lord" (Ether 3:6; see Ether 3:1–6). The same thing has happened in modern times. Joseph Smith recorded that after dropping the veils of the Kirtland Temple around the pulpit (see the preface to D&C 110) on 3 April 1836, he and Oliver Cowdery offered prayer and "the veil was taken from our minds, and the eyes of our understanding were opened. We saw the Lord" (D&C 110:1–2). Significantly, it is only after prayer that the veil is uncovered. This is symbolic of the uncovering of the heavenly veil, which also occurs after prayers.

According to 1 Enoch 9:10, prayers go to the gate of heaven. In 3 Baruch 11:1–9, we also learn that the gates of heaven are opened to receive prayers, an idea confirmed in Testament of Adam 1:10. A prayer in Sepher Raziʾel 441 asks God to open "the gates of light and prayer."[52] Rabbi Ishmael reported that it was only after prayer that he was ushered by an angel into the presence of God (see 3 Enoch 1:1–6).

The symbolism of the veil extends to women during temple prayer. Paul wrote that the woman's head should be covered during prayer (see 1 Corinthians 11:4–7, 13–15), which led to the practice of women covering their heads in the Catholic and Eastern churches (traditionally with a veil), though the practice is also known in orthodox Judaism.

We noted earlier that ancient temple prayer was symbolic of the crucified Christ. It is in this light that we must understand some of the teachings found in the Epistle to the Hebrews. In Hebrews 10:19–20 we read that the veil is the flesh of Jesus, who went ahead as a forerunner for us. The veil, then, is mortality, or our present carnal state. Jesus submitted the flesh to the will of the spirit and was thus able to pass beyond the carnal or earthly state into the celestial, where he now stands as the eternal high priest of the church and as our advocate with the Father. Having entered through the veil into the heavenly holy of holies, Christ desires that we, too, should pass by the veil into the presence of God. Hebrews 6:19–20 speaks of the "hope [which] we have as an anchor of the soul, both sure and stedfast, and which entereth into that within the veil; Whither the forerunner is for us entered, even Jesus, made an high priest for ever after the order of Melchisedec."

Prayer is also tied to the opening of the heavenly door in the Sermon on the Mount, in which Jesus admonished, "Ask, and it shall be given you; seek, and ye shall find; knock, and it shall be opened unto you: For every one that asketh receiveth; and he that seeketh findeth; and to him that knocketh it shall be opened" (Matthew 7:7–8).[53]

Conclusions

From the preceding discussion, we can see that ancient temple prayer was a symbol of Christ. From the wearing of the *tallith* (symbolizing the Lamb of God) to the raised arms with spread fingers (symbolizing the crucified Christ and, in Judaism, the cloven hoof of the sacrificial lamb) to the veil that opens when prayers are uttered, everything points to the Savior. It is altogether fitting, therefore, that we are commanded to pray to the Father in the name of Christ (see 2 Nephi 32:9; 3 Nephi 20:31).[54]

Notes

1. In Doctrine and Covenants 88:119 and 109:8, the Lord calls the temple a "house of prayer" (compare D&C 59:9; 88:137). Indeed, prayer is one of the more important activities performed in today's temples.

2. See M *Berakhot* 4:4–6.

3. The Jews prostrate themselves in prayer on the Day of Atonement, or Yom Kippur. In *3 Maccabees* 1:16, we have an example of the priests, dressed in their sacred vestments, prostrating themselves to ask God for help.

4. Koran 22:27 requires alternate standing, bowing, and prostration during prayer. Abū Jaʿfar Muḥammad b. Jarīr al-Ṭabarī (A.D. 839–923), in his *Taʾrīkh al-rusul waʾl-mulūk*, noted that when Abraham delivered his wife to "the tyrant" (either Pharaoh or Abimelech), he "stood up to pray." William M. Brinner, trans., *The History of al-Ṭabarī*, Prophets and Patriarchs, vol. 2 (Albany: State University of New York Press, 1987), 63.

5. See *Conflict of Adam and Eve* I, 5:1, 4; 23:4; 26:18–19; 27:8; 28:3; 32:7–8; 33:2; 34:3; 39:4; 41:8; 45:1; 47:6; 48:14; 50:1, 3; 52:3, 11; 54:1; 58:1, 3, 5; 61:13, 16; 63:6; 64:3, 8; 65:1; 66:2, 6; 68:10, 18; 69:2, 10; 71:6; 72:13, 15, 19–20; 73:6; and 77:4. Adam's immediate family also prayed in this manner (see *Conflict of Adam and Eve* II, 6:10; 9:8; 11:3; 18:12), as did their descendants (see *Conflict of Adam and Eve* II, 17:3, 43; *Conflict of Adam and Eve* III, 5:18; 7:15; 19:2, 8; 20:3; 21:5; and *Conflict of Adam and Eve* IV, 11:11).

6. See *Conflict of Adam and Eve* I, 26:5; 28:3; and 58:1. For the same practice among Adam's immediate family, see *Conflict of Adam and Eve* II, 17:43.

7. The exception is Yom Kippur, when one is expected to prostrate oneself on the ground.

8. Maurice Simon and Paul P. Levertoff, trans., *The Zohar* (New York: Bennet, 1958), 4:119.

9. See *Testament of Moses* 4:1; *Joseph and Aseneth* 11:15, 19.

10. See *Exegesis on the Soul*, II, 6, 136; *Second Apocalypse of James*, V, 4, 62.

11. Elisabeth S. Drower, trans., *The Canonical Prayerbook of the Mandaeans* (Leiden: Brill, 1959), 34.

12. W. Lowndes Lipscomb, *The Armenian Apocryphal Adam Literature* (West Philadelphia, Pa.: University of Pennsylvania, 1990), 160; compare 271.

13. See chapter 13 of *Kebra Negast* ("The Glory of Kings" of Ethiopia), in E. A. Wallis Budge, *The Queen of Sheba and Her Only Son Menyelek* (London: Medici Society, 1922), 10.

14. See Book II ("The Death of Joseph") of *Zênâhu La-Yosêf*, a manuscript from the Dabra Bizon monastery, cited in E. Isaac, "The Ethiopic *History of Joseph:* Translation with Introduction and Notes," *Journal for the Study of the Pseudepigrapha* 6 (April 1990): 112.

15. The text is cited in Ernest A. Wallis Budge, *The Book of the Bee* (Oxford: Clarendon, 1886), 98 n. 1.

16. Alexander Roberts and James Donaldson, eds., *Ante-Nicene Fathers* (1886; reprint, Peabody, Mass.: Hendrickson, 1995), 8:563.

17. See Martin McNamara, trans., *Targum Neofiti 1: Exodus,* and Michael Maher, trans., *Targum Pseudo-Jonathan: Exodus,* The Aramaic Bible, vol. 2 (Collegeville, Minn.: Liturgical Press, 1994), 40, 184.

18. Gerald Friedlander, trans., *Pirḳê de Rabbi Eliezer* (New York: Hermon, 1965), 347.

19. Aryeh Kaplan, trans., *The Bahir* (York Beach, Maine: Weiser, 1979), 52.

20. Harry Sperling, Maurice Simon, and Paul P. Levertoff, trans., *The Zohar* (New York: Bennet, 1958), 3:206–7.

21. Kaplan, *The Bahir,* 49.

22. *Zohar* Genesis 65a quotes Rabbi Simeon as saying, "When praying, I raise my hand on high; . . . my mind is concentrated on the highest." Harry Sperling and Maurice Simon, trans., *The Zohar* (New York: Bennet, 1958), 1:212. In *Zohar* Genesis 94b, we read that Rabbi Abba "lifted up his hands and blessed them [some who studied the Torah]" (ibid., 1:310). *Zohar* Exodus 9a says that "R. Simeon then lifted up his hands in prayer to the

Holy One" (ibid., 3:26). *Zohar* Exodus 57a notes that "when a man raises up his hand in prayer, his purpose is to bless God" (ibid., 3:177). *Zohar* Exodus 67a–b speaks of spreading the hands and lifting them to heaven in prayer and blessing. *Zohar* Deuteronomy 260a says that he who "offers his prayer before his Master . . . must stand like the heavenly angels, who are also called 'those who stand.'" Maurice Simon and Harry Sperling, trans., *The Zohar* (New York: Bennet, 1958), 5:342. That standing is ordinary for prayer is also noted in *Zohar* Deuteronomy 260b (ibid., 5:342–43).

23. Simon and Sperling, *The Zohar*, 5:60.

24. Friedlander, *Pirḳê de Rabbi Eliezer*, 58.

25. In the Keret text from Ugarit (KTU 1.14.II.22–24), lifting the hands to heaven parallels the offering of sacrifice. In his celestial vision, John saw the prayers of the saints rise before God from the hands of an angel, along with the incense he offered (Revelation 8:3–4). He also wrote of the odors from the vials held by the four beasts and the twenty-four elders being "the prayers of the saints" (Revelation 5:8; the idea corresponds to Psalm 141:2, "Let my prayer be set before thee as incense"). In *3 Baruch* 14:2, Michael brings the prayers of men to God as an offering (compare 12:8). Michael offers sacrifice in the heavenly temple in the fourth of seven heavens, according to TB *Ḥagigah* 12b (compare *Seder Rabba de-Bereshit* 24; *Hadar*, Leviticus 9:2), while in other Jewish traditions, it is the angel Metatron who ministers as high priest in the heavenly tabernacle (*Midrash Rabbah Numbers* 12:12).

26. Florentino García Martínez, trans., *The Dead Sea Scrolls Translated* (Leiden: Brill, 1996), 308.

27. See Donald W. Parry, "Temple Worship and a Possible Reference to a Prayer Circle in Psalm 24," *BYU Studies* 32/4 (1992): 57–62.

28. Compare Doctrine and Covenants 88:74: "purify your hearts, and cleanse your hands and your feet before me, that I may make you clean." Doctrine and Covenants 88 contains many temple elements. Also note one of Jesus' beatitudes, "Blessed are

the pure in heart: for they shall see God" (Matthew 5:8), which reminds us that, in ancient Israel, God frequently appeared to the prophets in his temple. Returning to Psalm 24, we note that verse 6 speaks of those who seek the face of the Lord.

29. The Book of Mormon teaches that God will judge us on the basis of our actions, our words, and our thoughts (see Mosiah 4:30; Alma 12:14; compare D&C 18:38; 88:109; 137:8–9; Isaiah 55:7; Matthew 12:36–37; 15:19; Mark 7:21; Acts 8:22). According to *2 Enoch* (J) 71:10, one can sin before God by word and thought, while in *3 Enoch* 45:1, we read that the deeds and thoughts of all mankind are written on the curtain that hangs before God. The *Testaments of the Twelve Patriarchs* indicate that we should love in deeds and thoughts, in the heart (see *Testament of Gad* 6:1, 3; 7:7; compare *Testament of Joseph* 4:6).

30. James H. Charlesworth, ed., *The Old Testament Pseudepigrapha* (Garden City, N.Y.: Doubleday, 1985), 2:759.

31. Ibid., 2:770.

32. See D. Plooij, "The Attitude of the Outspread Hands ('Orante') in Early Christian Literature and Art," *Expository Times* 23 (1912): 265–69, cited in John W. Welch, *Illuminating the Sermon at the Temple and Sermon on the Mount* (Provo, Utah: FARMS, 1999), 94–95.

33. See Budge, *The Queen of Sheba*, 181–82.

34. See M *Berakhot* 5:4; *Megillah* 4:3, 5–7; TB *Taʾanit* 26a–b; *Targum Pseudo-Jonathan* on Genesis 12:3. The spreading of the hands in priestly blessing is also noted in *Zohar* Exodus 232b, Leviticus 35a, and Numbers 147b. *Bahir* 123–24 and 138 discuss the raising of the priest's hands during blessing, saying that the ten fingers represent the Ten *Sefirot* and the Ten Commandments.

35. Before Jesus ascended to heaven, "he lifted up his hands, and blessed" his apostles (Luke 24:49–51). The lifting of hands by the rabbis when blessing people is noted in *Zohar* Numbers 186a. In his new year greeting of 1 January 1901, President Lorenzo Snow declared, "I lift my hands and invoke the blessing of heaven upon the inhabitants of the earth." James R. Clark, ed., *Messages of the First Presidency* (Salt Lake City: Bookcraft, 1966),

3:335. The lifting of hands to heaven in blessing was a feature of the Kirtland and Nauvoo Temples (see *History of the Church,* 2:386–87; compare *History of the Church,* 3:352; 4:557; 5:333; 7:271). In the revelation commanding the construction of the Kirtland Temple, the Lord told the Saints to "establish a house, even a house of prayer, a house of fasting, a house of faith, a house of learning, a house of glory, a house of order, a house of God; that your incomings may be in the name of the Lord; that your out-goings may be in the name of the Lord; that all your salutations may be in the name of the Lord, with uplifted hands unto the Most High" (D&C 88:119–20). He further commanded that the formal greeting in the school of the prophets be made "with up-lifted hands to heaven" (D&C 88:132, 135). Formerly, in the church, hands were raised during the blessing of the sacrament; the right hand is still raised when reciting the baptismal prayer.

36. The *Zohar,* describing the practice following the destruc-tion of the Jerusalem temple, notes that when the priests spread their hands to bless the people, the right hand is held higher than the left (see *Zohar* Exodus 225a; *Zohar* Numbers 146a). *Zohar* Numbers 195b notes the following statement by Rabbi Eleazar: "I lift up my hand in prayer before the Holy King, for we have learnt that it is forbidden for a man to raise his hand above him save in prayer and blessing and supplication, since the fingers of man have an important significance—and so I do now, and say that if any man shall arrange his service thus before his Master and sincerely carry out this purpose, his prayer shall not return unanswered. At first he must make himself a servant to arrange a service of praise and song before Him. Again he becomes a ser-vant to recite the standing-up prayer, and once more after saying his prayer." Simon and Sperling, *The Zohar,* 5:279.

37. Ernest G. Clarke, trans., *Targum Pseudo-Jonathan: Numbers,* The Aramaic Bible, vol. 4 (Collegeville, Minn.: Liturgical Press, 1995), 205.

38. C. D. Yonge, *The Works of Philo* (Peabody, Mass.: Hendrick-son, 1993), 431.

39. Theodor Reik, *Pagan Rites in Judaism* (New York City:

Farrar, Straus, 1964), 154. The spreading of the priest's fingers during the blessing is noted in *Zohar* Numbers 186b. Reik noted that he had disobeyed the injunction to refrain from looking at the priests during the blessing. The prohibition against looking at the priests' fingers during the blessing is noted in TB Ḥagigah 16a and in the *Zohar* (Exodus 66b, Leviticus 84a, Numbers 147a).

40. Reik, *Pagan Rites in Judaism*, 155. *Zohar* Genesis 87a, referring to the blessing of Abraham by Melchizedek, adds, "After this model it behoves [*sic*] the priest on earth to intertwine his fingers when blessing in the synagogue in order that he may be linked with the Right and that the two worlds may be linked together." Sperling and Simon, *The Zohar*, 1:290.

41. See Reik, *Pagan Rites in Judaism*, 155.

42. See "The Day of Atonement," in Karl Abraham, *Selected Papers* (London: Hogarth, 1955), 145, cited in Reik, *Pagan Rites in Judaism*, 155–56.

43. For a brief discussion and illustration of the *tallith*, see John A. Tvedtnes, "Priestly Clothing in Bible Times," in *Temples of the Ancient World: Ritual and Symbolism*, ed. Donald W. Parry (Salt Lake City: Deseret Book and FARMS, 1994), 659–60.

44. These are the "fringes" mentioned in Numbers 15:37–39 and Deuteronomy 22:12 and the "hem" of the garment mentioned in Matthew 9:20, 36.

45. See Reik, *Pagan Rites in Judaism*, 110–11.

46. Ibid., 141.

47. See ibid., 141–51.

48. Compare John 1:36; 1 Nephi 10:10; 11:21, 27, 31–32; 12:6, 10–11, 18; 13:24, 28–29, 33–34, 38, 40–41; 14:1–3, 6–7, 10, 12–14, 25; 2 Nephi 31:4–6; 33:14; Alma 7:14; Mormon 9:2–3; and D&C 88:106. In the early Christian document known as the *Shepherd of Hermas*, those who take upon themselves the name of Christ are also expected to take upon them certain virtues, which are represented by articles of clothing. See the discussion in Tvedtnes, "Priestly Clothing in Bible Times," 672–75. In *1 Jeu* 4, an early Coptic document from Egypt, Christ tells his apostles that those

who bear his good qualities and his garment without understanding blaspheme his name.

49. The text does not specify that these must be adult males, but that is the intent of the passage. The number ten is based on the fact that God told Abraham that he would not destroy Sodom and Gomorrah if he found ten righteous persons therein (Genesis 18:32). One of the Dead Sea Scrolls, the *Manual of Discipline*, requires that wherever there are ten men of the community, there should also be a priest to bless the wine and bread and a man to interpret the law (1QS 6.3–6). In orthodox Judaism, all males who have received their bar mitzvah initiation (usually at age 13) qualify for the count.

50. For ancient Christian prayer circles, see Hugh W. Nibley, "The Early Christian Prayer Circle," *BYU Studies* 19/1 (1978): 41–78, reprinted as chapter 3 in Hugh W. Nibley, *Mormonism and Early Christianity* (Salt Lake City: Deseret Book and FARMS, 1987), 45–99; and Hugh W. Nibley, *Old Testament and Related Studies* (Salt Lake City: Deseret Book and FARMS, 1986), 161–66, 183. For LDS prayer circles, see D. Michael Quinn, "Latter-day Saint Prayer Circles," *BYU Studies* 19/1 (1978): 79–105, and Bruce H. Porter, "Altar," and George S. Tate, "Prayer Circle," in *Encyclopedia of Mormonism*, 1:36–37, 3:1120–21. The reader should note, however, that Todd Compton was correct when he wrote that "some of the examples cited by Nibley are not really group prayers, or are not really circles, and so on, though there are some similarities to prayer circles." Todd Compton, review of *The Sermon at the Temple and the Sermon on the Mount*, by John W. Welch, *Review of Books on the Book of Mormon* 3 (1991): 322.

51. Nibley, *Mormonism and Early Christianity*, 75.

52. Martin S. Cohen, *The Shiʿur Qomah: Texts and Recensions* (Tübingen: Mohr, 1985), 120.

53. Welch, in *Illuminating the Sermon at the Temple*, 90, has noted the threefold petition involved in asking, seeking, and knocking and ties this aspect of prayer and of the opening of the door to the temple.

54. I have noted elsewhere that the word *amen*, with which we

conclude our prayers, is a title of Christ. See John A. Tvedtnes, "Faith and Truth," *Journal of Book of Mormon Studies* 3/2 (1994): 114–17.

CHAPTER 5

SACRED TEMPLES ANCIENT AND MODERN

Richard O. Cowan

Latter-day Saints affirm the antiquity of temples and temple ordinances. From the beginning, mortals have felt the need to establish sacred sanctuaries where they can get away from worldly concerns and receive instruction pertaining to the eternities. John A. Widtsoe believed that "all people of all ages have had temples in one form or another."[1] Joseph Fielding Smith likewise explained that the Lord taught the fulness of the gospel to Adam and his posterity. However, lamented Elder Smith, as men spread over the earth, they began to depart from the truth and to pervert the ordinances originally revealed to Adam. Nevertheless, he concluded, "heathen temples" and their ceremonies "grew out of," and to some extent reflected, the true concepts the Lord had revealed earlier.[2] Thus even a study of these temples may provide some valuable insights into the true nature of temples and temple worship.

Most Latter-day Saints think of temples primarily as buildings where sacred ordinances or ceremonies take place. Yet not all temples, even in the restored church, fit this particular definition. There is another and perhaps more basic function. Hugh Nibley has spent years researching what various ancient religions understood temples to be. That which makes a temple different from other buildings is not just its sacredness, he concluded, but rather its unique form and function. The earliest temples were regarded as "meeting places at which men at specific times attempted to make contact with the powers above."[3] These ancient peoples thought of the temple as being the highest point in their world, the best place from which to observe and learn the ways of the heavens. Consequently many ancient temples were built atop mountains, but even if they were physically in the valley they were still regarded as spiritual peaks where one could be closest to God. In a very real sense, the temple represented a halfway place between heaven and earth.[4]

Ancient Temples as Places of Revelation

The physical design of ancient temples often reflected their role as places of contact between heaven and earth. Ziggurats in Mesopotamia provided a platform on which temples were constructed, bringing the people who worshiped in them closer to heaven. Consequently, the prominent stairways up their sides symbolized the pathway leading from the human to the divine world. Perhaps the best known of the Mesopotamian ziggurats was the Tower of Babel (see Genesis 11:1–9). Although the builder's motives were materialistic and selfish, the name of this tower does reflect a true function of temples: In the ancient Babylonian language (as well as in modern Arabic) the first syllable *Bab-* meant gate, while the suffix *-el* was a widely recognized reference to deity. Hence the name *Babel* literally means "gate of God."

Similarly, when Jacob saw his dream of the ladder (or stairway) reaching into heaven and received great promises from the Lord, he named the place *Bethel* (which in Hebrew literally means "the house of God") and referred to it as "the gate of heaven" (Genesis 28:10–19).

The first biblical reference to a temple comes from the time of Moses (see Exodus 25:1–7). While the children of Israel were still in the wilderness of Sinai, Jehovah directed that they should construct a sanctuary where they might worship him. Because of their migratory status, this structure had to be portable. Nevertheless, it was to be made of the finest materials and workmanship available. It was to be the house of the Lord.

The tabernacle that the Lord commanded Moses to build was to serve both purposes mentioned above. First, the Lord directed his people to "make me a sanctuary that I may dwell among them." He promised to reveal himself there and give instructions to them (see Exodus 25:8, 22). He subsequently kept this promise: "And it came to pass, as Moses entered into the tabernacle, the cloudy pillar descended, and stood at the door of the tabernacle. . . . And the Lord spake unto Moses face to face, as a man speaketh unto his friend" (Exodus 33:9–11). Second, the Lord intended to reveal sacred ordinances to his people in that tabernacle (see D&C 124:38).

In all ages the Savior has revealed the patterns according to which his sacred houses were to be built.[5] Exodus chapters 25–30 contain the divine revelation of the tabernacle's design and functions.

The location of the tabernacle emphasized its sacredness and separation from the world. As the Israelites pitched their camps in the wilderness, the twelve tribes were arranged around the tabernacle like a protective shield from the outside world. Innermost was the tribe of

Levi, which included those with priestly authority (see Numbers 2–3). The 75' x 150' court of the tabernacle represented an additional protection. Note how admission was progressively more restricted as one approached the holiest precincts: While anybody could be out in the world, only Israelites were to be in the camp. Only the worthy could enter the courtyard, and only priests were permitted in the tabernacle's outer room or "holy place." Only one individual, the high priest, was to enter the "most holy place" or "holy of holies," and then only once each year—on the Day of Atonement, or Yom Kippur (see Leviticus 16:29–34).

The tabernacle's furnishings and ordinances further taught the children of Israel how they must prepare in order to return to the presence of God. The altar of sacrifice was the most prominent object in the tabernacle's courtyard. Here the people complied with the Lord's commands to make animal and other sacrifices, which served as a reminder of his great future atoning sacrifice and reemphasized the vital principles of obedience and sacrifice. Between the altar and the tabernacle was the laver, or large bronze water basin, in which the priests washed their hands and feet before entering the tabernacle or before officiating at the altar (see Exodus 30:18–21). The laver was thus a reminder of the principle that becoming clean is a key step on our path back to God's presence.

The tabernacle itself was a tent measuring about 15' x 45'. Its framework was of the most precious wood available, overlaid with gold, and covered by fine linens and costly skins. Like many other ancient temples, the tabernacle's entrance faced east—toward the rising sun (see Exodus 27:13–16). The main room was separated from the "holy of holies" by a beautiful veil of pure white, "fine twined linen" adorned with cherubim and other figures embroidered in blue, purple, and scarlet (see Exodus 26:31). A latter-day revelation speaks of angels as guardians along the way to exaltation in the kingdom of God (see D&C 132:19). Hence the veil may have symbolized the division between God and man.

Like the portable tabernacle in the wilderness, the permanent temple in the promised land was made of the finest possible materials and craftsmanship. The temple was set apart from the outside world by "great," "middle," and "inner" courts (1 Kings 7:12; 2 Kings 20:4).

The temple was related to the special covenant that existed between God and his people. In the midst of construction, the Lord reminded Solomon that if he would keep the commandments, the Lord would dwell among the people and never forsake them (see 1 Kings 6:11–13; compare Exodus 25:8). After seven and one-half years, the temple was completed. Its dedication was a milestone in the history of Israel and a spiritual feast for the people. "I have surely built thee a house to dwell in," King Solomon prayed, "a settled place for thee to abide in forever." He concluded his dedicatory prayer by petitioning: "The Lord our God be with us, as he was with our fathers: let him not leave us, nor forsake us: That he may incline our hearts unto him, to walk in all his ways, and to keep his commandments" (1 Kings 8:13, 57–58).

Features of other ancient temples were similar. For example, the noted Egyptian temple at Karnak (commenced a thousand years before Solomon's) was also entered through a large, walled court; one then needed to pass through the many-columned "hypostyle hall" (corresponding to the outer "holy place") before reaching the sacred shrine of the god Amun (paralleling the holy of holies).

Greek temples, such as the world-famed Parthenon built several centuries later, were similarly divided into two rooms.

Like its predecessors, Herod's Temple featured a series of courts to which admittance was increasingly restricted as one approached the holy sanctuary.[6] All nationalities were permitted in the Court of the Gentiles, but within it was a balustrade containing warnings to non-Israelites to go no farther. The Court of the Women was so named because both sexes were permitted there, while only men were allowed in the next area. Finally, the temple was immediately surrounded by a court open only to the priests. Ascending stairs from one court to another heightened the sense of the temple's sacredness.

Temples among the Lord's people were not limited to the Old World. The Book of Mormon contains the history of a righteous colony that left Jerusalem just before the Babylonians captured the city and destroyed the temple there. Within a few years of arriving in their new promised land in the Western Hemisphere, these people erected a temple in the land of Nephi. This edifice was constructed "after the manner of the temple of Solomon, save it were not built of so many precious things," which were not available in that land. Nevertheless, "the workmanship thereof was exceeding fine" (2 Nephi 5:16). The temple was the gathering place for religious worship and instruction (see Jacob 1:17; 2:2, 11). Some four centuries later, another temple in the land of Zarahemla filled a similar function (see Mosiah 1:18). Then, following the three days of terrible destruction at the time of the Savior's crucifixion, "a large multitude" of the righteous survivors gathered around yet another temple in the land Bountiful (see 3 Nephi 1:18). Here the resurrected Lord instructed and blessed them.

These Book of Mormon temples may have set the pattern for temples built by later inhabitants of ancient America. Maya temples, for example, were located at the center of their cities. Like Mesopotamian ziggurats, these early American structures provided elevated platforms that drew the people closer to heaven in sacred places of worship.

Ordinances in Ancient Temples

Modern revelation affirms that both the Tabernacle of Moses and the Temple of Solomon were built so that "those ordinances might be revealed which had been hid from before the world was" (D&C 124:38). Hence the Lord's people in these Old Testament times had access to at least some of the temple ordinances that would be restored in the latter days. Sidney B. Sperry reasoned that the Lord's requirements for exaltation, and therefore the need for temples, were the same then as they are now.[7]

Joseph Fielding Smith was convinced that Old Testament "washings" included baptisms.[8] Although vicarious service for the dead was not inaugurated until New Testament times, ordinances for the living were available during earlier dispensations. Furthermore, the explanations of Facsimile 2 in the Book of Abraham suggest that elements of what we now call the temple endowment were known anciently (see Fac. 2, figs. 3 and 8). Finally, a revelation given through Joseph Smith affirms that the ancient patriarchs and prophets held the sealing power (see D&C 132:39).

The nature and extent of these ancient ordinances and the exact location in the temple buildings where they were performed have been the subjects of much fruitless speculation. The Old Testament describes in detail the sacrifices and other performances associated with the lesser priesthood and the Mosaic law but says almost nothing about any higher ordinances. "Because such ordinances are sacred and not for the world," Joseph Fielding Smith explained, no detailed account of them has been made available. "There are, however, in the Old Testament references to covenants and obligations under which the members of the Church in those days were placed, although the meaning is generally obscure."[9]

The scriptures do emphasize, however, that those who participated in temple worship needed to be prepared. Specifically, the priests who officiated had to be ordained or consecrated. Each time they entered the temple, they were washed with water and then anointed with olive oil. This oil was used not only in cooking but also in lamps as a source of light and warmth; many ancient peoples associated the olive tree with the "tree of life."[10] The priests were also clothed in "holy garments" of white linen, including a cap, robe, sash, and trousers (see Exodus 28–29).[11]

The *Temple Scroll*, which dated from just before the time of Christ, also emphasized the importance of personal purity for those entering the temple. Elaborate laws of purification governed the temple and its surroundings. Even the whole city where the temple was located was to be kept holy and pure.[12] This was consistent with the Lord's desire that his people should be "a kingdom of priests, and an holy nation" (Exodus 19:6).

Nibley has presented evidence from ancient papyri showing that sacred ceremonies were also an essential feature of Egyptian temple worship. Following the traditional initiation of washing, clothing, and anointing,[13] an individual would enter the temple itself. Here he would receive instructions on returning to the presence of God. Moving from room to room symbolized his increasing understanding and progress.[14]

Members of the New Testament church did not receive their sacred ordinances in Herod's Temple, since, as the Master lamented, this holy house had been defiled by money changers and others (see John 2:14–16; Matthew 21:12–13). Heber C. Kimball affirmed that the early apostles received their blessings at the hands of the Savior himself.[15] Joseph Fielding Smith believed that Peter, James, and John received the endowment on the Mount of Transfiguration.[16] The New Testament confirms that some sacred truths taught to the faithful disciples were not appropriate for the world to have. Jesus specifically charged the three apostles to speak to no one concerning the events on the mount (see Matthew 17:9).

In recent decades a large body of apocryphal literature dating from early Christian times has been discovered and published. Particularly significant was the uncovering of a library of books written by fifth-century Christians at Nag Hammadi, a settlement on the Nile River in central Egypt.[17] Much of this material focuses on Christ's "forty-day ministry," especially in Galilee. According to these nonscriptural texts, the Lord performed sacred ordinances and gave his disciples teachings that Latter-day Saints associate with the temple endowment. In the middle of the fourth century, Cyril of Jerusalem described how the faithful had "entered the Annex of the baptistry, . . . [and] removed [their] street clothes," which act represented "putting off the old man and his works." They were then washed in a "tank of holy running water," anointed, and received a new garment.[18]

The early Christians came together in a circle to pray.[19] References in the New Testament itself describe how even in public worship the disciples prayed in the spirit of unity with uplifted hands (see 1 Timothy 2:8)[20] and how women prayed with their heads covered or veiled (see 1 Corinthians 11:5 RSV).

The writer of the *Gospel of Philip*, one of the apocryphal documents in the Nag Hammadi library, believed that the most sacred part of the temple was what he called the "bridal chamber," where a "woman is united to her husband" and "will no longer be separated." If a person does not receive these blessings in this world, he asserted, they cannot be received elsewhere (compare D&C 132:15–18).[21]

A significant development during the New Testament period was the introduction of temple ordinances for the dead. "The inauguration of this work among the dead," declared James E. Talmage, "was wrought by Christ in the interval between His death and resurrection."[22]

During the three days his body lay in the tomb, the Lord went to the spirit world and organized the work of preaching the gospel there (see 1 Peter 3:18–20; 4:6). During his brief stay, the Savior did not preach to everyone personally; rather, from among the righteous spirits he authorized messengers to carry the gospel truth to all (see D&C 138:28–30).

Even though it thus became possible to hear and accept the gospel in the spirit world, such essential ordinances as baptism could not be received there. It was necessary for living proxies to receive them on earth in behalf of those who had died without the opportunity. Just as the Savior atoned vicariously for the sins of mankind, early Christians, in the same spirit of love, performed saving ordinances in behalf of the dead. Paul used the accepted practice of baptizing in behalf of the dead as an argument in favor of there being a resurrection. Why do you baptize for the dead, he asked, if the dead will not live again? (see 1 Corinthians 15:29).[23] Sperry suggested that these Saints must have had temples where such ordinances could be properly performed, but these "sacred structures" may have been small and nothing is known about them.[24]

Hence in ancient times temples were places of contact between heaven and earth as well as places where sacred ordinances were performed. Both of these functions would need to be restored as part of "the dispensation of the fulness of times" (Ephesians 1:10).

The Restoration of Temple Worship

As the nineteenth century entered its fourth decade, the early Latter-day Saints eagerly proclaimed their faith that the long-anticipated "times of restitution of all things" (see Acts 3:21) had finally arrived. At this time the Saints were gathering at Kirtland in northeastern Ohio, where they built the first latter-day temple. Even though the fulness of temple ordinances was not restored until later on, the Lord's house in Kirtland nevertheless provided the setting for remarkable spiritual experiences and for the conferring of vital priesthood keys. Like ancient temples, it truly was a place of contact between heaven and earth.

In the weeks preceding the Kirtland Temple's dedication in 1836, the Saints witnessed remarkable spiritual manifestations to an unusual degree. They reported seeing heavenly messengers in at least ten different meetings. At five of these meetings, participants testified that they had beheld the Savior himself. Many received visions, prophesied, or spoke in tongues.[25]

On Thursday afternoon, 21 January 1836, the First Presidency were washed "in pure water." That evening they met with others in the west room of the temple attic where they anointed one another with consecrated oil and pronounced blessings and prophecies. Then, "the heavens were opened," the Prophet recorded, and he "beheld the celestial kingdom of God, and the glory thereof." The Lord declared: "All who have died without a knowledge of this gospel, who would have received it if they had been permitted to tarry, shall be heirs of the celestial kingdom of God" (D&C 137:1–4, 7).

In his history Joseph Smith declared that "this was a time of rejoicing long to be remembered."[26] Elder Orson Pratt later added:

> God was there, his angels were there, the Holy Ghost was in the midst of the people, the visions of the Almighty were opened to the minds of the servants of the living God; the vail [*sic*] was taken off the minds of many; they saw the heavens opened; they beheld the angels of God; they heard the voice of the Lord; and they were filled from the crown of their heads to the soles of their feet with the power and inspiration of the Holy Ghost.[27]

Some of the most memorable spiritual experiences occurred on Sunday, 27 March 1836, the day the temple was dedicated. The climax of the day was the dedicatory prayer, which had been given to the Prophet by revelation. After expressing gratitude for God's blessing, the Prophet, with hands raised to heaven and tears flowing freely, prayed that the Lord would accept the temple that had been built "through great tribulation . . . that the Son of Man might have a place to manifest himself to his people" (D&C 109:5). The dedication concluded with the entire congregation standing and shouting: "Hosanna, Hosanna, Hosanna, to God and the Lamb, Amen, Amen, and Amen," repeated three times.[28]

A transcendently important spiritual manifestation occurred on Sunday, 3 April 1836, just one week after the dedication. At the close of the afternoon worship service, Joseph Smith and Oliver Cowdery retired to the Melchizedek Priesthood pulpits in the west end of the lower room of the temple. Joseph Smith testified that "the veil was taken from our minds" (D&C 110:1) and that he and Oliver beheld a series of remarkable visions.

The Lord Jesus Christ appeared, accepted the temple, and promised to manifest himself therein "if my people will keep my commandments, and do not pollute this holy house." Moses then appeared and bestowed "the keys of the gathering of Israel and the leading of the ten tribes from the land of the north." Elias next conferred "the dispensation of the gospel of Abraham." Finally, in fulfillment of Malachi's prophecy (see Malachi 4:5–6), Elijah committed "the keys of this dispensation" in preparation for the "great and dreadful day of the Lord" (D&C 110:16). Through the sealing keys restored by Elijah, priesthood ordinances performed on earth can be "bound" or "sealed" in heaven.

Though accompanied by marvelous spiritual experiences, the ordinances as administered in the Kirtland Temple were not as complete as they would be in later times. Speaking in 1853 at the cornerstone-laying ceremonies for the Salt Lake Temple, President Brigham Young declared that in Kirtland the "first Elders" received only a "portion of their first endowments, or we might say more clearly, some of the first, or introductory, or initiatory ordinances, preparatory to an endowment."[29] "The prime purpose in having such a temple," Elder Harold B. Lee believed, "seems to have been that there could be restored the keys, the effective keys necessary for the carrying on of the Lord's work." He therefore concluded that the events of

3 April 1836 (as recorded in D&C 110) were "sufficient justification for the building of [this] temple."[30]

Plans for Temples in the City of Zion

While the temple at Kirtland was under construction, the Latter-day Saints were also looking forward to building another in Missouri. A revelation during the summer of 1831 identified Independence in Jackson County as the place for the future temple (see D&C 57:1–3). Almost from the beginning, the Saints were fired with the vision of establishing Zion on earth. Enthusiasm for building the temple increased in June 1833 when the Prophet Joseph Smith drafted his plan for the future City of Zion (see fig. 6). This plan set forth the pattern of wide streets crossing at right angles, which would in later decades become a familiar and welcome characteristic of Mormon settlements. Just seven weeks before, Joseph had received a revelation specifying that the temple, together with buildings for the Presidency and for printing, were to be located at the center of Kirtland (see D&C 94). Each structure in this complex was to have the same dimensions and was to be preserved as holy and undefiled.

The envisioned plan for Zion expanded this concept from three to twenty-four buildings. These "temples" were to be assigned to the various priesthood quorums and were to serve a variety of functions.[31] Hence, as had been the case with the Tabernacle of Moses and the Temple of Solomon, the Lord's house would once again be at the heart of the latter-day holy city. Because all its inhabitants were expected to be living on a celestial level (see D&C 105:5), all these buildings could be regarded as "temples"—places of communication between heaven and earth. Unfortunately, another outbreak of persecution prevented these plans from being carried out.

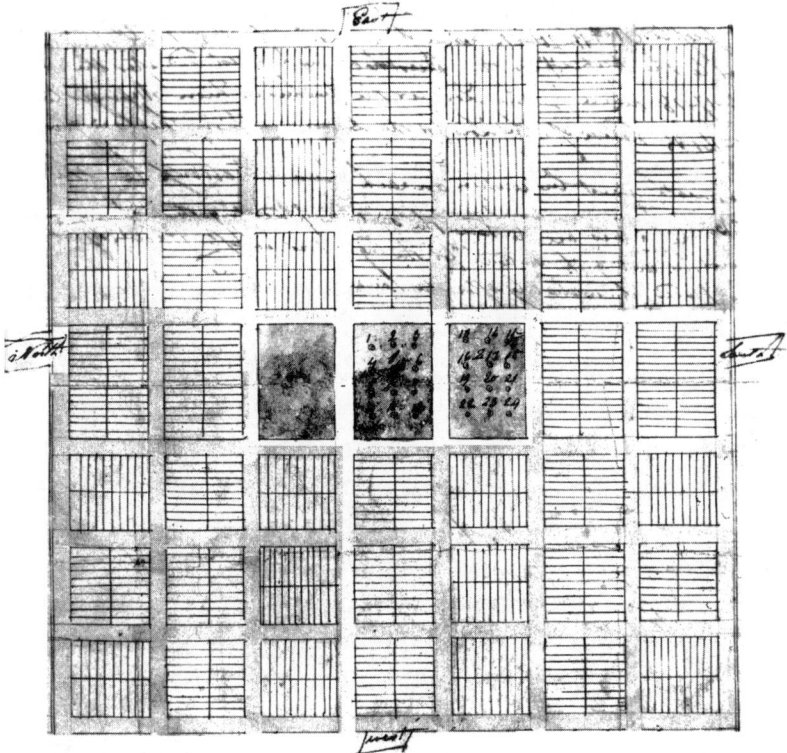

Figure 6. In this 1833 plat of the City of Zion, the two central blocks contain the twenty-four temples that were assigned to various priesthood quorums. These temples, like the ancient Israelite temples, were oriented to the rising sun in the east, designated at the top of the map.

The Restoration of Temple Ordinances

As the Latter-day Saints fled from their persecutors in Missouri, they turned eastward to Illinois, where in 1839 they established a new community named Nauvoo, from a Hebrew word meaning "beautiful." Within two years they would begin construction there on yet another temple. Before this sacred structure was completed, the restoration of holy ordinances would have far-reaching significance.

The practice of vicarious baptisms for the dead was

taught for the first time in the present dispensation on 15 August 1840.[32] Until November 1841, when a font was dedicated in the partially completed temple, church members participated in this ordinance in the Mississippi River. The Saints eagerly took advantage of the opportunity to make gospel ordinances and blessings available to their departed loved ones. By 1844, the year of the Prophet's martyrdom, 15,722 baptisms had been performed in behalf of the dead.

Meanwhile, the Saints had already turned their attention to building the temple. Early in August 1840 the First Presidency declared that "the time has now come, when it is necessary to erect a house of prayer, a house of order, a house for the worship of our God, where the ordinances can be attended to agreeably to His divine will."[33]

A revelation, received 19 January 1841, specifically pointed out the need for the temple: Echoing instructions given to Moses concerning the ancient tabernacle, the Lord now commanded his Latter-day Saints to gather precious materials from afar and build a house "for the Most High to dwell therein. For there is not a place found on earth that he may come to and restore again that which was lost unto you, or which he hath taken away, even the fulness of the priesthood" (D&C 124:27–28; compare Exodus 25:8, 22). Specifically, the Lord declared that the ordinance of baptism for the dead "belongeth to my house." He therefore commanded them to provide an appropriate font in the temple. He would grant them "a sufficient time" (D&C 124:31) to accomplish this, during which period he would continue to accept their baptisms performed in the river (see D&C 124:29–33). Hence the Nauvoo Temple, like holy sanctuaries in former dispensations, was to serve the dual purpose of being a place of contact between God and man where sacred priesthood ordinances are also performed.

While the Saints had received a preliminary or partial endowment in Kirtland, the time had now come to unfold these blessings more fully. Elder James E. Talmage described the temple endowment as a "course of instruction,"[34] reviewing key events in the history of mankind—the creation, fall of Adam, apostasy, restoration, and our eventual reunion with God—giving emphasis to the plan of redemption and to our living according to the high standards of the gospel. Hence these instructions outlined the way back to the presence of God—the path that had been symbolized by the prominent stairway up the sides of ancient pyramids and outlined in early Egyptian temple ceremonies.

On 4 May 1842, the first endowments were given in the large assembly room on the second floor of the Red Brick Store because the temple was not yet completed.[35] The brethren were washed, anointed, and given other initiatory ordinances, and then the instructions of the endowment were unfolded as the group moved from one area to another. Concerning this significant event, Joseph Smith recorded:

> I spent the day . . . in council with [seven brethren] instructing them in the principles and order of the Priesthood, attending to washings, anointings, endowments and the communication of keys pertaining to the Aaronic Priesthood, and so on to the highest order of the Melchizedek Priesthood, setting forth the order pertaining to the Ancient of Days, and all those plans and principles by which any one is enabled to secure the fullness of those blessings which have been prepared for the Church of the First Born, and come up and abide in the presence of the Eloheim in the eternal worlds. . . . The communications I made to this council were of things spiritual, and to be received only by the spiritual minded: and there was nothing made known to these

men but what will be made known to all the Saints of the last days, so soon as they are prepared to receive, and a proper place is prepared to communicate them, even to the weakest of the Saints; therefore let the Saints be diligent in building the Temple.[36]

By the time of the Prophet's martyrdom, over fifty individuals had received the blessings of the endowment.

Among the other blessings unfolded during these years was eternal marriage. During his earthly ministry, the Master had stressed the sanctity of the family. "What therefore God hath joined together, let no man put asunder" (Mark 10:9; see also 10:6–8). The apostle Paul similarly insisted: "Neither is the man without the woman, neither the woman without the man, in the Lord" (1 Corinthians 11:11). During the present dispensation a revelation had affirmed that "marriage is ordained of God" as the means of providing earthly tabernacles for the spirits that had lived before the world was made (see D&C 49:15–17).

In May 1843 Joseph Smith instructed the Saints that in order to attain the highest degree of the celestial kingdom, one must enter "the new and everlasting covenant of marriage" (D&C 131:2). Two months later he recorded a revelation which, among other things, declared: "If a man marry him a wife in the world, and he marry her not by me nor by my word, and he covenant with her so long as he is in the world and she with him, their covenant and marriage are not of force when they are dead, and when they are out of the world" (D&C 132:15). Following these instructions, which echoed the ancient apocryphal *Gospel of Philip*, the number of marriages for eternity increased.

In September 1842 the Prophet instructed that there must be "a welding link" established from generation to generation (see D&C 128:18). To this end ordinances began to be performed to seal children to their parents.

Even following Joseph Smith's martyrdom on 27 June 1844, the Saints pressed forward in building the temple. By December of the following year, the attic story was completed, furnished, and dedicated for presenting the endowment instructions. Even though during the next several weeks the Saints were making feverish preparations for their forced exodus, more than five thousand eagerly took the time to receive their temple blessings.

Temple Worship Today

Latter-day Saint temples have many of the qualities of those built in ancient times. For example, emblematic stones on the Salt Lake Temple and some other temples depict gospel teachings, as did the arrangement and furnishings at the Tabernacle of Moses. Also, many Latter-day Saint temples face east, perhaps in anticipation of the second coming of the Savior. Prophecies describe Christ's future coming as being like the dawning of a new day in the east (see Matthew 24:27; D&C 45:36–39).

Just as the ancients looked to the temple as a place to get out of the world and come closer to God, likewise we find temple worship to be a source of enriched spirituality. "In the temple we can receive spiritual perspective," affirmed Elder Boyd K. Packer.

> There, during the time of the temple service, we are out of the world.
>
> A large part of the value of these occasions is the fact that we are doing something for someone that they cannot do for themselves. As we perform the endowment for someone who is dead, somehow we feel a little less hesitant to pray fervently to the Lord to assist us. . . . There is something cleansing and clarifying about the spiritual atmosphere of the temple.[37]

Notes

1. John A. Widtsoe, "Temple Worship," *Utah Genealogical and Historical Magazine* 12 (April 1921): 52.

2. Joseph Fielding Smith, *Doctrines of Salvation* (Salt Lake City: Bookcraft, 1955), 2:237.

3. Hugh W. Nibley, "What Is a Temple?" in *Mormonism and Early Christianity* (Salt Lake City: Deseret Book and FARMS, 1987), 359.

4. See Hugh W. Nibley, "The Idea of the Temple in History," *Millennial Star* 120 (August 1958): 228–37, 247–49; this article was republished in pamphlet form by BYU Press in 1963 under the title "What Is a Temple?" and under the same title in *The Temple in Antiquity: Ancient Records and Modern Perspectives,* ed. Truman G. Madsen (Provo, Utah: BYU Religious Studies Center, 1984), 19–37; and in *Mormonism and Early Christianity* (Salt Lake City: Deseret Book and FARMS, 1987), 355–90.

5. See Stephen D. Ricks and Michael A. Carter, "Temple-Building Motifs: Mesopotamia, Ancient Israel, Ugarit, and Kirtland," in *Temples of the Ancient World,* ed. Donald W. Parry (Salt Lake City: Deseret Book and FARMS, 1994), 152–76.

6. For an illustration, see Donald W. Parry, "Demarcation between Sacred Space and Profane Space: The Temple of Herod Model," in *Temples of the Ancient World,* 418–19, fig. 41.

7. See Sidney B. Sperry, "Some Thoughts concerning Ancient Temples and Their Functions," *Improvement Era,* November 1955, 814.

8. See Joseph Fielding Smith, "Was Temple Work Done in the Days of the Old Prophets?" *Improvement Era,* November 1955, 794.

9. Ibid.

10. Stephen D. Ricks, "Olive Culture in the Second Temple Era and Early Rabbinic Period," in *The Allegory of the Olive Tree: The Olive, the Bible, and Jacob 5,* ed. Stephen D. Ricks and John W. Welch (Salt Lake City: Deseret Book and FARMS, 1994), 464–66.

11. John A. Tvedtnes, "Priestly Clothing in Bible Times," in *Temples of the Ancient World*, 649–704.

12. See Yigael Yadin, "The Temple Scroll," in *New Directions in Biblical Archaeology*, ed. David Noel Freedman and Jonas C. Greenfield (Garden City, N.Y.: Doubleday, 1969), 156–66; and Jacob Milgrom, "The Temple Scroll," *Biblical Archaeologist* 41 (September 1978): 105–20.

13. See Hugh W. Nibley, *Message of the Joseph Smith Papyri: An Egyptian Endowment* (Salt Lake City: Deseret Book, 1975), 96–99, 123, 267. See also John L. Gee, "The Requirements of Ritual Purity in Ancient Egypt" (Ph.D. diss., Yale University, 1998).

14. See Nibley, *Message of the Joseph Smith Papyri*, 118–19.

15. See Heber C. Kimball, in *Journal of Discourses*, 10:241 (27 June 1863).

16. See Smith, *Doctrines of Salvation*, 2:165.

17. See James M. Robinson, *The Nag Hammadi Library*, 2nd ed. (New York: Harper and Row, 1989), and Bentley Layton, *The Gnostic Scriptures* (New York: Doubleday, 1987).

18. Cyril of Jerusalem's Lectures on the Ordinances, in Nibley, *Message of the Joseph Smith Papyri*, 280.

19. See, for example, Hugh W. Nibley, "The Early Christian Prayer Circle," *BYU Studies* 19/1 (1978): 41–78.

20. See John A. Tvedtnes, "Temple Prayer in Ancient Times," in this volume, pages 79–98.

21. *Gospel of Philip* 69:14–25; 70:17–20; 86:3–7; see R. McL. Wilson, trans., *The Gospel of Philip* (New York: Harper & Row, 1962), 45–46, 62.

22. James E. Talmage, *The House of the Lord* (Salt Lake City: Bookcraft, 1962), 91 (1974 ed., 77).

23. See John A. Tvedtnes, "Baptism for the Dead in Ancient Christianity," in this volume, pages 55–78.

24. Sperry, "Ancient Temples," 827.

25. See Milton V. Backman Jr., *The Heavens Resound* (Salt Lake City: Deseret Book, 1983), 285.

26. *History of the Church*, 2:392.

27. Orson Pratt, in *Journal of Discourses*, 18:132 (9 October 1875).

28. On the hosanna shout, see Lael J. Woodbury, "The Origin and Uses of the Sacred Hosanna Shout," in *Sperry Lecture Series* (Provo, Utah: Brigham Young University, 1975), 18; and Lael J. Woodbury, "Hosanna Shout," in *Encyclopedia of Mormonism*, 2:659.

29. Brigham Young, in *Journal of Discourses*, 2:31 (6 April 1853).

30. Harold B. Lee, "Correlation and Priesthood Genealogy," address at Priesthood Genealogical Research Seminar, 1968 (Provo, Utah: BYU Press, 1969), 60.

31. See *History of the Church*, 1:358–59.

32. See *History of the Church*, 4:179; see also Doctrine and Covenants 124:132.

33. *History of the Church*, 4:186.

34. Talmage, *House of the Lord*, 99 (1974 ed., 83).

35. See Lucius N. Scovil letter in *Deseret News Semi-Weekly*, 15 February 1884, 2, quoted in *BYU Studies* 19/2 (1979): 159 n. 77.

36. *History of the Church*, 5:1–2.

37. Boyd K. Packer, *The Holy Temple* (Salt Lake City: Bookcraft, 1980), 180–81.

CHAPTER 6

SEVEN PROMISES TO THOSE WHO OVERCOME: ASPECTS OF GENESIS 2–3 IN THE SEVEN LETTERS

Richard D. Draper and Donald W. Parry

The Garden of Eden account (Genesis 2–3) is composed of several powerful symbols that look forward to or anticipate later temple systems. Biblical scholar Gordon Wenham categorizes this as "a type of archetypal sanctuary."[1] For instance, the text of Genesis 2–3 explicitly identifies items directly connected to Israelite sanctuaries (including the Mosaic Tabernacle and Solomon's Temple), such as the tree of life, cherubim, sacred waters, sacred vestments, Eden's eastward orientation, and divine revelation. The Eden story also contains words and phrases used in later biblical texts that refer to the temple.[2] John the Revelator used many of these same temple symbols and skillfully wove them into his letters to the seven churches (Revelation 2–3).

In this paper we compare and contrast the temple symbolism common to both Genesis 2–3 and Revelation 2–3. We point out the parallels between the two sections and then attempt to explain why John, in Revelation 2–3, used elements from the Eden story in his letters to the seven churches.

The Literary Structure of the Seven Letters

John structures the seven letters to the churches in a balanced and symmetrical configuration, comprising a seven-part pattern: (1) divine commission, (2) description of the speaker, (3) formal recognition, (4) criticism, (5) admonition, (6) call to hear, and (7) promise and blessing.[3] Each of these seven parts is presented to each of the seven churches (see table 1, pp. 124–27).

Of particular concern in our paper is the seventh part: promise and blessing. Each of the seven promises and blessings begins with the anaphoric expression *to him that overcometh,* and each features one or more temple images directed to those who do overcome. These temple images do not simply recall Israelite temple systems as advanced in the Old and New Testaments, but they also anticipate the end time when the elect will gain access to the temple in heaven (compare Revelation 7:15; 14:15, 17; 16:17).

Seven key themes listed in the promise and blessing sections of Revelation 2–3 correspond to the Garden of Eden story in Genesis 2–3:

1. the tree of life (Genesis 2:17; Revelation 2:7)
2. physical death (Genesis 2:17; 3:3) and the second death (Revelation 2:11)
3. bread (Genesis 3:19) and hidden manna (Revelation 2:17)
4. dominion (Genesis 1:28; Revelation 2:26)
5. sacred vestments (Genesis 3:21; Revelation 3:5)
6. expulsion (Genesis 3:23–24) and return (Revelation 3:12)
7. receiving names (Genesis 2:23; 3:20; 5:2; Revelation 2:17; 3:12)[4]

These promises and blessings to the seven churches clearly apply to the church in John's day as well as to our church today. "The whole church seems to be meant. . . . The instruction to each church was universal for it tells 'what the Spirit is saying to the churches'—all the churches."[5] We will now examine these seven key themes.

1. The Tree of Life (Genesis 2:17; Revelation 2:7)

God placed many trees in the Garden of Eden, including the trees of life and knowledge. According to the record, "out of the ground made the Lord God to grow every tree that is pleasant to the sight, and good for food; the tree of life also in the midst of the garden, and the tree of knowledge of good and evil" (Genesis 2:9). According to an ancient source, the tree of knowledge was also known as the tree of death,[6] for it brought death to Adam and Eve when they partook of the fruit: "And the Lord God commanded the man, saying, Of every tree of the garden thou mayest freely eat: But of the tree of the knowledge of good and evil, thou shalt not eat of it: for in the day that thou eatest thereof thou shalt surely die" (Genesis 2:16–17).

Once Adam and Eve partook of the fruit of the tree of death, God did not allow them to partake of the fruit of the tree of life:

> And the Lord God said, Behold, the man is become as one of us, to know good and evil: and now, lest he put forth his hand, and take also of the tree of life, and eat, and live for ever . . . the Lord God . . . placed at the east of the garden of Eden Cherubims, and a flaming sword which turned every way, to keep the way of the tree of life. (Genesis 3:22–24)

Table 1. Seven-Part Pattern in Letters to Seven Churches

Division	Ephesus (Rev. 2:1–7)
1. Divine Commission	Unto the angel of the church of Ephesus write;
2. Description of the Speaker	These things saith he that holdeth the seven stars in his right hand, who walketh in the midst of the seven golden candlesticks;
3. Formal Recognition	I know thy works. . . .
4. Criticism	Nevertheless I have somewhat against thee, because thou hast left thy first love.
5. Admonition	Remember therefore from whence thou art fallen, and repent, and do the first works. . . .
6. Call to Hear	He that hath an ear, let him hear what the Spirit saith unto the churches;
7. Promise and Blessing	To him that overcometh will I give to eat of the tree of life, which is in the midst of the paradise of God.

Smyrna (Rev. 2:8–11)	Pergamos (Rev. 2:12–17)
And unto the angel of the church in Smyrna write;	And to the angel of the church in Pergamos write;
These things saith the first and the last, which was dead, and is alive;	These things saith he which hath the sharp sword with two edges;
I know thy works . . .	I know thy works. . . .
and I know the blasphemy of them which say they are Jews, and are not . . .	But I have a few things against thee. . . .
be thou faithful unto death. . . .	Repent. . . .
He that hath an ear, let him hear what the Spirit saith unto the churches;	He that hath an ear, let him hear what the Spirit saith unto the churches;
He that overcometh shall not be hurt of the second death.	To him that overcometh will I give to eat of the hidden manna, and will give him a white stone, and in the stone a new name written, which no man knoweth saving he that receiveth it.

Table 1. *Continued.*

Thyatira (Rev. 2:18–29)	Sardis (Rev. 3:1–6)
And unto the angel of the church in Thyatira write;	And unto the angel of the church in Sardis write;
These things saith the Son of God, who hath his eyes like unto a flame of fire, and his feet are like fine brass;	These things saith he that hath the seven Spirits of God, and the seven stars;
I know thy works. . . .	I know thy works. . . .
Notwithstanding I have a few things against thee. . . .	. . . For I have not found thy works perfect before God.
. . . But that which ye have already hold fast till I come.	Remember therefore how thou hast received and heard, and hold fast, and repent. . . .
He that hath an ear, let him hear what the Spirit saith unto the churches.	He that hath an ear, let him hear what the Spirit saith unto the churches.
And he that overcometh, and keepeth my works unto the end, to him will I give power over the nations: And he shall rule them . . . : even as I received of my Father. And I will give him the morning star.	He that overcometh, the same shall be clothed in white raiment; and I will not blot out his name out of the book of life, but I will confess his name before my Father, and before his angels.

Philadelphia (Rev. 3:7–13)	Laodicea (Rev. 3:14–22)
And to the angel of the church in Philadelphia write;	And unto the angel of the church of the Laodiceans write;
These things saith he that is holy, he that is true, he that hath the key of David, he that openeth, and no man shutteth; the creation of God; and shutteth, and no man openeth;	These things saith the Amen, the faithful and true witness, the beginning of the creation of God;
I know thy works. . . .	I know thy works. . . .
Behold, I will make them of the synagogue of Satan, which say they are Jews, and are not. . . .	Because thou sayest, I am rich, and increased with goods, and have need of nothing. . . .
. . . Hold that fast which thou hast, that no man take thy crown.	. . . Be zealous therefore, and repent. . . .
He that hath an ear, let him hear what the Spirit saith unto the churches.	He that hath an ear, let him hear what the Spirit saith unto the churches.
Him that overcometh will I make a pillar in the temple of my God, and he shall go no more out: and I will write upon him the name of my God, and the name of the city of my God, which is new Jerusalem . . . : and I will write upon him my new name.	To him that overcometh will I grant to sit with me in my throne, even as I also overcame, and am set down with my Father in his throne.

Although Adam and Eve transgressed and were denied access to the tree of life, we learn that those who overcome the world will be able to partake of the fruit. The Lord promised the Saints of Sardis, "He that hath an ear, let him hear what the Spirit saith unto the churches; To him that overcometh will I give to eat of the tree of life, which is in the midst of the paradise of God" (Revelation 2:7). By overcoming the world, church members could return to life, but they first had to reach the tree, which was in the midst of sacred space. For the modern Saint to get to the tree, he or she must first visit the temple and partake of its glorious ordinances.

The tree of life icon in Israelite temple society is evident in the tabernacle menorah, or seven-branched lamp stand.[7] The menorah was a stylized tree of life.

> And thou shalt make a candlestick of pure gold: of beaten work shall the candlestick be made: his shaft, and his branches, his bowls, his knops, and his flowers, shall be of the same. And six branches shall come out of the sides of it; three branches of the candlestick out of the one side, and three branches of the candlestick out of the other side: Three bowls made like unto almonds, with a knop and a flower in one branch; and three bowls made like almonds in the other branch, with a knop and a flower: so in the six branches that come out of the candlestick. And in the candlestick shall be four bowls like unto almonds, with their knops and their flowers. And there shall be a knop under two branches of the same, and a knop under two branches of the same, and a knop under two branches of the same, according to the six branches that proceed out of the candlestick. Their knops and their branches shall be of the same: all it shall be one beaten work of pure gold. And thou shalt make the seven lamps thereof: and they shall light the lamps thereof, that they may give light over against it. (Exodus 25:31–37)

The menorah must have looked like a tree, possessing seven branches (a number of symbolic significance to the Israelite community)[8] and a number of flowers (almond blossoms?).

The tree of life was present in the garden, and a symbolic representation of the tree of life—in the form of a seven-branched lamp stand—was present in the Israelite temples. John's imagery suggests that the only way to reach this tree and thus eternal life is by going to the temple. In effect, the tree of life suggests that the fall of Adam has been surmounted; spiritual death can no longer claim the individual who obeys God.

2. Physical Death (Genesis 2:17; 3:3) and the Second Death (Revelation 2:11)

Physical death results in the "body without the spirit" (James 2:26). The "second death" (Jacob 3:11)—called "spiritual death" (Helaman 14:18) or "everlasting death" (Alma 12:32)—pertains to those who die in sin (see Alma 12:16), who "die as to things . . . of righteousness" (Alma 40:26), or who are "cut off from the presence of the Lord" (Alma 42:9). This second death is the penalty for doing evil (see Alma 12:32). As President Joseph F. Smith explained,

> Thanks be to the eternal Father, through the merciful provisions of the gospel, all mankind will have the opportunity of escape, or deliverance, from this spiritual death, either in time or in eternity, for not until they are freed from the first can they become subject unto the second death, still if they repent not "they cannot be redeemed from their spiritual fall," and will continue subject to the will of Satan, the first spiritual death, so long as "they repent not, and thereby reject Christ and his gospel."[9]

After partaking of the fruit of the tree of knowledge, Adam and Eve brought both physical and spiritual death into the world. Alma instructed his son that "it was appointed unto man to die—therefore, as they [Adam and Eve] were cut off from the tree of life they should be cut off from the face of the earth— . . . And now, ye see by this that our first parents were cut off both temporally and spiritually from the presence of the Lord" (Alma 42:6–7). This fall "brought upon all mankind a spiritual death as well as a temporal" (Alma 42:9; see D&C 29:40–43).

Death in the Garden of Eden corresponds to a statement in John's letter to the church of Smyrna: the Revelator promises that "he that overcometh shall not be hurt of the second death" (Revelation 2:11). Through Christ's atoning sacrifice and resurrection, all mankind will receive a resurrection, or a reuniting of body with spirit. This resurrected body will be immortal. Also through Christ's atonement, repentant individuals overcome spiritual death. Alma summarizes: "the atonement bringeth to pass the resurrection of the dead; and the resurrection of the dead bringeth back men into the presence of God; and thus they are restored into his presence" (Alma 42:23).

Note that in 1 Corinthians 15:22, Adam and Christ are connected but contrasted: "For as in Adam all die, even so in Christ shall all be made alive." Similarly, a relationship between Adam and Christ is identified in Mormon 9:12–13:

> Behold, he created Adam, and by Adam came the fall of man. And because of the fall of man came Jesus Christ, even the Father and the Son; and because of Jesus Christ came the redemption of man. And because of the redemption of man, which came by Jesus Christ, they are brought back into the presence of the Lord.

In 1 Corinthians 15:45, Adam is called the "first man Adam" and Christ is referred to as the "last Adam," again linking the two.

In the primal temple (the Garden of Eden), Adam and Eve did not overcome the temptations of Satan and consequently subjected themselves and their posterity to physical death; in the last temple (heavenly), however, all who overcome through Christ will not remain subject to the second death.

3. Bread (Genesis 3:19) and Hidden Manna (Revelation 2:17)

Bread, sometimes called the staff of life, was a vital foodstuff for sustaining life in the biblical world, and for that matter in many parts of the world through all ages. It is a common and important symbol of both physical and spiritual sustenance, as many scriptures testify. Every Sabbath in the Israelite temple (see Leviticus 24:5–9), priests consumed twelve loaves of bread (called *shewbread;* see Exodus 25:30). This bread anticipated the Lord's sacrament, which is composed of broken bread, signifying Christ's body ("Take, eat; this is my body," Matthew 26:26), and water or wine, symbolizing Christ's blood. The shewbread, the cereal offering in the temple, "the manna which fed the Israelites in the desolate deserts of Sinai, the . . . bread [fed] to the multitudes on the shores of Galilee, and the bread of the sacrament are but figures of the 'true bread,' which is the body of the Savior."[10] To his Old World disciples Jesus taught, "The bread that I will give is my flesh" (John 6:51), and to the Nephites, "He that eateth this bread eateth of my body to his soul" (3 Nephi 20:8).

Jesus explained, "I am the bread of life: he that cometh to me shall never hunger; and he that believeth on me shall never thirst" (John 6:35). Also, "if any man eat of this bread, he shall live forever," he shall be raised "up at the last day," he shall have "eternal life" or "everlasting life," and "he that eateth me, even he shall live by me" (John 6:51, 44, 54, 47, 57). The parallels between physical bread made of yeast and flour and spiritual bread are clear: one sustains physical life and the other provides eternal life.

Manna, which was "like coriander seed, white; and the taste of it was like wafers made with honey" (Exodus 16:31), was called "the corn of heaven," "angels' food" (Psalm 78:24–25), and "bread" (Exodus 16:15). Manna, like bread, typified the eternal life that Jesus Christ provides to repentant souls through his atonement. Jesus explained to his followers, "I am [the] bread of life. Your fathers did eat manna in the wilderness, and are dead. This is the bread which cometh down from heaven, that a man may eat thereof, and not die. I am the living bread which came down from heaven: if any man eat of this bread, he shall live for ever" (John 6:48–51). Note that the wilderness manna and Christ both "came down from heaven" and both provide life to partakers; one provides physical life and the other spiritual.

God commanded Moses to place a jar of manna in the temple's ark of the covenant (see Exodus 16:32–34; Hebrews 9:4) where, hidden from view, it became a memorial of God's sustaining Israel in the wilderness. Manna is mentioned in John's seven letters to the seven churches, where the Lord told the Saints of Pergamos: "To him that overcometh will I give to eat of the hidden manna" (Revelation 2:17). Christ is the manna for those who overcome.

The parallels between the wilderness manna and the hidden manna of Revelation are apparent. The first was hidden from view in the tabernacle's holy of holies; the second is hidden from view in the celestial holy of holies. The wilderness manna provided physical life to those who partook; the hidden manna provides spiritual life to those who repent and accept the atonement.

After their transgression, Adam and Eve were removed from the Edenic temple setting and were required to work the ground in order to obtain bread for sustenance. The Lord told Adam that after his transgression the ground was cursed for his sake, that he would eat foods produced from the ground "all the days of [his] life" or "till [he] return[s] unto the ground," and that he "in sorrow" would "eat bread" in the "sweat of [his] face" (Genesis 3:17, 19). The atonement of Christ reverses this process for those who repent, and Jesus thus becomes eternal sustenance to the righteous, who will return to the temple of heaven to dwell eternally.

4. Dominion (Genesis 1:28; Revelation 2:26)

When God contemplated the creation of humankind, he determined that dominion would be theirs.

> And God said, Let us make man in our image, after our likeness: and let them have dominion over the fish of the sea, and over the fowl of the air, and over the cattle, and over all the earth, and over every creeping thing that creepeth upon the earth. So God created man in his own image, in the image of God created he him; male and female created he them. And God blessed them, and God said unto them, Be fruitful, and multiply, and replenish the earth, and subdue it: and have dominion over the fish of the sea, and over the fowl of the air, and over every living thing that moveth upon the earth. (Genesis 1:26–28)

Adam began to exercise that dominion while yet in the primal temple setting. "Out of the ground the Lord God formed every beast of the field, and every fowl of the air; and brought them unto Adam to see what he would call them: and whatsoever Adam called every living creature, that was the name thereof" (Genesis 2:19). By naming the animals, Adam demonstrated his ascendancy. This dominion continued, to an extent, when this couple was driven from the garden into the telestial sphere.

What does *dominion* mean in these verses? Hugh Nibley, in his article "Man's Dominion," explains that "the ancients taught that Adam's dominion was nothing less than the priesthood, the power to act for God and in his place."[11] This agrees with Brigham Young's teaching that "the Spirit of the Lord and the keys of the priesthood hold power over all animated beings."[12] Nibley summarizes that "man's dominion is a call to service, not a license to exterminate."[13]

This earthly and temporal dominion is a type or shadow that points forward to the eternal dominion that exalted souls will possess. John wrote to the church of Thyatira: "to him who overcometh, and keepeth my commandments unto the end, will I give power over many kingdoms" (Revelation 2:26 JST). The dominion of the Saints is no longer limited to the animal kingdom. It spreads to the human kingdom as well. In the heavenly temple God expands the authority given in the primal temple.

5. Sacred Vestments (Genesis 3:21; Revelation 3:5)

The fifth parallel between the garden story and John's promise and blessing to the various congregations grows out of God's last act shortly before expelling Adam and Eve from the garden. "Unto Adam also and to his wife did the Lord God make coats [garments] of skins, and clothed them" (Genesis 3:21). Note God's careful attention to the sacred clothing—he does not delegate the making of the garments and the dressing of the couple to an angel or another but carries out these divine acts himself.

There are two chief connections between the garments

of skins and Christ's atoning sacrifice. First, ancient tradition suggests that the skin garments were made of sheep's wool.[14] Wool reminds us of Jesus Christ and his atonement, for the scriptures refer to sacrificial lambs that typify Jesus' death.[15] Christ also is called "our passover" (1 Corinthians 5:7), the "Lamb of God, which taketh away the sin of the world" (John 1:29), and the "lamb without blemish" (1 Peter 1:19). Other scriptural images also relate the lamb to Christ's sacrifice (see, for example, Isaiah 1:18). Second, the English word *atonement* (at-one-ment) originated from the Hebrew word *kaphar*, which means "to cover." When the Lord covered Adam and Eve with garments of skin, he was, as it were, covering or protecting them by the power of his atonement. Though leaving the presence of God, they were not leaving his protection.[16]

The apostle Paul perhaps had the idea of *kaphar* or "covering" in mind when he wrote the following statements: "For as many of you as have been baptized into Christ *have put on* Christ" (Galatians 3:27); "let us *put on* the armour of light" (Romans 13:12); "this corruptible must *put on* incorruption, and this mortal must *put on* immortality" (1 Corinthians 15:53); and "*put on* the new man" (Ephesians 4:24, emphasis added in each instance).

The garments of skin may be for this world only (compare JS—H 1:31), but the Lord promised the church at Sardis, "He that overcometh, the same shall be clothed in white raiment; and I will not blot out his name out of the book of life, but I will confess his name before my Father, and before his angels" (Revelation 3:5). The color of the garment is important. The Greek *leukos* denotes brilliance, the state of heavenly splendor, the state of innocence and purity. The brilliant, white garment covers those who enter the sacred space of God. As God clothed Adam and Eve for their journey through mortality, he now clothes those who overcome the world for their journey through eternity.

6. Expulsion (Genesis 3:23–24) and Return (Revelation 3:12)

The sixth parallel centers on the expulsion of Adam and Eve from the garden, because "the man is become as one of us [the gods], to know good and evil: and now, lest he put forth his hand, and take also of the tree of life, and eat, and live for ever: Therefore the Lord God sent him forth from the garden of Eden" (Genesis 3:22–23). Adam's punishment for his transgression was death, so he was forced to leave the Garden of Eden, where he "must have remained forever, and had no end" (2 Nephi 2:22). But not all was lost. To the Saints of Philadelphia, the Lord promised, "Him that overcometh will I make a pillar in the temple of my God, and he shall go no more out" (Revelation 3:12). Again John emphasizes that the key to reentering God's sacred dwelling is overcoming the world. In this covenant, however, God promises the Saints more than a "place" in his heavenly kingdom, for they become a part of sacred space, never to leave its environs.

7. Receiving Names (Genesis 2:23; 3:20; 5:2; Revelation 2:17; 3:12)

The seventh and final parallel between Genesis 2–3 and Revelation 2–3 deals with the reception of sacred names for Adam and Eve (in Genesis) and for those who overcome the world (in Revelation). It was God who gave to Adam and Eve—that is, to the man and the woman—their names while yet in their paradisiacal setting. According to Genesis, "This is the book of the generations of Adam. In the day that God created man, in the likeness of God made he him; Male and female created he them; and blessed them, and called their name Adam, in the day when they were created" (Genesis 5:1–2). This title not only designated the first pair, but also their descendants. Thus God named humankind at the beginning of the world, giving it the name Adam.

At the end of world, God will give a new name to those who overcome. Indeed, he who overcomes shall receive a threefold name: "I will write upon him the name of my God, and the name of the city of my God, which is new Jerusalem, which cometh down out of heaven from my God: and I will write upon him my new name" (Revelation 3:12). No longer will the Saint be *Adam,* but he or she shall possess the very name of the Father and the Son, the name of God's city, the New Jerusalem (meaning they will be inhabitants of that city), and the new name. This new name, however, is that of the Lord, and thus it identifies the recipient with him. In this way they become heirs of God and Christ, receiving the full power and glory with the Son.

John referred to the new name (see Revelation 2:17; compare D&C 130:9–10) and promised that the name of the righteous would not be blotted out of the book of life (see Revelation 3:5).

Conclusion

Having listed the parallels (see table 2), we can now postulate why these correlations exist between the garden story and the letters to the seven churches. John drew his readers' attention to the temple esoterica found in Genesis 2–3. The letters were to sound a warning to the church as a

Table 2. Key Themes Common to Genesis 2–3 and Revelation 2–3

Key Theme	Primal Temple (Eden)	Temple of Heaven
1. Tree of Life	Adam and Eve are forbidden to eat the fruit of the tree of life (see Gen. 2:17).	The elect will partake of the fruit of the tree of life (see Rev. 2:7).
2. Death	Death enters the world because of the transgression of Adam and Eve (see Gen. 2:17; 3:3).	The elect will not be hurt by the second death (see Rev. 2:11).
3. Bread/Manna	Adam and Eve eat bread by sweat (see Gen. 3:19).	The elect will eat of the hidden manna (see Rev. 2:17).
4. Dominion	Adam and Eve replenish and subdue the earth and have dominion over the animal kingdom (see Gen. 1:28).	The elect will have power over the nations (see Rev. 2:26).
5. Sacred Vestments	God made coats of skins and clothed Adam and Eve (see Gen. 3:21).	The elect will be clothed in white raiment (see Rev. 3:5).
6. Expulsion/Return	The Lord "sent [Adam and Eve] forth from the garden"; he "drove out" the man and the woman (Gen. 3:23–24).	The elect will reenter the temple and become (symbolically) pillars in the temple; i.e., they will possess eternal access to the temple (see Rev. 3:12).
7. Receiving Names	God "called their name Adam ['humankind,' 'man and woman'] in the day when they were created" (Gen. 5:2).	The elect of God will receive the name of God and Christ's new name (see Rev. 3:12).

whole. Apostasy was running full steam, fueled by false prophets and apostles. Entire branches were ignorantly or willfully being overrun by it. The message to the churches sounded a clear warning that God would abandon them unless they returned to him. Each congregation was responsible to stop the spread of heresy, hold on to the truth, and thereby gain salvation. The book *Opening the Seven Seals* explains:

> From the context of the letters, the Church's spiritual life foundered in six areas. Two were external: a willingness to compromise with paganism and a denial of Christianity due to Jewish harassment. Four were internal: the acceptance of unauthorized leaders, approval of false doctrine promulgated by pseudo-prophets, halfheartedness and indifference, and a loss of love for the Church and her Master. Succumbing to any one of these would have sounded the death knell for the Church.[17]

John reached out to warn and hold them, choosing the most powerful imagery he could—temple imagery. The trial of the Saints in Asia Minor became a kind of microcosm for the problem the Saints faced everywhere: overcoming the world while facing forces that would take them away from God. John's readers lived in the fallen world and felt the effects of that fall. John encouraged them by promising a return to sacred space. After having left the divine temple of Eden, humankind could, by overcoming the world, once more enter into sacred space and enjoy the blessings of the eternal paradise, the temple in heaven. Our contemporary temples, of course, serve to reverse the direction of our (Adam and Eve's) path toward the second death and destruction. Our temples assist us in partaking of the power of Christ (the hidden manna), gaining dominion in the eternal world, acquiring the sacred vestments, receiving the sacred name, and returning to the tree of life and to God's presence.

Notes

1. Gordon J. Wenham, *Genesis 1–15*, Word Biblical Commentary, vol. 1 (Waco, Tex.: Word Books, 1987), 86. On the temple symbols in the Garden of Eden, see Donald W. Parry, "Garden of Eden: Prototype Sanctuary," in *Temples of the Ancient World: Ritual and Symbolism,* ed. Donald W. Parry (Salt Lake City: Deseret Book and FARMS, 1994), 126–51.

2. Examples of three phrases used in connection with the temple are found in Parry, "Garden of Eden," 143–45.

3. We have simplified certain elements in this seven-part pattern.

4. We could, of course, present other parallels between these two texts, but in the context of this paper we will examine only these seven.

5. Richard D. Draper, *Opening the Seven Seals: The Visions of John the Revelator* (Salt Lake City: Deseret Book, 1991), 37.

6. See Ingvild S. Gilhus, "The Tree of Life and the Tree of Death: A Study of Gnostic Symbols," *Journal of Religion and Religions* 17 (1987): 337–53. Gilhus writes that the "Tree of Knowledge is here made equivalent to a Tree of Death," and this Tree of Death "created death for those who ate of it" (p. 341).

7. See Carol L. Meyers, *The Tabernacle Menorah: A Synthetic Study of a Symbol from the Biblical Cult* (Missoula, Mont.: Scholars Press, 1976), 165–79. Note that in Revelation 1:12–13, John "saw seven golden candlesticks; And in the midst of the seven candlesticks one like unto the Son of Man." These seven golden candlesticks, John is informed, represent the "seven churches" (Revelation 1:20).

8. See John W. Welch, "The Temple in the Book of Mormon," in *Temples of the Ancient World*, 353, 384 n. 85.

9. Joseph F. Smith, *Gospel Doctrine* (Salt Lake City: Deseret Book, 1986), 15.

10. Joseph Fielding McConkie and Donald W. Parry, *A Guide to Scriptural Symbols* (Salt Lake City: Bookcraft, 1990), 25.

11. Hugh W. Nibley, "Man's Dominion, or Subduing the Earth," in *Brother Brigham Challenges the Saints* (Salt Lake City: Deseret Book and FARMS, 1994), 7.

12. Elden J. Watson, *Manuscript History of Brigham Young 1846–1847* (Salt Lake City: Watson, 1971), 142 (26 April 1846).

13. Nibley, "Man's Dominion," 18.

14. See Stephen D. Ricks, "The Garment of Adam," in *Temples of the Ancient World,* 706. Latter-day Saint scholars have pointed out that these sacred vestments may be garments of "light" rather than "skin," based on ancient writings, and because the two Hebrew words are homonyms, differing only in the initial character 'ôr (skin) and 'ôr (light). See ibid., and John A. Tvedtnes, "Priestly Clothing in Bible Times," in *Temples of the Ancient World,* 651–54. Ricks, "The Garment of Adam," 706, explains, "Probably the oldest rabbinic traditions include the view that God gave garments to Adam and Eve before the Fall but that these were not garments of skin . . . but instead garments of light."

15. See McConkie and Parry, *A Guide to Scriptural Symbols,* 141–42: "In six ways the sacrificial lamb was a type of Jesus Christ. 1) No bones of the lamb were to be broken (Ps. 34:20; Ex. 12:46; John 19:36). 2) The lamb must be perfect (Mal. 1:7–14; 3 Ne. 12:48). 3) The lamb must be without blemish (Ex. 12:5; Heb. 7:26–27; 1 Pet. 2:22). 4) The flesh of the lamb was to be eaten (Ex. 12:8; John 6:53–55). 5) The lamb must be the firstborn (Ex. 13:2; D&C 93:21). 6) The lamb must be a male (Ex. 12:5; Matt. 1:21)."

16. For the physical and spiritual protection offered to the wearer by the garments, see Tvedtnes, "Priestly Clothing in Bible Times," 659–61.

17. Draper, *Opening the Seven Seals,* 37.

Figure 7. John A. Widtsoe's testimony of temple work began at Harvard in 1892. Sixty years of hallowed service generated immeasurable contributions to the work performed in LDS temples today. Photo used by permission, Utah State Historical Society, all rights reserved. Photo no. C-92 Box 1 Folder 1.

CHAPTER 7

MODERN TEMPLE WORSHIP THROUGH THE EYES OF JOHN A. WIDTSOE, A TWENTIETH-CENTURY APOSTLE

Alan K. Parrish

John A. Widtsoe's Temple Conversion

Since the Quorum of the Twelve Apostles was restored in 1835 nearly one hundred exemplary men have been called to the office of apostle. From that noble group, John A. Widtsoe and Joseph Fielding Smith have been the most deeply involved in the developments of genealogy, family history, and modern temple work. Their contributions are well documented in the many lessons, addresses, books, and articles that detail the developments of that branch of the church's mission. They also dominate the recent centennial history of the Genealogical Society of the Church.[1] Widtsoe's attachment to modern temple work steadily deepened throughout his life, even though he was one of Utah's foremost citizens with unusually heavy demands on his time and abilities. Building on his distinguished training at Harvard and Göttingen (Germany), he became a teacher and scientist of international renown. While still a young man, he became president first of the Utah Agricultural College, 1907–1916, and then of the

University of Utah, 1916–1921, before being ordained an apostle of the Church of Jesus Christ of Latter-day Saints. That modern temple work rose to such prominence amid the strains of his demanding life is compelling evidence of his conversion to it. This chapter reviews his teachings about modern temple worship and his activities associated with facilitating its efficient accomplishment.

In an address to the Genealogical Society, following a historic six-year mission to Europe, Widtsoe reminisced over an early acquaintance that kindled his interest in temple service. He was a student at Harvard in 1892 when Susa Young Gates visited Boston on a genealogical research trip. Her remarks, public and private, gave an emphasis to temple work that profoundly shaped his life. Five years later Widtsoe married Gates's daughter Leah after finding more common interests that grew out of that same research trip. Widtsoe recalled of Susa Young Gates:

> I first met Sister Gates in 1893 [1892], in Boston, Massachusetts. She was there then to gather genealogy for the Young family, and she discovered a number of things with respect to that genealogy which has made the extension of that family record possible. Ten years or more after that time, illness overtook Sister Gates. She was ready to die, or at least we thought so. A servant of the Lord, later the President of the Council of the Twelve, declared that her time to go had come, and then, under the power of inspiration, he said in substance, "No, the edict of death had been revoked, on the condition that you dedicate the remainder of your life to the cause of salvation for the dead." She accepted life and the challenge, and as far as I know, and as Brother Smith has expressed himself, she never faltered in helping to establish this work. She was the one who turned my interest in the direction of genealogy. Her fiery faith lighted my faith and gave me courage to undertake the work.[2]

Widtsoe developed strong feelings that the most vital element in modern temple work was expressed in the words of Moroni and Malachi when they spoke of turning the hearts of children and fathers to each other. Mutual concern for the ultimate happiness of each family member was the divine intent behind gathering family data and performing sacred temple ordinances. It was so in Widtsoe's own family, and in his early years he had a rich conversion experience to temple work. His mother, Anna, and his Aunt Petroline spent almost a year in Norway collecting their family genealogy. After finishing the essential temple ordinances for almost one hundred ancestors with whom they had established a direct link, some discouragement set in and interest waned because they were unable to establish further adequate relationships. That disappointment, however, was soon overcome by a remarkable spiritual experience that Widtsoe remembered to the end of his life. He wrote:

> One Sunday morning when I awoke I had a distinct impulse to examine the book the sisters had brought with them, containing the list of blood relatives that they had collected. Obedient as I have always been to spiritual messages, I sought out the book, and studied it for five hours. I found that morning the key which has enabled me to secure thousands of desired names.[3]

Widtsoe became an ardent believer in divine assistance that comes to diligent temple workers: "I feel so strongly that the work of the dead must be done in the very best manner possible, but I have no fear about ultimately finding means of any nature whatsoever with which to accomplish the work."[4] Despite the work he had done for his family, Widtsoe shared with a fellow officer in the Genealogical Society his fear of inadequacy: "The limitations in my life [were] such as to make it difficult for me to do the amount of temple work that my long list of dead required of me."[5] Because Widtsoe was not able to do all the work for his deceased ancestors, he enlisted the service of others to help him. To one of them, he wrote: "I have been so caught by circumstance[s] the last few years as to make it very difficult to do the temple work that is really required of me, and this generous action of yours has done much to make amends for that which I myself have failed to do."[6]

A shared love between ancestors and descendants is the heartbeat in binding the entire human family to eternal life in the kingdom of the Father. To obtain it will take more time than this life for most. Agency and opposition, the elements that guide man's progression, require time to master and perfect. The opportunity of perfection extends beyond mortality; thereby, the doctrine of universal salvation became the foundation of modern temple emphasis.

The Doctrine of Universal Salvation

Widtsoe understood the intimate connection between the powers of heaven and modern temple work. It was his testimony that temple work is the very center of the plan God devised for the happiness and progression of all his children. Although there are many intricacies in God's plan, underlying it all is the doctrine of universal salvation. This doctrine extends the blessings of eternal life to all mankind if they choose to accept it, but that choice, assured by the doctrine of agency, remains with the individual. To Widtsoe, this doctrine was the root out of which the work of ancient and modern temples grew and the effectual core of the restoration of gospel doctrines through the Prophet Joseph Smith. Work for the salvation of the dead is of supreme importance in the Prophet's teachings. Widtsoe relied on the assurances of Joseph Smith that without turning our hearts to temple ordinances in redeeming our dead kinsmen, we cannot be made perfect (see D&C 128:18). The Prophet further said, "The greatest responsibility in this world that God has laid upon us is to seek after our dead."[7] He also warned that, "Those Saints who neglect it in behalf of their deceased relatives, do it at the peril of their own salvation."[8] Widtsoe himself emphasized the significance of work for the dead:

The basic reason for the importance of the work for the dead, is that the Lord would save all his children. The plan of salvation is absolutely universal. The work of the Lord will not be completed until all who come on earth have had a full and fair chance to accept or reject the gospel. The power to do so remains with the dead in the spirit world, where the gospel will be preached to them.

However, the possible blessings of salvation are conditioned upon obedience to the principles and ordinances of the plan. The dead as well as the living must comply with the requirements for salvation. These requirements are of a two-fold nature. Those that can be met in the life after this, in heaven, and those that must be performed on earth. Faith and repentance may be developed in the spirit world. Baptism with water (strictly an element of earth), a necessary ordinance of the gospel, can be performed only on earth.

This makes the dead dependent on us, the living, for help. Since the dead cannot themselves submit to ordinances, which are specifically of the earth, yet by divine edict are requisite for entrance into the kingdom of heaven, the only thing that can be done, since the law must not be broken, is for someone living on earth to perform these ordinances in behalf of the dead. Such vicarious work, of course, becomes effective only when the dead accept the work thus done for them. This provides a way, by which, with the help of the living, the faithful dead can attain their full destiny.[9]

Continual progression after death and vicarious ordinance work, the nature of most of the work performed in modern temples, were addressed by Widtsoe:

> Temple work rests on the principle of the Great Plan that all must be saved, or at least given the opportunity of salvation. Those who have been unable to accept the Gospel ordinances on earth, are not necessarily denied the privileges of membership in the Church or refused the blessings which come to those who accept the truth. For such dead persons vicarious work must be done in all the essential ordinances of the Church. Vicarious work is not new, for it has been practiced in various forms from the first day. . . . The work of Jesus Christ was essentially vicarious, for he atoned for the act of Adam.[10]

The scriptural passage "For behold, this is my work and my glory—to bring to pass the immortality and eternal life of man" (Moses 1:39) echoes through all of Widtsoe's teachings on temple work. Because that work extends through all eternity, temples are universally the shrines of God's plan for the eternal life of man and the workstations for bringing about his work and glory. Widtsoe taught that salvation for the dead is the great keystone in the gospel arch that holds all other parts of the gospel together: "We shall not progress very far here or hereafter, until we are tied to our fathers back through our natural family lines to Father Adam. We cannot move on to our full exaltation until this is done. Let everyone help in this work."[11] Widtsoe further spoke about the worth of redeeming the souls of the dead in furthering one's own eternal development and advancement. A seldom-considered, yet impassioned viewpoint concerning their worth was revealed when he wrote:

The foundation of this work is love, born and nurtured and developed in sacrifice. The worth of a soul now becomes great to me. I go into the temple, and give a half day to opening the doors of salvation for a dead person; or I spend many precious hours searching for, planning, gathering genealogy in order that he and his brothers—my brothers—may have those saving ordinances done for them by my fellow-workers who have access to the Temples of the Lord. I only know him by name, and never shall know him nearer on this earth; but out of my own understanding love of the cause, no matter how humble it may be, and out of my willingness to sacrifice to prove that love, I take a step toward the likeness of my Father in heaven. It is a tremendous thing—this soul for whom I labour. Without that soul I might not find the same opportunity of approaching the likeness of my Father. That soul is of immense worth to me. . . .

. . . A soul becomes of indescribable value, since it offers a means of service by which we ourselves may rise to the position and power of godhood.

The worth of a soul can best be measured in its effect upon man's realization of his highest ideal. Without my brother I cannot attain my highest. Without loving him I cannot look forward to the highest place. Without sacrificing for him I cannot hope to win the fullest recognition. Without him I cannot achieve my likeness to the Lord. We are bound together, one great human family, moving on to a glorious destiny.[12]

Encompassed in God's plan of universal salvation is every man's upward progression toward eternal life. The divine desire of a loving Heavenly Father for the eternal life of every child is unquestioned. That very desire underscores the divine worth of every soul born into mortality, for each is bound up in the love of an infinite Redeemer who fulfilled the sacred atonement. Further, when men and women accepted the great plan of God in the grand council in the premortal world, they became parties to the salvation of every person under that plan. Thus the immortality and eternal life of every man and woman became the work and glory of each mortal brother and sister.

Because temples are a vital link between the here and the hereafter, Widtsoe taught that they are places for cementing eternal relationships in the world to come and in allowing every soul to receive the great blessings associated with his or her highest hopes in eternity. Through temple work, the great mysteries of eternity are laid open to the minds of men and women who prepare themselves for the revelations of God given there. Anyone who has the opportunity to participate in the divine work performed in modern temples and refrains from doing so deprives himor herself of some of God's greatest blessings. Widtsoe emphasized the missed opportunities of not performing temple work when he explained:

> The instructions and all other parts of the endowment ceremonies are of such a nature as to exalt the spirit of man. The sealing powers of the priesthood, exercised in the temples, uniting parents and children, and husband and wife, for time and eternity, give indescribable satisfaction to the soul. The vast meaning of the temple ordinances opens the human understanding to the mysteries of eternity. . . .
>
> Those who fail to receive their endowments and sealings, who enter into marriage outside of the temple, are losers beyond expression. Those who have had their endowments but who do not work for the dead fail to receive the refreshing of their souls that comes by repeated communion with the Spirit of God so abundantly manifested in the temple.[13]

In a 1921 address in the Assembly Hall on Temple

Square, while serving as president of the University of Utah, Widtsoe described man's voluntary choice to place himself under the plan, to fulfill part of the plan by performing temple work, and to participate in the onward and upward progression encompassing the universal salvation of mankind. He taught that through modern temple work both man's premortal and mortal existences are connected to his future potential for exaltation:

> To understand the meaning of temple worship, it is necessary to understand the plan of salvation and its relation to temple worship. The human race were "in the beginning with God," and were created spiritual beings in a day before the[ir] arrival upon this earth. Mankind is here because of its acceptance of the Plan of Salvation, and satisfactory pre-existent lives. We have won the right to be here; we have not been forced to come here; we have won our place upon the earth. We shall pass into another sphere of existence, and shall continue upward and onward forever and forever, if we obey the high laws of eternal existence.
>
> The plan of salvation for eternal beings involves the principle that God's work with respect to this earth will not be complete until every soul has been taught the Gospel and has been offered the privilege of accepting salvation and the accompanying great blessings which the Lord has in store for his children. Until that is done the work is unfinished.[14]

Behind the various beliefs surrounding eternal life and universal salvation of mankind lay some of the greatest religious battles. Such beliefs were at the heart of the religious excitement that Joseph Smith encountered around Palmyra, New York, the very spark that led him into the Sacred Grove. Widtsoe described the tension over this doctrine as it festered in Joseph's youth:

The vicious doctrine had been preached for generations that only a few men and women were destined to be saved in the presence of God. In that battle, questions were asked. Is there power of repentance beyond the grave? At death does nothing remain of the old life? Is memory blotted out? Is the power of free will then a thing of the past? Around such questions, asked by intelligent men, a great battle was waged. That was after the Lord had turned the key, through the Prophet Joseph Smith, and laid bare the doctrine of universal salvation, which declares that all who repent, either here or in the hereafter, may achieve salvation in one or the other of the great glories that the Lord has prepared for His children.[15]

Widtsoe also taught: "The fact that such corruptions of ordinances and ceremonies have always existed is a strong evidence of the continuity of temple worship, under the Priesthood, from the days of Adam."[16] He made further reference to this in his Assembly Hall address:

Let me suggest that the reason why temple building and temple worship have been found in every age, on every hand, and among every people, is because the Gospel in its fullness was revealed to Adam, and that all religions and religious practices are therefore derived from the remnants of the truth given to Adam and transmitted by him to the patriarchs. The ordinances of the temple in so far as then necessary, were given, no doubt, in those early days, and very naturally corruptions of them have been handed down [through] the ages. Those who understand the eternal nature of the gospel—planned before the foundations of the earth—understand clearly why all history seems to revolve about the building and use of temples.[17]

The mysteries that lie behind the means of man's attaining eternal life make up the mystique of the world's temples, a fascination that has intrigued mankind for centuries.

The work of temples centers on the duties of men and women in this world and the influence of their labors on the degrees of glory to be attained in the worlds beyond. Thus temples are an undisputed intersection between the mortal world and the worlds of glory that extend even to God's own habitation. The varied views of man's immortal salvation are evident in the work of the world's temples. Such temples, from whatever century or sect of religious thought, were raised in acknowledgment of God and his plan for the eternal life of mankind. The great shrines built by men throughout the ages connect ancient and modern temple work and provide evidence that obtaining eternal life is the shared duty of mortal kinsmen. Over the ages, men have tried to maintain the correct form and meaning of revealed temple ordinances, even at times when God had withdrawn the necessary power and guidance for correct performance. These attempts in all ages gave rise to the corruption of temple ordinances. Awareness of this corruption sheds important light on the history of revealed temple work and is essential to any consideration of modern temple work.

Some Historical Developments in Modern Temple Work

The seeds Susa Young Gates planted in Widtsoe developed early roots. Throughout his busy academic career, many years prior to his apostolic appointment, Widtsoe maintained a constant vigilance in matters of modern temple work. The Utah Genealogical Society was organized a few months after his graduation from Harvard in 1894. He followed the society closely for many years and was an active participant by 1910, when their publication, the *Utah Genealogical and Historical Magazine,* began. At that time he was on the Committee on Preparation of Genealogical and

Historical Papers, Lectures, etc., chaired by his brother, Osbourne.[18] On 6 October 1910, a paper written by Widtsoe for the quarterly meeting of the society was read by his brother while John was in Washington, D.C., on business for the Agricultural College. In the address, John described some key theological elements embodied in the work of the society that culminated in vicarious temple ordinances. He lucidly described God's plan for the exaltation of man as an ongoing, upward spiral. He also described the restoration of priesthood keys that ushered in the sacred temple ordinances to be administered before the sons of Levi could make their offering as prophesied by John the Baptist (see D&C 13:1). Widtsoe taught that their offering was based on the restoration of modern temple work:

> Dr. Widtsoe declared that the life of man began with loving sacrifice, and received its crowning mission in the work of redemption for his dead kindred. The mystic allusion in the Doctrine and Covenants which refers to the time when the sons of Levi will offer an offering in righteousness would be clear and beautiful in the light of the principle of vicarious salvation; for the sons of Levi would offer upon the altar, which the Prophet Joseph Smith declared was the acceptable offering in righteousness—the books containing the records of their dead, who had received vicarious salvation at their hands. Man's endeavor throughout the history of the world has been a constant search for joy. Whatever his work, however diligently he pursues one line of endeavor or another, the purpose is always the same—the circular line of upward progress leading him ever back to the quest for joy. As all other activities in the great and grand plan of the world work by upward evolution, so the course of God is an eternal round of love.[19]

In 1915, at the request of David O. McKay, then a member of the Quorum of the Twelve, Widtsoe wrote a lesson manual that became the Melchizedek Priesthood quorum textbook for that year. In a lesson on temple work, he wrote of temple ordinances and symbols performed on earth in tandem with ordinances and realities accomplished in heaven:

> The earthly ordinances of the Gospel are themselves only reflections of heavenly ordinances. For instance, baptism, the gift of the Holy Ghost and temple work are merely earthly symbols of realities that prevail throughout the universe; but, they are symbols of truths that must be recognized if the Great Plan is to be fulfilled. The acceptance of these earthly symbols is part and parcel of correct earth life, but being earthly symbols they are distinctly of the earth, and cannot be accepted elsewhere than on earth.[20]

In several addresses Widtsoe discussed the instrumental role of the Prophet Joseph Smith in restoring modern temple work and the thoroughgoing importance he attached to it. Almost the first and last interests in the administrative ministry of the Prophet Joseph Smith centered on the building of temples. From the dedication of the temple site in Independence shortly after the church was organized to the preparations for the temple in Nauvoo just before his death, Joseph held a constant vision of the importance of building temples and getting temple work underway. Joseph's attention to the dedication of temple sites and his many revelations about temples all point to his deep understanding of the necessity of temple work and the redemption of the dead.[21]

> The main concern of the Prophet Joseph Smith in the restoration of the Gospel in these latter days was the

founding, building, and completion of temples in which the ordinances "hid from before the foundation of the world" might be given. In fact, the Lord declared repeatedly to the Prophet that unless temples were built and used, the plan of salvation could neither be in full operation nor fully accomplished.[22]

Widtsoe taught that the revelations Joseph received and the work he caused to be performed in early temples indicate the hand of the Lord in restoring temple work to his children.

Widtsoe studied the inspired teachings of Joseph Smith throughout his lifetime and became the church's leading scholar on the revelations of the Prophet as recorded in the Doctrine and Covenants. In addition to the first extensive concordance on the Doctrine and Covenants, Widtsoe wrote two books and many articles about the Prophet; through it all he shared the Prophet's enthusiasm for the fundamental role of temple work. In an address to the Genealogical Society nearly a year before his call to the Twelve, he declared:

> For myself, I can simply say that I doubt whether association with any other organization would give me greater joy than this one, because it seems to me that the work in charge of the Genealogical Society is the very keystone of the Gospel arch. If the work entrusted to us in this organization is well done, the Lord's work is safe, and will go onward, according to the will of the Lord; but if it be poorly done or slighted, the work of the Lord to that degree will be hindered.[23]

In addition to the necessity of the sacred ordinances performed in the temples, Widtsoe had a strong testimony of personal revelations received there. He learned this firsthand numerous times. One particularly valuable insight illustrates the kind of revelation available. "For seve-

ral years, under a Federal grant with my staff of workers
we had gathered thousands of data in the field of soil mois-
ture; but I could not extract any general law running
through them. I gave up at last. My wife and I went to the
temple that day to forget the failure. In the third endowment room, out of the unseen, came the solution, which has
long since gone into print."[24] Such revelations were answers to the greatest problems that vexed the lives of righteous men and women. Another statement illustrates the
depth of this belief:

> I have spent my life in endeavoring to save souls,
> chiefly the souls of young people. As a school teacher,
> that has been my responsibility. My own children were
> nearly all taken from me, and that made it important that
> I devote myself to the children of other people. I have
> had many experiences in life, having been in public serv-
> ice all my life since I was a lad. And I want to tell you, as
> my individual testimony, that I know no sweeter joy, I
> know of nothing that has given me more assistance of
> spirit, more courage to go on in life, than to try to make
> use of my fellow men in saving my own soul, by helping
> them save theirs. It is the sweetest work one can be en-
> gaged in. . . . I have had so many experiences, both in and
> out of the temple, in seeking the names of my own dead,
> in gathering books for the genealogical library, that I
> know that the powers of heaven follow the person who
> unselfishly gives himself to this work, as perhaps no
> other class of workers within the Church.[25]

Those who enter the temple to perform a service for the
dead may be the recipients of blessings and revelations as a
consequence of that service. "That is the gift that comes to
those who enter the temple properly, because it is a place
where revelations may be expected. I bear you my personal
testimony that this is so."[26] Further,

Does it mean that once in a while God may come into the temples, and that once in a while the pure in heart may see God there; or does it mean the larger thing, that the pure in heart who go into the temples, may, there, by the Spirit of God, always have a wonderfully rich communion with God? I think that is what it means to me and to you and to most of us.[27]

Apostolic Leadership and Teachings

Though he had been a stalwart and able contributor to the Genealogical Society for many years before his call to the Twelve, Widtsoe was able to devote more time and attention to it as one of the duties of his apostolic appointment. Bearing the apostolic mantle, his spiritual conviction of modern temple work grew even deeper. Soon after his call to the Twelve, he was made a director of the Genealogical Society. As an apostle he carried a stronger driving influence on the policies and directions the society would take. After a few months as one of the Twelve, Widtsoe shared with his longtime friend Maude May Babcock a glimpse of the significance he attached to the restoration of temple work begun with the Prophet Joseph Smith:

I haven't the slightest doubt that unseen forces all about us are guiding us into the proper performance of the important work for the dead. In fact, the longer I study the Gospel of Jesus Christ the more convinced I am that salvation for the dead is the cementing principal which holds together all the other doctrinal divisions of the Church. . . .

. . . It seems to me that [the] spirit of temple work is growing by leaps and bounds among the people.[28]

Widtsoe's experience in the state college and university set him apart as an unusually adroit administrator. As an apostle this had a substantial impact. In 1995, in commemoration of the one-hundred-year anniversary of the Utah Genealogical Society, a detailed history was published by three reputable historians. Of Widtsoe's appointment, they noted: "A respected scholar and academician, Widtsoe brought broad perspective and foresight into guiding the direction of the society for the thirty years he served on the board."[29]

Origin of the Temple Index Bureau

In 1921 a substantial and divisive problem arose because of duplication in research efforts and ordinance work. Harry H. Russell, an energetic servant in the library of the Genealogical Society, became the leading voice in the urgency of the duplication problem. An incident from his own temple activity illustrates the magnitude of the problem. Being one of the most ardent research and ordinance workers in the church, Russell was progressing well with work on one of his family lines. After spending 360 days in performing the proxy ordinances for those ancestors, he discovered that other members of his family were doing work on that same family line in St. George. Elated by the discovery of further family involvement, he quickly arranged a trip to St. George to celebrate and compare notes: "To his dismay, he discovered that they had the same book and had been doing work for the same names he had done in the Salt Lake Temple. His training as an accountant and businessman led him to quickly calculate the hours lost if such duplications were taking place in all the Church's temples."[30] Though Russell was one of the church's most conscientious genealogists, he refused, at least for a significant time, to perform further endowments for his own ancestors, though he continued his work as a temple officiator.

Widtsoe reported similar aggravations among other diligent church members:

> I heard of a sister recently who said she had quit doing Temple work because she had just expended $500 in Temple work only to find afterward that someone had preceded her in doing it. She became discouraged. Another sister expressed herself along the same lines for the same reasons. This should not be, but we should strive to overcome such possibilities. . . . I may say also in this connection that a plan is being devised, in connection with the Genealogical Society, to reduce the possibility of duplication by a card index system containing the names of those whose work has been done, and which will be valuable, and available to everyone who is interested.[31]

Attempts to resolve this problem began in the 1890s, but it wasn't until Widtsoe chaired the society's Activities and Programs Committee that the problem was solved.[32] In 1921 Widtsoe and his committee set their sights on finding a solution. Russell devised a plan for an index bureau to act as a clearinghouse to approve all names before essential temple ordinances could be performed.[33] Widtsoe approved Russell's plan and brought it to the attention of Anthon H. Lund, president of the Genealogical Society, and Joseph Fielding Smith, then church historian and recorder.[34] The idea was endorsed, and Widtsoe was left to work out the details with Elders Joseph Fielding Smith and Joseph Christenson. A meeting with temple presidents and recorders was held during the October 1921 general conference to refine the plan. On 3 November 1921 Widtsoe explained the system and outlined the steps to the board of directors of the Utah Genealogical Society who, after some discussion, instructed Widtsoe and his committee to finish their plans and bring their final recommendations with an estimate of the costs of operation before members of the board and the First Presidency. Later in November Widtsoe outlined the proposal in a letter to President Heber J. Grant. His eloquent justification gives a clearer view of the problem and why they diligently sought to resolve it:

> The work in our temples has grown to such proportions that a knowledge of the work done in the temples is called for by very many people to avoid duplication, and to guide in the preparation of family records. The financial loss due to duplication is large; the discouragement that follows duplication is larger, but the fewer spirits provided with the blessings of the endowment when duplication occurs is the most serious consequence. To make the records furnish this protection, an index is necessary. . . . The Directors of the Society, the presidents and recorders of the temples, and the committee on classwork and activities are unanimous in the opinion that the time has come when the index should be made.[35]

Widtsoe stressed the urgency of forming the index and recommended that young people familiar with the typewriter be called on short-time missions to get the project in place. The cost of the cards—which he estimated at $1,500–2,000—was about all that was required. Two months later Widtsoe wrote to the First Presidency suggesting that stakes in temple districts call qualified women to serve six-month missions to complete the cards and establish a central filing office where work could be checked to avoid duplication. He also recommended that Harry H. Russell be called to supervise and oversee the work.[36] The recommendations were approved, and Russell was made director of the Temple Index Bureau.

Fundamental Principles behind Temple Work

In major addresses to the Genealogical Society, Widtsoe frequently spoke of fundamental principles of Mormon doctrine that are firmly established by temple and genealogical work. The following excerpts briefly capture his view of the most important principles of church doctrine around which temple work centers.

The Eternal Existence of Man

Every person who goes into the temple tacitly admits his belief in the principle of the eternal existence of man. This is the first thought that must possess any intelligent worker in the temple, otherwise why spend time on the work.

The Eternal Life of Man

Man is not only indestructible, but is subject to growth. . . . Every time we go into the temple we accept the doctrine that not only shall man live forever, but he shall either grow or retrograde.

The Free Agency of Man

The eternal spirit of man is characterized by its free agency. . . . Certainly we could not conceive of the true meaning of temple work, unless we accept the eternal principle of man's free agency; and that the dead as well as the living may receive or reject the opportunities of the Gospel.

Judgment of Man according to Works

The spirits sent to this earth will be judged by their works. . . . Moreover our punishment stands, at least measurably, throughout the endless ages, because, as we go onward, those above us go onward also, and the relative positions remain the same. . . . Temple work . . . assumes this principle of eternal justice.

The Love of God for Man

My spirit and yours, and the spirit of every man or woman are guided and will be guided by a loving Father. . . . In the presence of His love we grew and developed in our spiritual existence, as today we live out our physical existence, and as in the hereafter we shall continue our eternal life. Temple work best represents the quality of the infinite love of God for his children. . . . Unless we know the eternal love of our Father for His children we gather only a partial meaning of temple work. God's plan is to save His children.

The Authority of God and the Great Plan

Then, also, to perform these ordinances of the earth officially, and to make them valid, God has delegated authority to His servants on earth, whereby the work of the Great Plan, as pertaining to the earth, can be consummated. . . . Hence, living men and women may act for and in behalf of the dead under the direction of the Priesthood. Those who die in unbelief, but who later obtain belief, must have the chance to go on, otherwise justice is not satisfied.[37]

Guided by these fundamental gospel principles, Widtsoe often spoke of the accountability all men share for their dead. In general conference, 3 April 1927, he taught: "We have been told by the Prophet Joseph Smith that without our dead we cannot be saved; or, as he stated it, 'Their salvation is necessary and essential to our salvation.'"[38] In remarks he was invited to make in a meeting of the Roberts Family Organization, he stressed that family members currently on the earth cannot progress to eternal life until their family lines are tied back to Adam. Guided by this conviction, Widtsoe wrote:

I believe the Lord requires of us that we all set our houses in order in this respect, that each man and woman, every family, set about to secure just as completely as may be possible a record of their dead, so that thereby the genealogies of the human family may be gathered and increased in number, and we may have ample material with which to labour in the Temples of the Lord.[39]

All these fundamental principles underscore the larger ideas of man's universal salvation and obtaining eternal life. They are the core truths around which modern temple work has developed.

Popularizing Modern Temple Work

To help place all organizations in close touch with the Genealogical Society and to educate members about genealogy and modern temple work, Widtsoe headed a committee that included representatives from the Sunday School, the Young Men's and Young Women's Mutual Improvement Associations, the Primary, Church Education, and Brigham Young University.[40] He wrote to Adam S. Bennion, superintendent of Brigham Young University, to inquire about having instruction in genealogy and temple work added to some of the curriculum.[41] In a letter to the general Primary president, he wrote, "I feel that you are sowing seed on very fertile soil. If our children can be taught some of the elements of Temple work, however small, it will mean much to the Temple workers of a generation hence when these little boys and girls shall be grown men and women."[42]

The *Utah Genealogical and Historical Magazine* had carried some brief outlines for lessons on genealogy. Topics centered on record keeping, the Genealogical Society, the doctrine behind genealogy, and the history of genealogy. With his educational background and his reputation as a gifted teacher, it is little wonder that Widtsoe was almost constantly on the committees that were assigned to formulate genealogical lessons. In February 1923, in a letter to George D. Kirby, Widtsoe shared some personal wishes regarding the lessons: "Some day I hope that the central office will have complete study courses for the genealogical societies of the Church."[43] Some lessons on genealogy were being taught throughout the church at the time, but no universal system was followed. His wish for a study course from the central office was fulfilled in 1925 when a three-year course on genealogy and temple work was begun. The lessons, published in the *Utah Genealogical and Historical Magazine,* were designed for weekly study classes. The foreword explained the intent behind the lessons:

> The lesson work presented herewith is the beginning of a three years' course in genealogical and temple work, based upon the new genealogical handbook, published by the Genealogical Society of Utah.
>
> Each lesson is grouped into four parts, designed for weekly class study for genealogical workers, and others interested in the work of redemption of the dead.
>
> The outlines and lesson-statements have been purposely left brief to enable the class to work out its own details and otherwise delve into the work in a manner best suited to the conditions at hand. With the handbook of easy access and an abundance of material in the Scriptures to supplement its teachings, there is now at the disposal of all Latter-day Saints sufficient material to give them a working knowledge of genealogical procedure, if they will but devote the necessary time to master the intricacies of this wonderful art. Even those who do not desire to become practical genealogists will find much satisfaction in a careful study of the doctrine presented.[44]

The signature beneath the foreword reads: "Genealogical Society of Utah, Lesson Committee, Dr. John A. Widtsoe, Chairman. Salt Lake City, Utah. Dec. 1, 1924."[45] These lessons focused on the fundamental doctrine behind genealogical and temple work. They included frequent examples from scripture and an emphasis on world history and world society. A notable difference between these lesson outlines and previous ones was that about every third lesson was devoted to genealogical procedures. This allowed every student to gain an appreciation for and understanding of genealogy and the skills needed to perform his or her own genealogy in the process of redeeming their dead. Lesson topics included indexing, the Temple Index Bureau, filming, and record keeping. Students also learned how to use various sources of genealogical information and how the Genealogical Society functioned. Widtsoe was determined to teach every church member about the importance of temple work and how to proceed with that work for his or her own family.

Building a Central Genealogical Library

While traveling through Europe with Senator Reed Smoot in 1923, Widtsoe assessed the work required by each country to maintain accurate genealogical records and surveyed their sources and repositories. As Widtsoe visited Great Britain, Denmark, Sweden, Norway, Germany, France, Belgium, and Holland, he found out how to obtain genealogical information from them. He carefully observed what procedures they followed and tried to secure as much information as he could for the Utah Genealogical Society's library.[46] At the conclusion of his trip he submitted his observations and recommendations:

It is very clear that in all the countries visited there has been for some time an active interest in genealogical research. Our missionaries, following the suggestion of Brother Morton, could help greatly in locating such collections. Selections of books and other materials should be made, however, only by some one who is experienced with books and who has a deep interest in genealogy. My Frankfurt [Germany] experience was confirmation of this view.

Clearly also there is quite as much genealogical material in Scandinavia as in any other country, if it only may be made available. The Society should proceed vigorously to supply its library with all valuable printed material on genealogy. The collections made on this trip will make a good foundation. Such library facilities will do much for the cause here at home, and will furnish leads for more detailed work abroad.

Our genealogical work abroad is done in a very haphazard manner. I fear that some of it is inaccurate. It seems to me that steps must be taken to organize for this work. Competent men should be placed in Scandinavia for genealogical purposes. There is work enough to support them. It may be the wisest plan to form some organization at home, a genealogical bureau, which will undertake to act as a medium between the person seeking the names of his dead and the expert worker who will collect the names. The system as now practiced is not commensurate with the cause, or with the provision made for temple work.[47]

Subsequent visits brought significant improvements in genealogical work in all European countries.

Whenever Widtsoe was on assignment in Europe, he conscientiously sought to purchase worthy genealogical books and already published family histories. In the 1931 Genealogical Convention, Elder Joseph Fielding Smith announced that the purchases made by Widtsoe had kept the society nearly broke. President Widtsoe responded, "I regret that, of course, but I am not very sorry. Nearly every book will be of value to us in the course of time."[48] In many of his endeavors to obtain important books, he had felt the direction of the Holy Spirit. He shared one of his most memorable experiences:

> I know of no work that I have done in the Church which has been so filled with testimonies of the divinity of this work as the little I have done in behalf of the salvation of our dead. I could tell you a number of experiences, but the one that impressed me most happened a few years ago when I accompanied Brother Reed Smoot to Europe. We came to Stockholm; he had his work to do; I decided to see what I could do in the way of finding books on Swedish genealogy. I knew the names of the two big bookstores in Stockholm. I went to the one, made my selections, and then started across the city to the other bookstore in the hope that I might find some more suitable books. As I hurried along the street filled with people, I was stopped suddenly by some voice which said to me: "Go across the street and down that narrow side street." I looked across the street and saw a little narrow street. I had not been in Stockholm before. I thought: This is all nonsense, . . . I have to do my work, and I walked on. Almost at once the voice came again, as distinctly as any voice I have ever heard. Then I asked myself: What is your business in this city? Are you not on the Lord's errand? And I crossed over; went down the little narrow street, and there, half-way down, found a little bookstore that I had known nothing about. When I asked for books on genealogy the lady said: "No, we do not carry books on genealogy. When we get such books we send them to the bookstore"—naming the store for which I was headed. Then, just as I was leaving in disap-

pointment, she said: "Stop a minute. A leading book col-
lector, a genealogist, died about a month ago, and we
bought his library. Many of his genealogical books are in
the back room ready to be sent to the bookstore, but if
you want to buy them you may have them." Thus we se-
cured the foundation of Swedish genealogy in our
library.[49]

From these inspired beginnings, the Genealogical Library of the church has become the largest and most useful
repository of genealogical information in the world.

A Program for Genealogical Exchange

The European trip with Senator Smoot deepened
Widtsoe's conviction of the need of church members and
interested genealogists to coordinate and share their research. Travel to distant lands to research ancestral lines
was too costly for most to consider, but in almost all of
those distant lands were fellow church members or interested professionals who could exchange research information for work on their lines in yet another part of the world.

The emphasis given temple work from the beginning
of the restoration of the gospel to the Prophet Joseph Smith
underscores the importance of making genealogical information and temple ordinances available to everyone as ex-
peditiously as possible.[50] This was the underlying message
of an address on the beginnings of modern temple work by
Widtsoe.[51] In 1928 he published the names of key workers
and the addresses of the significant archives and libraries
of genealogical information in the Scandinavian countries.
From each library or archive he requested information
on local researchers who could be employed on an individual basis to do research for church members who wished
to obtain their information but could not travel to these

countries. The information was most helpful in furthering the work.[52] Yet this was not enough; the need for greater success drove Widtsoe to find more successful ways of accomplishing the work.

From 1928 to 1934 Widtsoe was the president of the European Mission, which consisted of ten to eleven missions across the various capitals of Europe. He became starkly aware of the feelings of deprivation among European church members who were without a temple in which they could receive their own endowments and sealings or in which they could do the work for their dead ancestors. Under the leadership of President Widtsoe, the mission presidents in Europe established a program for genealogical research and exchange. Each branch of members organized a genealogical class in which they studied the best-known manuals on genealogy in the church. A mission genealogical agent was called to coordinate the classes and the research results. Within each country, church members could aid each other; for example, a member in Liverpool, England, could do research for someone in Glasgow, Scotland, and thereby eliminate travel and lodging costs for the Saint from Scotland. In exchange, someone from Glasgow could do local research for the Liverpool member or someone else from their branch with family roots in Glasgow. Global exchanges were even more intriguing. Without a temple, the only work European Saints could participate in was gathering genealogical data. On the other hand, they had an advantage that those in Utah did not have—they were in the very lands from which the Utah members or their ancestors had come and could readily research the family records. The following excerpt is from a reprint of one of Widtsoe's *Millennial Star* editorials:

> It is further proposed that Latter-day Saints of European descent, living in temple districts, may be willing to do

work in the temples for the dead of those who live in Europe, in exchange for genealogical help. Such valuable mutual assistance could be arranged with profit through the mission genealogical agent. A definite basis for exchange will probably be suggested, as, for example, three new names in a given family line or four hours of actual research work done by someone in Europe would pay for the endowment of one person in one of the temples.[53]

This editorial includes an excerpt from a letter President Widtsoe wrote to the Genealogical Society to report the success of the exchange program in missions that had undertaken it. This same editorial, later reprinted in the *Utah Genealogical and Historical Magazine,* instructed Saints in the United States to send their research requests to President Widtsoe's office. The mission genealogical agent would then process the requests and forward them to someone who could assist the American Saints. Widtsoe's mailing address in Liverpool was included as well as a description of the information needed from all who wished to obtain research help in Europe. To assure fairness in the program, the editorial included a standard basis on which the users could plan:

> Members living in Temple Districts will do ordinance work for names of those living in Missions at the standard rate of 50c for a female and 75c for a male.
>
> Members living in Missions will copy information from parish or probate registers at the rate of 25c per hour.
>
> Thus two hours research will pay for the endowment of one woman and three for that of a man.[54]

In April 1931 Widtsoe, though still living in Europe, spent time in Salt Lake City to attend general conference. His attendance was requested by the First Presidency because he had not attended for three years while residing in

Europe. Held in connection with the conference was a convention of the Genealogical Society. Responding to their request, he gave a moving report of genealogical interest among the Saints in the missions of Europe. He reported that it was a matter of great lament to many Saints in Europe, especially those of second- or third-generation church membership, that they must live their lives without the benefit and blessings of temple ordinances. Moreover, they lamented that they didn't have the privilege of enjoying the blessings of regular temple attendance. He spoke of their concern about the thousands of Saints who had faithfully lived the principles set forth in the restoration and who had gone on to a splendid reward beyond the grave but who most often were required to wait substantial periods for their temple work to be done. They waited in the spirit world with those who had rejected the gospel or never had it. The living descendants of these faithful Saints were, of course, anxious that temple ordinance work become more efficient with unnecessary delays eliminated. Widtsoe requested that the society take this matter up and, through the Index Bureau, get the temple work of deceased members efficiently accomplished. He reported disappointment that the work of the Exchange Bureau had developed very slowly, yet he spoke with confidence and urged patience and greater effort to make it successful. As a result of this interest and at his recommendation, the Research Bureau of the Genealogical Society was established. Despite his sincerity and the intrinsic merit of the idea, it did not flourish.

> The Society did not adopt the worldwide supervisory program Elder Widtsoe had in mind, but it did establish the Research Bureau, which supervised all research done at the library, hired researchers, made contacts with for-

eign researchers, transferred money to foreign countries
when needed, conducted classes in genealogical research,
assisted in obtaining information not available in the library, and acted as a general clearinghouse in coordinat-
ing research activities.[55]

An Apostle for Modern Temple Work to the End

In 1923 Widtsoe was asked to attend the dedication
services of the Alberta Temple. The experience seemed to
invigorate him further and intensify his advocacy of temple
work. He was particularly moved by the spiritual impact
temple work had on the rest of the gospel work in the latter
days:

> The Alberta Temple . . . is an architectural gem, beautiful
> inside and out. The architects have produced an exquisite
> harmony such as I think I have never known before in
> any structure whether in the new or old world. The dedi-
> catory exercises were very impressive. There were eleven
> sessions and the spirit which actuates the great latter-day
> work known as "Mormonism" was present abundantly
> so that every person present was touched by it.[56]

Widtsoe continually strove to deepen the appreciation
and understanding of church members regarding temple
work. He was convinced of the "need to lay out with great
care a general plan for the future development of this work,
having in mind the tremendous importance of it according
to our faith."[57] Additional concern arose over those in the
mission field who did not have the knowledge to do their
own genealogical work:

> I do think that the Saints residing in the mission field
> would be greatly benefited if some definite help could be
> tendered them. They need to know something about the
> sources of genealogical information, often lying near at

hand, and the methods of building their genealogy for Temple work.[58]

Through the remainder of his life, Widtsoe participated in the developments and decision making that guided the society and the church in matters of temple and genealogical work and salvation of the dead. In 1935 he taught that of all the gospel principles, probably none contributed more toward developing one's spiritual power and strength than work associated with salvation of the dead. From his own experience and the experiences of his friends, he assured church members that "those who give themselves in wisdom and with propriety to this work will round out their spiritual experiences, enrich their lives, and find a new and abiding joy in all duties pertaining to life under the Gospel of Jesus Christ."[59] During Leadership Week at BYU in 1935, he spoke of the doctrine of universal salvation again: "If the Gospel is not for all men—if God has a few chosen spirits whom He loves and who, irrespective of their labors in the past, in mortality, and in the hereafter, shall be brought into His presence—then the whole latter day work falls to the ground as a set of separate and distinct unorganized principles."[60]

In 1937 he described the urgency with which the church must proceed with temple work: "The dead are so many that we cannot hope, unless we use the utmost expedition, to keep pace with the gathering of names made available in our genealogical research."[61] In 1939 and 1940 he prepared outlines for lessons that were carried in the society's magazine. From 1940, when the church ceased publication of the *Utah Genealogical and Historical Magazine*, through 1954, a genealogical section was included in the *Improvement Era*.[62] From 1935 to 1952 Widtsoe was editor of the *Improvement Era*. In 1943 an editorial in the *Improvement Era* carried Widtsoe's ideas further:

To give glory to the Lord, members of the Church must seek the blessings offered by the temples. To build with a flaming faith, and then, when the building is completed, to fail to use it, is folly and unacceptable to the Lord. The flame of faith must not burn low. Every member of the Church should so conduct himself as to be worthy of receiving the ordinances offered within temple walls. Further, he should seek opportunities to labor there for the dead, so that they, if the work is accepted by them, may also win membership in the kingdom of God. Then we do honor to the Lord, and win blessings for ourselves and our ancestry.[63]

In moving remarks growing out of the worldwide horrors of the Great War, especially its devastation among beloved European countries, Widtsoe gave a sobering challenge to church members. His address in general conference of April 1943 was given in recognition of the fiftieth anniversary of the dedication of the Salt Lake Temple:

These are trying days, in which Satan rages, at home and abroad, hard days, evil and ugly days. We stand helpless as it seems before them. We need help. We need strength. We need guidance. Perhaps if we would do our work in behalf of those of the unseen world who hunger and pray for the work we can do for them, the unseen world would in return give us help in the day of our urgent need. There are more in that other world than there are here. There is more power and strength there than we have here upon this earth. We have but a trifle, and that trifle is taken from the immeasurable power of God. We shall make no mistake in becoming collaborators in the Lord's mighty work for human redemption.[64]

The great emphasis Widtsoe and other society officials put on gathering family names and performing temple work in time created a serious dilemma. Inflexible policies of proving familial relationships in the clearance process for names submitted to the temple, combined with increases in temple attendance, led to a shortage of names for temple work. Elders Joseph Fielding Smith and John A. Widtsoe were the main advocates for processing names regardless of family connections to members of the church. Their views gave rise to the current name extraction program.

In September 1943, Elder Widtsoe anticipated the policy that eventually developed when he declared that the Society ought to obtain all published manuscript and microfilm records as fast as possible and use the names for temple work. "Why don't we use the names for temple work which cannot be tied to any Church families? . . . The Lord has provided these names by inspiring genealogists to compile and publish them. In an extremity like the present, why not use the names from such records? . . . For what purpose have these books been compiled, if not to make the names available for temple work?"[65]

The urgency Widtsoe had always expressed for this sacred work did not diminish as he neared the end of his life. Addressing the general conference in April 1950, he urged once again that the Saints turn their hearts steadily and forcefully toward the duty of laboring for the dead. He said: "We cannot be saved without doing so. The earth cannot continue to its destined end unless we so do."[66] As always, he pointed to the outstanding spiritual benefit that flows to all those who actively participate in the work:

Let us do our duty for ourselves and for the future of this earth upon which we live and which we hold so dear. And let us remember always that the spiritual forces centering in our temples are more powerful than atom rays or any earthly force discovered by man.[67]

In the last year of his life, he summarized his lifelong

view of temple work: "Temple work is the cement that holds together all gospel principles. Genealogy is the first step in universal salvation, as far as we on earth can contribute to this great human destiny."[68] The *Improvement Era* published excerpts from an article on the temples that Widtsoe was working on at the time of his death. Illustrating his article are color photographs of the interior and exterior of the St. George Temple. The essay reviewed many of the teachings about temple work Widtsoe had expounded over his lifetime. These final comments returned to the fundamental essence of the doctrine of modern temple work—the work and glory of God. Lifelong devotion to the salvation of the dead draws each one closer to those so served and to God whose work it is. Reminding readers that a person is not expected to comprehend the details of the temple in a single visit, he declared:

> Therefore, the Lord has provided means of repetition. Temple work must be done first by each person for himself or herself; then it may be done for one's dead ancestors or friends as frequently as circumstances will allow. This service will open the doors of salvation for the dead and will also help fix upon the mind of the living the nature, meaning, and obligations of the endowment. By keeping the endowment fresh in mind, we shall be better able to perform our duties in life under the influence of eternal blessings.[69]

> Wherever one turns in the revealed gospel of the Lord Jesus Christ, and particularly in the temple, the conviction grows that the work of God is re-established for his specific purposes in the latter days. Temple service is to aid and to help us in qualifying for this mighty work: ". . . to bring to pass the immortality and eternal life of man." (Moses 1:39)[70]

A strong testimony of an intimate connection between the powers of heaven and modern temple work illuminated the life and teachings of John A. Widtsoe. It began to burn its way into his heart while he was a young student at Harvard, and in those early years he developed unusually poignant feelings for temple work. Those feelings grew ever stronger until the day he himself passed through death's portal. His study of scripture and the revealed teachings of latter-day prophets brought conversion to the doctrine behind temple work, while personal experiences in gathering genealogical data and participating in vicarious temple ordinances brought conversion to the divinity of the work. Widtsoe's testimony deepened throughout his life, and he became one of the church's foremost spokesmen for modern temple work.

Notes

1. See James B. Allen, Jesse L. Embry, and Kahlile B. Mehr, *Hearts Turned to the Fathers: A History of the Genealogical Society of Utah, 1894–1994* (Provo, Utah: BYU Studies, 1995).

2. John A. Widtsoe, "The Opening of Our New Home," *Utah Genealogical and Historical Magazine* (hereafter *UGHM*) 25 (April 1934): 56.

3. *In a Sunlit Land: The Autobiography of John A. Widtsoe* (Salt Lake City: Deseret News, 1952), 176–77.

4. John A. Widtsoe to Nellie T. Taylor, 9 November 1921, John A. Widtsoe Collection, Archives Division, Historical Department, Church of Jesus Christ of Latter-day Saints (hereafter LDS Church Archives).

5. John A. Widtsoe to Harry H. Russell, 28 March 1923, Widtsoe Collection, LDS Church Archives.

6. John A. Widtsoe to Nellie T. Taylor, 27 March 1923, Widtsoe Collection, LDS Church Archives.

7. *Teachings of the Prophet Joseph Smith,* 356.

8. Ibid., 193.

9. John A. Widtsoe, "What Is Our Personal Obligation for the Salvation of the Dead?" in *Gospel Interpretations: More Evidences and Reconciliations* (Salt Lake City: Bookcraft, 1947), 98–99.

10. John A. Widtsoe, "Work for the Dead," *UGHM* 6 (January 1915): 33.

11. John A. Widtsoe, "Purpose of the Family Organization," *UGHM* 14 (June 1923): 81.

12. John A. Widtsoe, "The Worth of Souls," *Millennial Star* 96 (1 March 1934): 132–34.

13. John A. Widtsoe, "The Beginnings of Modern Temple Work," *Improvement Era*, October 1927, 1076, 1079.

14. John A. Widtsoe, "Temple Worship," *UGHM* 12 (April 1921): 54.

15. John A. Widtsoe, "Genealogical Activities in Europe," *UGHM* 22 (July 1931): 105.

16. Widtsoe, "Temple Worship," 62. A similar reference to temples in earlier ages and other cultures suggests an important connection to modern temple work:

> All people of all ages have had temples in one form or another. When the history of human thought shall be written from the point of view of temple worship, it may well be found that temples and the work done in them have been the dominating influence in shaping human thought from the beginning of the race. Even today political controversies are as nothing in determining the temper of a people, as compared with religious sentiments and convictions, especially as practiced in the temples of the people.
>
> In every land and in every age temples have been built and used. In China, age old with four thousand years of written history; in India; on the islands of the sea; in South America; in North America; in Africa and in Australia; everywhere there are evidences of the existence and use of temples. (Ibid., 52)

17. Ibid., 53–54.

18. See "The Biennial Meeting of the Genealogical Society of Utah," *UGHM* 1 (July 1910): 140.

19. John A. Widtsoe, "The Genealogical Society's Quarterly Meeting," *UGHM* 2 (January 1911): 46.

20. Widtsoe, "Work for the Dead," 33.

21. See Widtsoe, "Temple Worship," 54: "Those who understand the eternal nature of the gospel—planned before the foundation of the earth—understand clearly why all history seems to revolve about the building and use of temples."

22. Ibid., 53. The critical emphasis the Prophet Joseph Smith put on temple and genealogical work is further attested in an address by Widtsoe to the Liberty Stake Genealogical Convention, 24 May 1922: "It is sufficient for us to remember that temple work for the living and for the dead was the burden of the thought and labors of the Prophet Joseph Smith from the day when the Angel Moroni first stood before him and told him of the things that were to be, up to the last day of the Prophet's life. The principle of salvation for the dead received foremost consideration by the prophet because of its close and intertwining relationship to all other principles." John A. Widtsoe, "Fundamentals of Temple Doctrine," *UGHM* 13 (July 1922): 129.

An outstanding essay by Widtsoe reviewing Joseph's involvement in the beginnings of modern temple work was published in October 1927; see Widtsoe, "Beginnings of Modern Temple Work," 1073–79.

23. John A. Widtsoe, "The Meaning and Importance of Records," *UGHM* 11 (July 1920): 97.

24. *Sunlit Land*, 177.

25. Widtsoe, "Worth of Souls," 131.

26. Widtsoe, "Temple Worship," 64.

27. Ibid., 56.

28. John A. Widtsoe to Maude May Babcock, 14 December 1921, Widtsoe Collection, LDS Church Archives.

29. Allen, Embry, and Mehr, *Hearts Turned to the Fathers*, 95.

30. Ibid., 97.

31. Widtsoe, "Purpose of the Family Organization," 81.

32. See Allen, Embry, and Mehr, *Hearts Turned to the Fathers,* 98.

33. See ibid., 97–98.

34. See Archibald F. Bennett, "The Growth of the Temple Index Bureau: World-Wide Clearing-house," *Improvement Era,* April 1936, 218.

35. John A. Widtsoe to President Heber J. Grant, 15 November 1921, Widtsoe Collection, LDS Church Archives.

36. See Widtsoe to the First Presidency, 13 January 1922, Widtsoe Collection, LDS Church Archives.

37. Widtsoe, "Fundamentals of Temple Doctrine," 130–34. A powerful editorial by Widtsoe summarizing these same fundamental principles was published in the *Millennial Star* in 1929. "Salvation for the Dead," *Millennial Star* 91 (19 September 1929): 600–601.

38. John A. Widtsoe, "Serving Our Dead," *Millennial Star* 89 (4 August 1927): 483.

39. Ibid., 484.

40. See Allen, Embry, and Mehr, *Hearts Turned to the Fathers,* 112.

41. See John A. Widtsoe to Superintendent Adam Bennion, 13 May 1921, Widtsoe Collection, LDS Church Archives.

42. John A. Widtsoe to Louie B. Felt, 26 July 1922, Widtsoe Collection, LDS Church Archives.

43. John A. Widtsoe to George D. Kirby, 24 February 1923, Widtsoe Collection, LDS Church Archives.

44. John A. Widtsoe, "Lessons In Genealogy," *UGHM* 16 (January 1925): 33.

45. Ibid.

46. See John A. Widtsoe, "Report of Dr. John A. Widtsoe's Visit to Scandinavia," *UGHM* 15 (January 1924): 11–16.

47. Ibid., 15.

48. Widtsoe, "Genealogical Activities in Europe," 100.

49. Ibid., 101.

50. The church's recent move toward constructing many

smaller temples, in order to make the temple more accessible to all church members, is further evidence of this need.

51. See Widtsoe, "Beginnings of Modern Temple Work," 1079.

52. See John A. Widtsoe, "Obtaining Scandinavian Genealogies," *UGHM* 19 (January 1928): 1–8.

53. Editorial from the *Millennial Star*, "European Program for Genealogical Study, Research and Exchange," *UGHM* 21 (January 1930): 34.

54. Ibid., 35.

55. Allen, Embry, and Mehr, *Hearts Turned to the Fathers*, 105.

56. John A. Widtsoe to F. W. Smith, 13 September 1923, Widtsoe Collection, LDS Church Archives.

57. John A. Widtsoe to Susa Young Gates, 25 June 1925, Widtsoe Collection, LDS Church Archives.

58. John A. Widtsoe to Susa Young Gates, 8 August 1927, Widtsoe Collection, LDS Church Archives.

59. "Lesson Course: Methods of Genealogical Research," *UGHM* 26 (July 1935): 139.

60. John A. Widtsoe, "Elijah, the Tishbite," *UGHM* 27 (April 1936): 54.

61. John A. Widtsoe, "The Urgency of Temple Service," *UGHM* 28 (January 1937): 5.

62. See Allen, Embry, and Mehr, *Hearts Turned to the Fathers*, 133.

63. John A. Widtsoe, "The Temple Calls," *Improvement Era*, April 1943, 224.

64. John A. Widtsoe, "The Way of Salvation," *Improvement Era*, May 1943, 278–79.

65. Allen, Embry, and Mehr, *Hearts Turned to the Fathers*, 177.

66. John A. Widtsoe, "Universal Brotherhood Will Save the World," *Improvement Era*, May 1950, 429.

67. Ibid., 430.

68. *Sunlit Land*, 176.

69. John A. Widtsoe, "Looking toward the Temple," *Improvement Era*, October 1962, 710.

70. Ibid., 765.

CHAPTER 8

CONFLICTING ORDERS: ALMA AND AMULEK IN AMMONIHAH

Thomas R. Valletta

During the tenth year of the reign of the judges, enmity between two fiercely competing orders of Nephite society erupted into open violence in Ammonihah, a city in the land of Melek. The records describing these hostilities, appearing in Alma 8–14, provide considerable insight into the holy order of the Son of God and its spurious counterpart, the order of Nehor. The theology, priesthood, temple worship, legal practices, and monetary system of the Nephites during the first century B.C. are subjects generously illuminated in these chapters.[1] This paper focuses on the conflict between the holy order of the Son of God and the order of Nehor. The former was patterned after the Savior's life and was rooted in keeping sacred covenants centered in the temple as a symbol of eternity. The latter was patterned after an ambitious murderer and rooted in prideful competition in which individuals were resolute on attaining money as a means of power and riches. Important comparisons and contrasts between these two opposing orders emerge from these chapters; their sources of authority and power, heroes, centers and rituals of worship, doctrines and standards of behavior, and aspirations and purposes are a few of the most obvious.

The catalyst for the confrontation at Ammonihah occurred over a year earlier when Alma, concerned about increasing pride and wickedness among his people, "delivered up the judgment-seat to Nephihah, and confined himself wholly to the high priesthood of the holy order of God, to the testimony of the word, according to the spirit of revelation and prophecy" (Alma 4:20). Alma began a mission "to deliver the word of God unto the people, first in the land of Zarahemla, and from thence throughout all the land" (Alma 5:1).

Alma's preaching throughout the land met with mixed success. Ammonihah was one of the least receptive cities to the word of God. Mormon editorialized that "Satan had gotten great hold upon the hearts of the people of the city" (Alma 8:9). Alma had "labored much in the spirit, wrestling with God in mighty prayer, that he would pour out his Spirit upon the people who were in the city; . . . Nevertheless, they hardened their hearts" (Alma 8:10–11). Despite Alma's valiant efforts, many of the inhabitants of Ammonihah "withstood all his words, and reviled him, and spit upon him, and caused that he should be cast out of their city" (Alma 8:13).

Only by divine intervention and a visit from an angel of the Lord to Alma was Ammonihah given another chance to hear God's word through the prophet (see Alma 8:14–18). Returning to Ammonihah, Alma found a spiritually receptive Amulek readily confessing that he knew, also by angelic visitation, that Alma was "a holy prophet of God" (Alma 8:20). After spending "many days with Amulek" (Alma 8:27), presumably teaching and preparing him for the ministry, Alma received revelation that they both were to "go forth and prophesy" unto the people of Ammonihah (Alma 8:29).

The subsequent confrontation between these righteous men of God and the wicked leaders of Ammonihah involved far more than a disagreement between individuals or even a clash of personalities. It was the continuation of an age-old confrontation between priestcraft and true priesthood—in this case, between the keepers of the purse and the keepers of the mysteries of God. In this classic conflict between two competing orders of society, Alma and Amulek acted as agents of the Son of God, while Zeezrom and his comrades assumed the role of minions of Satan, claiming authority from a false priesthood called the order of Nehor.

The High Priesthood of the Holy Order of God

Alma's commission to teach and testify was "according to the holy order of God, which is in Christ Jesus" (Alma 5:44). During his mission, Alma variously refers to his authority as

* "the high priesthood of the holy order of God" (Alma 4:20; 13:6),
* "the holy order of God" (Alma 5:54; 7:22; 8:4),
* "the holy order" (Alma 6:8),
* "his holy order, which was after the order of his Son" (Alma 13:1),
* "the order of his/the Son" (Alma 13:2, 7, 9),
* "the high priesthood of the holy order" (Alma 13:8),
* "the holy order, or this high priesthood" (Alma 13:10),
* "the high priesthood according to the holy order of God" (Alma 13:18).

"The Holy Priesthood, after the order of the Son of God," is referred to in modern revelation as the Melchizedek Priesthood, "out of respect or reverence to the name of the Supreme Being, to avoid the too frequent repetition of his name" (D&C 107:3–4). It has long been convincingly reasoned, in my opinion, that the righteous Nephites functioned under the power and authority of the Melchizedek Priesthood rather than the Levitical order.[2]

That the Melchizedek Priesthood was present among the righteous Nephites is evident by the resulting effects and blessings of that priesthood. Modern revelation indicates that

> this greater priesthood administereth the gospel and holdeth the key of the mysteries of the kingdom, even the key of the knowledge of God. Therefore, in the ordinances thereof, the power of godliness is manifest. And without the ordinances thereof, and the authority of the priesthood, the power of godliness is not manifest unto men in the flesh; For without this no man can see the face of God, even the Father, and live. (D&C 84:19–22)

The Book of Mormon is replete with references to ordinances and blessings that relate to the higher priesthood, including the gift of the Holy Ghost[3] as well as the right to bestow that gift, the spirit of prophecy and revelation, ordinations, healing the sick, raising the dead, a knowledge of the mysteries of God, seership, sealing power, promises of eternal life, visitations of God, and the keys of the kingdom (see, for example, 1 Nephi 1:8; 2 Nephi 2:4; 11:2; Mosiah 8:13–18; 28:16; Alma 6:1; 9:20–21; 15:5; 17:2–3; 19:13; 31:36; 3 Nephi 7:22; 19:4). Joseph Fielding Smith declared that "all through the Book of Mormon we find references to the Nephites officiating by virtue of the Higher Priesthood after the holy order."[4] Elder Bruce R. McConkie concluded that "the Nephite branch of the house of Israel was subject to the higher priesthood during all its history."[5] The remainder of this paper is based on the assumption that righteous Nephites administered under the power and authority of the Melchizedek Priesthood.

High Priesthood and Temple Worship

Intimately connected with priesthood authority are the ordinances and covenants of the temple (see, for example, Numbers 1:48–53; 16:9; Hebrews 7; D&C 124:28, 39, 41–42). The Prophet Joseph Smith alluded to these connections in a talk given on 27 August 1843. He taught that "the Priesthood of Aaron . . . administers in outward ordinances, and the offering of sacrifices." That the ancient Israelites were limited to the Levitical Priesthood was the result of their refusing the "blessing or knowledge" that Moses offered them at Mt. Sinai. Joseph Smith explained that although the Levitical Priesthood was for performing temple service (see Numbers 1:48–53), it only allowed for "priests to administer in outward ordinances, made without an oath." To receive the higher orders of the priesthood, such as the "patriarchal authority," the Prophet admonished the Saints to "go to and finish the temple, and God will fill it with power, and you will then receive more knowledge concerning this priesthood." Those holding the "fulness of the Melchizedek Priesthood," according to Joseph, "are kings and priests of the Most High God, holding the keys of power and blessings." To receive this "anointing and sealing is to be called, elected and made sure."[6] Alma made it clear that these blessings were available to faithful believers if they would humble themselves before God and "bring forth fruit meet for repentance" (Alma 13:13; see Alma 13:10–19).

The Prophet Joseph Smith had learned early in his ministry of the strong relationship between priesthood and temple. In one of the earliest revelations of this dispensation, Joseph Smith was informed that the priesthood would be revealed by the "hand of Elijah the prophet"; otherwise, "the whole earth would be utterly wasted at [the Lord's] coming" (D&C 2:1, 3). The young Joseph soon discovered that this was "because he [Elijah] holds the keys of the authority to administer in all the ordinances of the Priesthood; and without the authority . . . , the ordinances could not be administered in righteousness."[7] Later, Joseph taught that "the spirit, power, and calling of Elijah is, that ye have the power to hold the key of the revelations, ordinances, oracles, powers and endowments of the fulness of the Melchizedek Priesthood and of the kingdom of God on the earth; and to receive, obtain, and perform all the ordinances belonging to the kingdom of God."[8] In addition, he explained that "if a man gets a fullness of the priesthood of God he has to get it in the same way that Jesus Christ obtained it, and that was by keeping all the commandments and obeying all the ordinances of the house of the Lord."[9]

Only a temple complete with all the ordinances and covenants can provide opportunity for a generation to receive the fulness of the priesthood. As previously noted, Alma's teachings in Ammonihah include several references to the holy order of the Son of God (see Alma 13:1, 2, 6–9, 16). Concerning this order, President Ezra Taft Benson taught: "To enter into the order of the Son of God is the equivalent today of entering into the fullness of the Melchizedek Priesthood, which is only received in the house of the Lord."[10] Alma's claim that his calling and authority was of "the high priesthood of the holy order of God" strongly suggests that he was intimately familiar with higher ordinances and covenants received in temples that included more than Levitical authority (see Alma 4:20; see also Alma 13:6, 8).

Importance of Temples in the Book of Mormon

In antiquity, "the Holy Temple was the very heart and soul" of God's chosen people.[11] According to Menahem Haran, the temple constituted "the most conspicuous and prominent of all cultic institutions in ancient Israel."[12] "As the ritual center of the universe," wrote Hugh Nibley, "the temple was anciently viewed as the one point on earth at which men and women could establish contact with higher spheres."[13] "The central rite of the temple was certainly the offering of sacrifice—the slaughtering of beasts; yet," according to Nibley, "the activities we read about in the Bible simply take that for granted and tell us of preaching, of feasting, and of music. The place seemed to be a general center of activity."[14] Joshua Berman agreed that,

> Contrary to the popular misconception that the Temple is solely a sacrificial center, the Temple needs to be construed as part of an organic whole and cannot be studied in isolation. As the center of Israel's national and spiritual life, it relates integrally to many of the institutional pillars of the Jewish faith—the Sabbath, the land of Israel, kingship, and justice, to mention just a few.[15]

"The presence of the temple represented stability and cohesiveness in the community," reported Stephen Ricks, "and its rites and ceremonies were viewed as essential to the proper functioning of the society."[16] "If there is no temple," stressed Nibley, "there is no true Israel; and where there is no true temple, civilization itself is but an empty shell."[17] As might be expected for a covenant people with direct claims to ancient Israel, "evidence in the Book of

Mormon indicates that temples were equally important among the Nephites, both in their religion and in their society."[18] As examined below, much of this evidence is provided in the account of Alma in Ammonihah.

The importance of temples in the Book of Mormon is demonstrated by the centrality of such holy places at each of the Nephite capitals (see 2 Nephi 5:16; Mosiah 1:18; 2:1; 7:17; 11:10, 12; Alma 16:13; 23:2; 26:29; Helaman 3:9, 14; 3 Nephi 11:1). The first order of business that Nephi undertook as he assumed leadership over the faithful was to "observe to keep the judgments, and the statutes, and the commandments of the Lord in all things, according to the law of Moses" (2 Nephi 5:10), and to initiate the construction of a temple (see 2 Nephi 5:16). Temples are noted in the Book of Mormon as places of sacrifice and offerings, special instruction, coronations, and covenant ceremonies (see 2 Nephi 5:10; Jacob 1:17; 2:2, 11; Mosiah 2:1–7, 37; 13:30; Alma 16:13; 23:2; 26:29; 30:3; 34:10; 3 Nephi 9:19–20).[19] Various sermons and writings in the Book of Mormon relate to the most sacred teachings associated with holy temples (see Mosiah 1–6, Alma 12–13, and 3 Nephi 11–18).[20] With references to ridding one's garments from people's sins (see Jacob 2:2), to the garments becoming "white through the blood of the Lamb" (Ether 13:10), and to God not dwelling "in unholy temples" (Alma 7:21; Helaman 4:24), temple imagery and allusion appear liberally in the text of the Book of Mormon. The temple and its related teachings are an important aspect of the Book of Mormon.

Nephites and the Higher Temple Ordinances

Since the Nephites had the fulness of the gospel and functioned under the direction of the high priesthood after the holy order of the Son, their temples were not likely limited to Levitical ordinances.[21] The Book of Mormon makes it clear that some Nephites, before the coming of Christ, entered into sacred ordinances pertaining to the holy order of the Son, were familiar with sacred garments, viewed great and wondrous revelations, received the mysteries of God, attained the sealing powers, and received promises of eternal life (see Jacob 2; Mosiah 26:20; Alma 13; Helaman 10). As Robert Millet expressed it:

> They were Former-day Saints who enjoyed transcendent spiritual blessings. They had the veil parted and saw the visions of heaven. They knew the Lord, enjoyed his ministration, and received from him the assurance of eternal life. They built temples (see 2 Nephi 5:16; Jacob 1:17; 2:2, 11; Mosiah 1:18; Alma 10:2; 16:13; 26:29; 3 Nephi 11:1), not to perform work for the dead, for such was not done until the ministry of Christ to the world of spirits, but to receive the covenants and ordinances of exaltation. During the Nephite "mini-millennium" and, we would suppose, during those prior periods of Nephite history when the people qualified themselves for such, "they were married, and given in marriage, and were blessed *according to the multitude of the promises which the Lord had made unto them*" (4 Nephi 1:11 italics added). These were the promises made to Abraham, Isaac, and Jacob, the promise of the gospel, the priesthood, and eternal life (see D&C 2; Abraham 1:2–3; 2:8–11).[22]

Some have questioned the Melchizedek nature of the Nephite temples prior to the ministry of Jesus Christ based on a misunderstanding of Nephi's declaration that he "did build a temple . . . [and] construct it after the manner of the temple of Solomon save it were not built of so many precious things; . . . it could not be built like unto Solomon's temple. But the manner of the construction was like unto the temple of Solomon; and the workmanship thereof was exceedingly fine" (2 Nephi 5:16). It should be realized that Nephi was not, in this verse, referring to the kind of ordinances that were being performed, but rather the manner of construction. "When Nephi said that the 'manner of construction' was the same as in Jerusalem," according to John L. Sorenson, "he could only have meant that the general pattern was similar. What was that pattern, and what was its function?" Sorenson explained:

> The temple of Solomon was built on a platform, so people literally went "up" to it. Inside were distinct rooms of differing sacredness. Outside the building itself was a courtyard or plaza surrounded by a wall. Sacrifices were made in that space, atop altars of stepped or terraced form. The levels of the altar structure represented the layered universe as Israelites and other Near Eastern peoples conceived of it. The temple building was oriented so that the rising of the sun on solstice day (either March 21 or September 21) sent the earliest rays—considered "the glory of the Lord"—to shine through the temple doors, which were opened for the occasion, directly into the holiest part.[23]

John W. Welch added concerning the Temple of Solomon:

> In the opinion of some scholars, Solomon's temple was distinctive in that it "consisted of three rooms one behind the other, with a narrow front. . . . What is characteristic of the Jerusalem Temple is rather that the three rooms stand one behind the other in a straight line, and that the building is the same width all along its length" with the middle room being the largest.[24]

Constructing such a temple would not restrict the ordinances performed therein to a Levitical order. Nor would a temple operating under the Melchizedek Priesthood prohibit the performance of Levitical ordinances. Welch wrote:

The Nephites clearly understood the gospel of Jesus Christ and the doctrines of the Messiah, but that understanding was superimposed on their observance of the law of Moses to give even further meaning to this already profoundly rich system of symbolism and religious devotion to the Holy One of Israel. Instead of abrogating the Israelite system, the Nephite understanding infused it with joy that brought its commandments more to life. Accordingly, it is important to allow room for all the ordinances of the law of Moses as well as the ceremonies of Christ's eternal gospel to operate concurrently in Nephite temples down to the coming of Christ.[25]

Evidence of Melchizedek Temple Ordinances in Alma 8 through 14

Many references in Alma 8–14 suggest that Alma, and probably some of his contemporaries, were familiar with the ordinances, covenants, and teachings associated with temple rites of the Melchizedek Priesthood. These include repeated mention of the holy order of the Son of God; the sacred manner of the calling and ordination with a holy ordinance to this high priesthood (see Alma 13:1–12); how the mysteries of God are known and imparted (see Alma 12:8–12); a caution that we will be judged by our hearts, words, works, and thoughts (see Alma 12:12–14); and a warning that those who once had the mysteries and rejected them will suffer a second death of everlasting destruction (see Alma 12:11–18).[26]

The presentation of God's eternal plan by Alma and Amulek while preaching in Ammonihah includes elements that compare to known temple themes, for example, the premortal existence (see Alma 13:3–5); Adam and Eve's partaking of the forbidden fruit (see Alma 12:21–23); cherubim

and a flaming sword guarding the way to the tree of life
(see Alma 12:21); the resulting death and mortal probation
as a time given when men should "prepare to meet God"
(Alma 12:24); angels being sent to converse with and teach
Adam and Eve (see Alma 12:29); angels teaching men to
"call on his [God's] name" and to make "known unto them
the plan of redemption" (Alma 12:30); men being given
commandments and warned of the penalty for doing evil
(see Alma 12:32); sacred ordinances given to cleanse one's
garments from sin through the blood of the Lamb (see
Alma 13:1–12); sanctification and entering into God's rest
through humility, repentance, and obedience (see Alma
13:13); the great King Melchizedek as an example (see Alma
13:14–18); and ordinances given to help one look forward
to and rely on Jesus Christ as a type of his order (see Alma
13:16). There seems to be a strong link between the pattern
of these teachings and the Nephite temple ceremony.

The Manner after Which They Are Ordained

One of the sacred ordinances discussed by Alma in
Ammonihah, which seems especially related to temple ritual, is the "holy ordinance" of ordination as priests to the
holy order of God. As noted earlier, entering this holy order in its fulness is intimately connected with the temple.
Alma may have been alluding to Nephite temple ceremony
and imagery as he discussed the calling, preparation, and
ordination to the holy order. As might be expected from
one who was steeped in ancient temple ceremony, Alma
initiated his discussion of this sacred ordinance by alluding to his earlier remarks concerning the beginning of time,
after Adam and Eve had been driven out from the Garden
of Eden (see Alma 12:28–34). He "cite[d their] minds forward" (Alma 13:1) to the forepart[27] of temporal history

when "God gave these commandments [of which he had been speaking] unto his children" and "ordained priests, after his holy order, which was after the order of his Son, to teach these things unto the people" (Alma 13:1). It is not clear from the text, but Alma may have had in mind a mental image of the temple, which, if patterned after Solomon's Temple (see 2 Nephi 5:16), would have had three main levels, symbolizing telestial, terrestrial, and celestial worlds.[28] For Alma to cite his hearers' minds "forward" when the commandments were first given may have had reference to the outer area of the Nephite temples. This first level, or forepart of the temple, might have represented the fallen or telestial world into which Adam and Eve were cast to begin their probationary state. In any case, Alma cited their minds forward to the time when God first gave commandments to his children and ordained priests.

These priests after his holy order, according to Alma, "were ordained after the order of his Son, in a manner that thereby the people might know in what manner to look forward to his Son for redemption" (Alma 13:2). It has long been understood by the Saints of this dispensation that "all the ancient prophets and all righteous men who preceded our Lord in birth were, in one sense or another, patterns for him."[29] Alma's point here is that those who were ordained into the "holy order of the Son of God" were ordained in a manner that was in similitude of the Son's redemption. He supported this by listing several points of comparison:

• They were "called and prepared from the foundation of the world" (Alma 13:3).

• This calling and preparation was according to the "foreknowledge of God, on account of their exceeding faith and good works" (Alma 13:3).

• In the first place, they were left to choose good or

evil, and they chose good and exercised exceedingly great faith (see Alma 13:3). Alma's reference to "the first place" is generally assumed to mean the first estate or premortal existence. He may have been alluding to an actual "place" in the temple that symbolized the premortal calling and preparation of those ordained after the order of the Son.

- Their holy calling was "prepared with, and according to, a preparatory redemption for such" (Alma 13:3). Among the Nephites, the holy calling to the high priesthood was accomplished in such a way as to typify the Lord's redemption as well as to rely on it. Verse three also suggests a preparatory or conditional aspect to the calling of a high priest, which somehow signified how the redemption was prepared. As an ordinance of the holy order, the calling was based on the redemption of Jesus Christ. Although the atonement was in the meridian of time, its effects are beyond the bounds of time. It is an infinite and eternal sacrifice (see Alma 34:10–14). As such, it is the basis and the model for the holy callings of those ordained priests after his holy order.

- These holy callings were prepared "from the foundation of the world for such as would not harden their hearts" (Alma 13:5).

- Their holy calling is "in and through the atonement of the Only Begotten Son, who was prepared" (Alma 13:5).

- They are called and ordained "to teach his commandments unto the children of men, that they also might enter into his rest" (Alma 13:6).

- "This high priesthood [is] after the order of his Son, which order was from the foundation of the world; or in other words, being without beginning of days or end of years, being prepared from eternity to all eternity, according to his foreknowledge of all things" (Alma 13:7).

- They are "called with a holy calling, and ordained with a holy ordinance, and taking upon them the high priesthood of the holy order, which calling, and ordinance, and high priesthood, is without beginning or end" (Alma 13:8).

A careful examination of these passages detailing the calling and ordination of those entering the holy order suggests that more than one comparison may be involved. Alma was, without question, revealing the similitude of the holy calling of priests of the holy order and "in what manner to look forward to his Son for redemption" (Alma 13:2). He also seemed to be alluding to the pattern of how the calling and ordaining of these priests was symbolized in the Nephite temple ceremony. In the words of Welch:

> After stating the fundamentals of the plan of salvation, Alma continued his discourse in words that apparently retrace the steps of a sacred Nephite rite that evidently involved an ordination to the priesthood (see Alma 13:1) and prepared the way for obedient people to "enter into the rest of the Lord" (Alma 13:16). This Nephite ordinance was evidently a symbolic ritual, since Alma says that it was performed "in a manner" that looked forward to the redemption of the Son of God (Alma 13:2). That manner, however, is mentioned by Alma only in veiled terms. At a minimum, it appears that the Nephite ceremony referred to a premortal existence, for the candidates were assured that they had been "called and prepared from the foundation of the world" with a "holy calling" (Alma 13:3, see also vv. 5, 8). That calling "was prepared with, and according to, a preparatory redemption for such," implying that it was provided by God before the world began (Alma 13:3); and it was patterned after, in, and through the preparation of the Son (see Alma 13:5). In this setting, the participants

were "ordained with a holy ordinance," "taking upon them the high priesthood of the holy order" (Alma 13:6, 8). Thereby they became "high priests forever, after the order of the Son." After these preparatory ordinances, and after making a choice "to repent and work righteousness rather than to perish," the candidate was sanctified by the Holy Ghost, his garments were washed white, and he "entered into the rest of the Lord" (Alma 13:9–10, 12).[30]

The Order of Nehor: An Imitative Priesthood

Since before the beginning of time, Satan has sought to destroy the eternal plan of God through any means, including lies and deception (Moses 4:1–3, 5). As a result of his rebellion in the premortal existence, "he became Satan, yea, even the devil, the father of all lies, to deceive and to blind men, and to lead them captive at his will, even as many as would not hearken unto my voice" (Moses 4:4). "The devil has great power to deceive," stated the Prophet Joseph Smith. "He will so transform things as to make one gape at those who are doing the will of God."[31] During this mortal probation of mankind, Satan's deception has included imitating and counterfeiting true religion. "In relation to the kingdom of God," taught Joseph Smith, "the devil always sets up his kingdom at the very same time in opposition to God."[32] Commenting on this satanic ploy, Bruce R. McConkie said:

> Since the kingdom of God or true church has been on earth from age to age, so also has the kingdom of the devil or the church of the devil. Adam and Abel had true worship and offered sacrifices in the way the Lord ordained. On the other hand, "Cain loved Satan more than God." That is, he chose to live after the manner of the

world, and it was Satan, not the Lord, who told Cain, "Make an offering unto the Lord." (Moses 5:18.) Thus the pattern was set for all ages. Satan tells men to worship the Lord, but the proposed worship that he gives them is false and without saving power.[33]

Satan's cunning artifice of imitation has successfully misled many throughout history. It is a tactic not to be underestimated. As President Joseph F. Smith warned:

> Let it not be forgotten that the evil one has great power in the earth, and that by every possible means he seeks to darken the minds of men, and then offers them falsehood and deception in the guise of truth. Satan is a skillful imitator, and as genuine gospel truth is given the world in ever-increasing abundance, so he spreads the counterfeit coin of false doctrine.[34]

Such warnings should be considered when pondering the influences driving the wicked leaders in Ammonihah in opposition to Alma and Amulek.

The order of Nehor was a schismatic apostate group that originated in the early years of the reign of the judges. Its name was derived from the heretic Nehor who introduced priestcraft into Nephite society (see Alma 1:12).[35] Nehor's doctrine and approach included "bearing down against the church; declaring unto the people that every priest and teacher ought to become popular; and they ought not to labor with their hands, but that they ought to be supported by the people" (Alma 1:3). His movement fits well within the broader rubric of priestcraft, which Nephi defined as "men preach[ing] and set[ting] themselves up for a light unto the world, that they may get gain and praise of the world; but they seek not the welfare of Zion" (2 Nephi 26:29). *Priestcraft*, a word not in most modern dictionaries, is defined by the 1828 *American Dictionary of the English*

Language by Noah Webster as "the stratagems and frauds of priests; fraud or imposition in religious concerns; management of selfish and ambitious priests to gain wealth and power, or to impose on the credulity of others."[36] This is in contrast to the same dictionary's definitions of *priesthood:* (1) "the office or character of a priest" and (2) "the order of men set apart for sacred offices; the order composed of priests."[37] From these definitions, it is clear that priestcrafts, including the order of Nehor, are counterfeits or frauds of priesthood or the sacred priestly order.

Fundamental to Nehor's dogma was his teaching that "all mankind should be saved at the last day, and that they need not fear nor tremble, but that they might lift up their heads and rejoice; for the Lord had created all men, and had also redeemed all men; and, in the end, all men should have eternal life" (Alma 1:4). As is evidently not uncommon among apostates, Nehor attempted to enforce his priestcraft by the sword in his murder of Gideon.[38] As a result, he was condemned to die according to the law set forth by King Mosiah (see Alma 1:13–14). The description of his execution suggests a ceremonial invoking of a covenantal cursing, and, as has been suggested by Nibley, may hark back to an ancient tradition of the fallen angel Shamhozai, who "repented, and by way of penance hung himself up between heaven and earth."[39] In the case of Nehor, he was carried to "the top of the hill Manti, and there he was caused, or rather did acknowledge, between the heavens and the earth, that what he had taught to the people was contrary to the word of God; and there he suffered an ignominious death" (Alma 1:15).

Nehor's confession and ritual execution "did not put an end to the spreading of priestcraft through the land; for there were many who loved the vain things of the world"

(Alma 1:16). Within five years Amlici, another scheming demagogue after the order of Nehor, arose to prominence. His cunning and worldly wisdom drew away many people and created a great contention among the Nephites. Amlici sought political power in an effort to deprive the people "of their rights and privileges of the church" and ultimately to "destroy the church of God" (Alma 2:4). Rejected by the voice of the people, Amlici's own followers consecrated him to be their king (see Alma 2:7–9). These dissenters marked themselves in such a way as to separate themselves from their brethren (see Alma 3:4). Following in the tradition of many apostates, the proclivities of Amlici and his followers turned violent (see Genesis 6:11–13; Ether 8–9; Moses 5:32, 47; 6:28; 8:28–30). Amlici's first order of business as a factional monarch was to command his followers to "take up arms against their brethren" that "he might subject them to him" (Alma 2:10). A terrible and bloody slaughter followed (see Alma 2:16–20). Though routed, the Amlicites refused to quit and eventually joined with the Lamanites (see Alma 2:21–24). A series of ferocious battles continued with an appalling loss of lives on both sides (see Alma 2:25–3:3).

The Order of Nehor at Ammonihah

Notwithstanding the violence and trouble that accompanied the order of Nehor, it thrived during this era of Nephite history. By the tenth year of the reign of the judges, Ammonihah was a hotbed of this order of dissidents. It is not clear from the scriptures whether Ammonihah had its own particular strain of the order or whether the descriptions of the order in Ammonihah can be generalized to the entire order. Specific details, however, are given in the scriptures concerning the order of Nehor in Ammonihah.

They were a hard-hearted people who were familiar with Alma and yet rejected his authority as the high priest, believing that he had no power over them (see Alma 8:11–12). Their disagreement with Alma was vehement to the point of bigoted derision and physical abuse (see Alma 8:13). The angel who appeared to Alma after his expulsion from Ammonihah described their wickedness as so serious that "except they repent the Lord God will destroy them" (Alma 8:16). This angel declared that the wicked in Ammonihah, in accordance with what Satan and his minions have historically sought, "do study at this time that they may destroy the liberty of thy people, (for thus saith the Lord) which is contrary to the statutes, and judgments, and commandments which he has given unto his people" (Alma 8:17; see Moses 4:3; Galatians 2:4 JST; 2 Peter 2:19; Helaman 1:8; 3 Nephi 6:30).

After Alma's return to Ammonihah and while he was spiritually preparing Amulek, the people "did wax more gross in their iniquities" (Alma 8:28). Again Alma "went forth," this time with Amulek, "to declare the words of God unto" the wicked of Ammonihah (Alma 8:30). Filled with the Holy Ghost, Alma and Amulek preached and prophesied "according to the spirit and power which the Lord had given them" (Alma 8:32). Alma was the first to speak, but his spirit and power seemed not to influence the people. They reacted contentiously (see Alma 9:1). Not yet realizing that Alma had proselytized a powerful ally, they scoffed at the notion that "we shall believe the testimony of one man" (Alma 9:2). In addition, having long since lost the Spirit and forgotten the power of God, "they knew not that the earth should pass away" (Alma 9:3); so they ridiculed the idea that their "great city should be destroyed in one day" (Alma 9:4). All this was because they "knew not that

God could do such marvelous works, for they were a hard-hearted and a stiffnecked people" (Alma 9:5). Like the apostates in all dispensations, the reaction of those in the order of Nehor is best described by the Prophet Joseph Smith when he taught that "the apostate is left naked and destitute of the Spirit of God. . . . When once that light which was in them is taken from them, they become as much darkened as they were previously enlightened, and then, no marvel, if all their power should be enlisted against the truth, and they, Judas like, seek the destruction of those who were their greatest benefactors."[40]

A Once-Enlightened People

Alma's response to the people at this juncture is revealing. He initially inquired: "O ye wicked and perverse generation, how have ye forgotten the tradition of your fathers; yea, how soon ye have forgotten the commandments of God" (Alma 9:8). Then he continued,

> Do ye not remember that our father, Lehi, was brought out of Jerusalem by the hand of God? Do ye not remember that they were all led by him through the wilderness? And have ye forgotten so soon how many times he delivered our fathers out of the hands of their enemies, and preserved them from being destroyed, even by the hands of their own brethren? (Alma 9:9–10)

Alma repetitively asked if they had "forgotten" or if they did not "remember." Alma spoke as though he was not teaching these people anything new, but reminding them of covenants and commandments with which they had once been conversant (see Alma 9:8–14). In a similar vein, Joseph Smith once told a member of the church that "When you joined this Church you enlisted to serve God. When you did that you left the neutral ground, and you never can

get back on to it. Should you forsake the Master you enlisted to serve it will be by the instigation of the evil one,
and you will follow his dictation and be his servant."[41] This
is the principle taught by Alma to these people who had
once been "such a highly favored people of the Lord; yea,
after having been favored above every other nation, kin-
dred, tongue, or people" because of their obedience to
covenants (Alma 9:20; see Alma 9:15–19).

Revelation in our own dispensation makes it clear
that "he who sins against the greater light shall receive the
greater condemnation" (D&C 82:3). Exactly how much light
and knowledge these Ammonihah apostates previously
received is not clear in the text, but considering the accessi-
bility of the higher priesthood and the Melchizedek temple
ordinances, it may be that they had at one time entered into
very sacred covenants of the holy order. Alma reminded
the people of many of their past blessings, such as "having
had all things made known unto them . . . ; Having been
visited by the Spirit of God; having conversed with angels,
and having been spoken unto by the voice of the Lord; and
having the spirit of prophecy, and the spirit of revelation,
and also many gifts" (Alma 9:20–21). He warned "that if
this people, who have received so many blessings from the
hand of the Lord, should transgress contrary to the light
and knowledge which they do have, . . . it would be far
more tolerable for the Lamanites than for them" (Alma
9:23). This caution resembles a later passage in the book
of Alma: "And thus we can plainly discern, that after a
people have been once enlightened by the Spirit of God,
and have had great knowledge of things pertaining to
righteousness, and then have fallen away into sin and
transgression, they become more hardened, and thus their
state becomes worse than though they had never known

these things" (Alma 24:30). Rather than repent, as Alma pled for them to do, "the people were wroth" with Alma because he told them "that they were a hard-hearted and a stiffnecked people" and "a lost and a fallen people." They became angry and "sought to lay their hands upon [Alma], that they might cast [him] into prison" (Alma 9:30–32).

Learned in All the Arts and Cunning Devices

When Amulek provided support for Alma's testimony, those of the order of Nehor in Ammonihah attempted to "question them, that by their cunning devices they might catch them in their words" (Alma 10:13). These men were "lawyers, . . . learned in all the arts and cunning of the people; and this was to enable them that they might be skilful in their profession" (Alma 10:15). A once-enlightened people of the Lord had degenerated to the level of marshaling all their secular skills and tactics in their efforts to destroy the representatives of God (see Alma 10:14).

Not realizing that he "perceived their thoughts," they began "to question Amulek, that thereby they might make him cross his words, or contradict the words which he should speak" (Alma 10:16–17). Amulek wisely employed this discernment to his advantage, emphatically declaring:

O ye wicked and perverse generation, ye lawyers and hypocrites, for ye are laying the foundations of the devil; for ye are laying traps and snares to catch the holy ones of God. Ye are laying plans to pervert the ways of the righteous, and to bring down the wrath of God upon your heads, even to the utter destruction of this people. (Alma 10:17–18)

"The guilty taketh the truth to be hard" (1 Nephi 16:2), and Amulek's words only enraged these people more. "They cried out, saying: This man doth revile against our laws which are just, and our wise lawyers whom we have selected" (Alma 10:24). Amulek

> stretched forth his hand, and cried the mightier unto them, saying: O ye wicked and perverse generation, why hath Satan got such great hold upon your hearts? Why will ye yield yourselves unto him that he may have power over you, to blind your eyes, that ye will not understand the words which are spoken, according to their truth? For behold, have I testified against your law? Ye do not understand; ye say that I have spoken against your law; but I have not, but I have spoken in favor of your law, to your condemnation. (Alma 10:25–26)

Cutting to the core issue of the debate, Amulek exclaimed, "I say unto you, that the foundation of the destruction of this people is beginning to be laid by the unrighteousness of your lawyers and your judges" (Alma 10:27).

Filthy Lucre

The unrighteousness of the Ammonihahite lawyers and judges consisted not so much in their chosen profession, but rather that "their hearts [were] set so much upon the things of this world" (D&C 121:35). The record is clear that it was their "sole purpose to get gain" (Alma 11:20). Their law and their lucre had become their God. Their craving for the things of this world was so intense that "they did stir up the people to riotings, and all manner of disturbances and wickedness, that they might have more employ, that they might get money according to the suits which were brought before them" (Alma 11:20). Possibly this emphasis on "gain" as a driving force of the order of Nehor was a major reason that Alma 11 includes the only extant scriptural account of the Nephite monetary system.[42] The interpolation of the Nephite monetary system at this point in the narrative fits well with the introduction of the characters representing the order of Nehor in Ammonihah. Zeezrom, who had just stepped forward to contend with Amulek, carried a name with a peculiar affinity to one of the units of silver employed as money (*ezrom*, in Alma 11:12). When his confidence waned, Antionah stepped in for the rescue. His name also exhibits a fascinating connection with one of the gold measures noted (*antion*, in Alma 11:19). The two characters representing the order of Nehor both seem to have names closely associated to the monetary system.[43]

It does not seem merely coincidental that immediately after the textual interpolation explaining the monetary system, Zeezrom offered Amulek a bribe if he would deny "the existence of a Supreme Being" (Alma 11:22). The only description in the Book of Mormon of a monetary system functions well to emphasize the greed in Ammonihah, as well as to accentuate the value of the bribe that Zeezrom subsequently offered to Amulek. Zeezrom's motivation for such a curious proposition is difficult to determine, but Amulek revealed that Zeezrom had no intent to pay the enticement even if it did succeed (see Alma 11:25). It is possible that Zeezrom, having been brought up in a society where anything and everything could be bought with money,[44] and knowing that Amulek had prospered in the same environment, figured that the ploy was workable. Amulek's terse response was damning: "O thou child of hell, why tempt ye me? Knowest thou that the righteous yieldeth to no such temptations? Believest thou that there is no God? I say unto you, Nay, thou knowest that there is a God, but thou lovest that lucre more than him" (Alma 11:23–24).

Doctrinal Conflicts of the Orders

Little is known concerning the behavior and doctrine of the order of Nehor in Ammonihah other than the fact that they were apostate, corrupt, contentious, and money hungry. Their theology is difficult to pin down because of limited information and the polemical nature of the material available. The interrogation of Amulek by Zeezrom in Alma 11:21–46 and the subsequent questioning of Alma by Antionah beginning in Alma 12:20 provide a few clues, however, to some of their false beliefs. Most of their questions concern aspects of the plan of salvation and teachings evidently related to the Nephite temple ceremony.[45]

The nature of Zeezrom's questions to Amulek suggests that he, and perhaps the entire order of Nehor in Ammonihah, had difficulty understanding the concept that the Son of God would redeem mankind from their sins (see Alma 11:34–40). Years earlier Nehor had taught "that all mankind should be saved at the last day, and that they need not fear nor tremble, but that they might lift up their heads and rejoice; for the Lord had created all men, and had also redeemed all men; and, in the end, all men should have eternal life" (Alma 1:4). This belief evidently persisted in the order of Nehor in Ammonihah. Alma 15:15 describes these people as "of the profession of Nehor, and did not believe in the repentance of their sins." It could logically follow in a belief system espousing that all are redeemed and automatically given eternal life that repentance would be unnecessary. This teaching may explain Zeezrom's challenge of Amulek's assertion that God "shall not save his people in their sins" (Alma 11:36; see Alma 11:35).

Amulek's response suggests that Zeezrom may have had a problem not only with believing in the consequences of sin and the need for repentance, but also with the fundamental doctrines of the resurrection and the judgment. Amulek reasoned that God declared "that no unclean thing can inherit the kingdom of heaven; therefore, how can ye be saved, except ye inherit the kingdom of heaven? Therefore, ye cannot be saved in your sins" (Alma 11:37). Amulek further explained that Christ "shall come into the world to redeem his people; and he shall take upon him the transgressions of those who believe on his name; and these are they that shall have eternal life, and salvation cometh to none else" (Alma 11:40). He got to the crux of the issue when he declared that "the wicked remain as though there had been no redemption made, except it be the loosing of the bands of death; for behold, the day cometh that all shall rise from the dead and stand before God, and be judged according to their works" (Alma 11:41). Amulek explained the doctrine of the restoration in the resurrection with emphasis on the fact that in the judgment "we shall be brought to stand before God, knowing even as we know now, and have a bright recollection of all our guilt" (Alma 11:43). There everyone will be restored to a perfect frame, brought before the bar of Christ, and judged according to his works (see Alma 11:44).

As Amulek completed his powerful testimony of the resurrection, the "people began again to be astonished, and also Zeezrom began to tremble" (Alma 11:46). The people's reaction may be partially explained by the power and truthfulness of Amulek's teachings. Also, Amulek was known among them previously as "a man of no small reputation," who had "acquired much riches" through his own industry (Alma 10:4). Like many of these people before him, Amulek had hardened his heart and "rebell[ed] against God" (Alma 10:6). But now he was here before them as one willing to consecrate "all his gold, and silver, and his precious things, which were in the land of Ammonihah," including his family and friends, "for the word of God" (Alma 15:16). He exhibited unusual integrity for a wealthy citizen of Ammonihah when he called the bluff on Zeezrom's bribe (see Alma 11:22–25). In addition, he proved himself a formidable foe even against a lawyer of the stature of Zeezrom (see Alma 10:31; 11:21). Zeezrom's specific reaction, on the other hand, arose because "he beheld that Amulek had caught him in his lying and deceiving to destroy him," as well as a "consciousness of his [own] guilt" (Alma 12:1). Zeezrom began to shrink from further confrontation. He was later healed, baptized, and taught the gospel (see Alma 15). The experience with Zeezrom is reminiscent of Alma's own dramatic conversion after having vehemently opposed the church (see Mosiah 27:8–32).

The Nehorite confusion concerning the consequences of sin, the resurrection, and the judgment were evidently widespread in Ammonihah. When Antionah stepped forward to question Alma, he seems to have been baffled by some of these same concerns. His questions suggest that he, and perhaps others of his order, confounded immortality with eternal life. On the other hand, Antionah may simply have been attempting to trap Alma into making a contradiction. His first question was "What is this that thou hast said, that man should rise from the dead and be changed from this mortal to an immortal state, that the soul can never die?" (Alma 12:20). In rapid-fire succession, Antionah immediately asked his second question: "What does the scripture mean, which saith that God placed cherubim and a flaming sword on the east of the garden of Eden, lest our first parents should enter and partake of the fruit of the tree of life, and live forever?" (Alma 12:21). His second question seems intended to cast doubt on what he assumed would be Alma's response to the first question. Rather than wait for Alma's response, Antionah gave his own conclusion: "And thus we see that there was no possible chance that they should live forever" (Alma 12:21). In other words, Antionah's evident purpose was not to learn from the prophet Alma but to snare him into a logical contradiction. His strategy seems to have included an attempt to show that Alma was teaching contrary to his own scriptures, a common tactic among apostates even today. If, on the other hand, Antionah's bewilderment was sincere, it reveals that he was doubting the possibility of eternal life, the fairness of the consequences of Adam and Eve's transgression, or even the justice of God.[46]

Alma's inspired response implied that he recognized Antionah's mixed motives in posing his questions. Alma asserted that the real contradiction would have arisen if Adam and Eve had been able to partake of the fruit of the tree of life immediately after their fall. Then "there would have been no death, and the word would have been void, making God a liar, for he said: If thou eat thou shalt surely die" (Alma 12:23). Alma then explained that temporal "death comes upon mankind," but that "a space [is] granted unto man in which he might repent; therefore," declared Alma, "this life became a probationary state; a time to prepare to meet God; a time to prepare for that endless state which has been spoken of by us, which is after the resurrection of the dead" (Alma 12:24). Alma taught that this was all part of the plan of redemption, and that if, in fact, "our first parents could have gone forth and partaken of the tree of life they would have been forever miserable, having no preparatory state" (Alma 12:26). "But behold," testified Alma, "it was appointed unto men that they must die; and after death, they must come to judgment, even that same judgment of which we have spoken" (Alma 12:27). Thus Alma showed that what he and Amulek were teaching was indeed consistent with the scripture that Antionah questioned and with the assertion that mortality is a preparatory state given in order to repent and prepare for the judgment and resurrection. Nothing in this scripture nor in what Alma and Amulek were teaching was inconsistent with the plan and justice of God.

In a presentation that easily could have been modeled after a sacred temple drama, Alma explained how God would use mortal probation to teach man about "the things whereof he had appointed unto them" (Alma 12:28). After death came upon man, God "sent angels to converse with them, who caused men to behold of his glory" (Alma 12:29). "From that time forth," declared Alma, they began "to call on his name; therefore God conversed with men, and made known unto them the plan of redemption, which had been prepared from the foundation of the world; and this he made known unto them according to their faith and repentance and their holy works" (Alma 12:30). Alma clarified that men, having chosen mortality, "plac[ed] themselves in a state to act" (Alma 12:31). "Therefore God gave unto them commandments, after having made known unto them the plan of redemption, that they should not do evil" (Alma 12:32). Doing evil, contrary to the commandments, would bring the penalty of "a second death, which was an everlasting death as to things pertaining unto righteousness; for on such the plan of redemption could have no power, for the works of justice could not be destroyed, according to the supreme goodness of God" (Alma 12:32). The eternal plan of God provided opportunity to repent (see Alma 12:33), according to Alma, "therefore, whosoever repenteth, and hardeneth not his heart, he shall have claim on mercy through mine Only Begotten Son, unto a remission of his sins; and these shall enter into my rest" (Alma 12:34). Alma here adds the stiff warning that "whosoever will harden his heart and will do iniquity, behold, I swear in my wrath that he shall not enter into my rest" (Alma 12:35).

Having answered Antionah's questions in the abstract, Alma now personalized his remarks to Antionah and his friends. He warned them directly "that if ye will harden your hearts ye shall not enter into the rest of the Lord" and reminded them that "your iniquity provoketh him that he sendeth down his wrath upon you as in the first provocation" (Alma 12:36), when the children of Israel led by Moses refused the higher law and the fulness of the blessings of the priesthood (see Psalm 95:8; Hebrews 3:8, 15; Jacob 1:7; D&C 84:23–26). With a knowledge of this impending punishment, Alma pled for the Ammonihahites to act: "And now, my brethren, seeing we know these things, and they are true, let us repent, and harden not our hearts, that we provoke not the Lord our God to pull down his wrath upon us in these his second commandments which he has given unto us; but let us enter into the rest of God, which is prepared according to his word" (Alma 12:37). Alma's plea suggests that the Nephites possessed what the ancient Israelites refused, but that they could also lose it and bring upon them the wrath of God in doing so.

Zeezrom Begins to Repent

Apostasy had so infected the people of Ammonihah that many had no understanding of the doctrines and principles of the gospel. At one time in the glorious past, they had been "a highly favored people of the Lord" (Alma 9:20).

They had "been visited by the Spirit of God; having conversed with angels, and having been spoken unto by the voice of the Lord; and having the spirit of prophecy, and the spirit of revelation" (Alma 9:21). But that was gone because they had transgressed "contrary to the light and knowledge" which they had (Alma 9:23). An earlier Book of Mormon prophet warned: "How unsearchable are the depths of the mysteries of him; and it is impossible that man should find out all his ways. And no man knoweth of his ways save it be revealed unto him; wherefore, brethren, despise not the revelations of God" (Jacob 4:8).

Now, Zeezrom, caught in his lies and conscious of his guilt, began the arduous path back into the light. He would become an example to future readers of the Book of Mormon that there truly is a way back (see Alma 15:1–12). Ammon, a contemporary of Zeezrom serving the Lord in another land, confirmed:

> Yea, he that repenteth and exerciseth faith, and bringeth forth good works, and prayeth continually without ceasing—unto such it is given to know the mysteries of God; yea, unto such it shall be given to reveal things which never have been revealed; yea, and it shall be given unto such to bring thousands of souls to repentance, even as it has been given unto us to bring these our brethren to repentance. (Alma 26:22)

Earlier, the prophet Nephi taught that "he that diligently seeketh shall find; and the mysteries of God shall be unfolded unto them, by the power of the Holy Ghost" (1 Nephi 10:19). Zeezrom "began to inquire of [Alma and Amulek] diligently, that he might know more concerning the kingdom of God" (Alma 12:8).

The Mysteries of God

"Alma began to expound" the things of the kingdom unto Zeezrom, but with an important caveat: "It is given unto many to know the mysteries of God; nevertheless," Alma warned, "they are laid under a strict command that they shall not impart only according to the portion of his word which he doth grant unto the children of men, according to the heed and diligence which they give unto him" (Alma 12:9). "He that will harden his heart," cautioned Alma, "the same receiveth the lesser portion of the word." On the other hand, Alma promised, "he that will not harden his heart, to him is given the greater portion of the word, until it is given unto him to know the mysteries of God until he know them in full" (Alma 12:10). And in an appropriate description of the wicked in Ammonihah, Alma declared that "they that will harden their hearts, to them is given the lesser portion of the word until they know nothing concerning his mysteries; and then they are taken captive by the devil, and led by his will down to destruction. Now this is what is meant by the chains of hell" (Alma 12:11).

The term *mysteries* is used in various ways in the scriptures.[47] It describes God and his eternal plan, as well as the sacred knowledge given to the faithful through divine revelation (see, e.g., D&C 76:1–10; compare 1 Nephi 10:17–19; Moses 1:5).[48] Significantly, given its context in Alma 12, it has also been used historically and scripturally to refer to priesthood and temple ordinances.[49] The King James Version of the New Testament employs the Greek word *musterion* which means "a 'secret' or 'mystery' (through the idea of *silence* imposed by *initiation* into *religious* rites). The word is from a derivative of the Greek 'muō' which meant 'to *shut* the mouth.'"[50] William Vine noted that "among the

ancient Greeks 'the mysteries' were religious rites and ceremonies practiced by secret societies into which any one
who so desired might be received. Those who were initiated into these 'mysteries' became possessors of certain
knowledge, which was not imparted to the uninitiated, and
were called 'the perfected.'"[51] Another scholar has clarified
that

> in ancient religions, for example from the Hellenistic
> world, the word *mysteries* was often used to describe
> "cultic rites . . . portrayed by sacred actions before a circle
> of devotees," who "must undergo initiation" and who
> are promised "salvation by the dispensing of cosmic
> life," which is sometimes "enacted in cultic drama," ac-
> companied by a strict "vow of silence."[52]

Strikingly similar to these Greek definitions are those
found in Webster's 1828 dictionary. Webster included several definitions for the word: "In *religion*, any thing in the
character or attributes of God, or in the economy of divine
providence, which is not revealed to man"; and "a kind of
ancient dramatic representation."[53]

In our own dispensation, the "keys of the mysteries,
and the revelations" (D&C 28:7) were given to the Prophet
Joseph Smith in connection with the Melchizedek Priesthood, which priesthood "administereth the gospel and
holdeth the key of the mysteries of the kingdom, even the
key of the knowledge of God" (D&C 84:19; see D&C 28:7;
35:18; 107:18–19). It is "in the ordinances thereof, [that] the
power of godliness is manifest" (D&C 84:20). And, as the
revelation emphasized, "without the ordinances thereof,
and the authority of the priesthood, the power of godliness
is not manifest unto men in the flesh; for without this no
man can see the face of God, even the Father, and live"

(D&C 84:21–22). These passages reveal a similar link between priesthood, knowledge, ordinances, temple, and mysteries, as is evident in Alma 12. Even if Alma was employing the term in a broader scriptural sense, it would not exclude a temple allusion. As President Benson explained:

> Everything we learn in the holy places, the temples, is based on the scriptures. These teachings are what the scriptures refer to as the "mysteries of godliness" [see 1 Timothy 3:16; D&C 19:10]. They are to be comprehended by the power of the Holy Ghost, for the Lord has given this promise to His faithful and obedient servants: "Thou mayest know the mysteries and peaceable things" (D&C 42:61).[54]

Those with Hearts Hardened against the Word

Alma forewarned concerning the awful state of those who have hardened their hearts "against the word." Not only will the word not be found within them, but their state will be awful, "for then [they] shall be condemned" (Alma 12:13). In the day of judgment, "if we have hardened our hearts against the word [of God], . . . our words will condemn us, yea, all our works will condemn us; we shall not be found spotless; and our thoughts will also condemn us" (Alma 12:13–14). And, cautioned Alma, "in this awful state we shall not dare to look up to our God; and we would fain be glad if we could command the rocks and the mountains to fall upon us to hide us from his presence" (Alma 12:14). To those who have rejected the word of God after having been such a highly favored and blessed people of the Lord, and who have lost the mysteries after having had a fulness, the day of judgment will bring "a death, even a second death, which is a spiritual death" (Alma 12:16). This is a time, declared Alma, "that whosoever dieth in his sins, as to a temporal death, shall also die a spiritual death; yea, he shall die as to things pertaining unto righteousness" (Alma 12:16). "Then is the time," explained Alma, "when their torments shall be as a lake of fire and brimstone, whose flame ascendeth up forever and ever: and then is the time," emphasized Alma, "that they shall be chained down to an everlasting destruction, according to the power and captivity of Satan, he having subjected them according to his will" (Alma 12:17).

Alma's harsh warning to these Ammonihahites of "a death, even a second death, which is a spiritual death . . . when their torments shall be as a lake of fire and brimstone, whose flame ascendeth up forever and ever" (Alma 12:16–17) can be understood in at least two ways. Alma may have been referring to the fate of those who are spiritually alienated from God and who will suffer for their sins until the second resurrection (see D&C 19:4–12; 76:99–109), or he may have had in mind the destiny of those who would become sons of perdition. To warn of such a dire fate for his audience would suggest that at least some in Ammonihah had once received the Holy Ghost, had the heavens opened unto them, knew God, and then turned against him.

As the Prophet Joseph Smith further explained: "He has got to say that the sun does not shine while he sees it; . . . [he has got] to deny the plan of salvation with his eyes open to the truth of it; and from that time he begins to be an enemy. This is the case with many apostates of the Church of Jesus Christ of Latter-day Saints."[55] Modern revelation has also revealed the fate of these "vessels of wrath, doomed to suffer the wrath of God" in language similar to that employed in Alma 12 (D&C 76:33; see D&C 76:31–38). Phrases such as *second death* and *lake of fire and brimstone* are used both in Alma's discourse and in latter revelation to refer to the sons of perdition. Still, it is difficult to determine exactly what Alma had in mind in this part of his discourse. He may have deliberately left his intent ambiguous, "that it might work upon the hearts" of those to whom he referred (D&C 19:7). In any case, Alma's discourse on the second death intimated that his listeners would be held accountable for having once been enlightened but subsequently hardening their hearts against the word, therefore losing the mysteries.

Entering into the Rest of the Lord

In contrast to the awful fate of whosoever will "harden his heart and will do iniquity" (Alma 12:35), Alma relayed the divine promise in his final major address to the people of Ammonihah that "whosoever repenteth and hardeneth not his heart, he shall have claim on mercy through mine Only Begotten Son, unto a remission of his sins: and these shall enter into my rest" (Alma 12:34). Entering into the rest of the Lord was the principal focus of this segment of Alma's discourse. He used a variation of the phrase *enter into the rest of the Lord* nine times between Alma 12:34 and 13:29.[56]

The phrase *rest of the Lord* is used in various ways in the scriptures. The Savior promised "rest" to all "that labour and are heavy laden" who "come unto [him]" (Matthew 11:28).[57] The word *rest* is also used in the scriptures to describe the reception of postmortal spirits of the righteous "into a state of happiness, which is called paradise, a state of rest, a state of peace, where they shall rest from all their troubles and from all care, and sorrow" (Alma 40:12; see Alma 60:13). Further, it is employed to describe eternal life after the resurrection and judgment (see Moroni 7:3).

Modern revelation sometimes equates the "rest" of the Lord with entering into the presence of God, or receiving the "fulness of his glory" (D&C 84:24). We learn that Moses

> sought diligently to sanctify his people that they might behold the face of God; But they hardened their hearts and could not endure his presence; therefore, the Lord in his wrath, for his anger was kindled against them, swore that they should not enter into his rest while in the wilderness, which rest is the fulness of his glory. Therefore, he took Moses out of their midst, and the Holy Priesthood also. (D&C 84:23–25; see Exodus 34:2 JST)

This interpretation of "the rest of God" is consistent with Alma's use of the phrase in his teachings in Ammonihah. Alma even evoked the memories of Israel's first provocation of God as he similarly pled with his people not to "pull down his wrath upon" them, but instead, to "enter into the rest of God" (Alma 12:37). Alma's plea was voiced in the hope that the people of Ammonihah could avert God's wrath by repenting and accepting what Israel earlier rejected—the greater priesthood and the ordinances thereof, in the which the power of godliness is manifest. Only then could they enter into the rest of God. Entering into the rest of the Lord is closely bound to the sacred ordinances connected with the holy order of God. At one point in his exhortation, Alma declared concerning the ancients:

> They were called after this holy order, and were sanctified, and their garments were washed white through the blood of the Lamb. Now they, after being sanctified by the Holy Ghost, having their garments made white, being pure and spotless before God, could not look upon sin save it were with abhorrence; and there were many, exceedingly great many, who were made pure and entered into the rest of the Lord their God. (Alma 13:11–12)

This, of course, can be understood on various levels, but as

Robert Millet reminded us, "we encounter the holy order of God through receiving the ordinances of the temple, through receiving the endowment and the blessings of eternal marriage."[58]

Melchizedek as a Model of Righteousness

In contrast with the wicked people of Ammonihah, who had chosen Nehor as their model, the faithful were admonished by Alma to "humble [themselves] even as the people in the days of Melchizedek, who was also a high priest after this same order which I have spoken" (Alma 13:14). Whereas Nehor was a lying murderer and a promoter of priestcraft, Melchizedek was a man of "mighty faith" who "received the office of the high priesthood according to the holy order of God" (Alma 13:18). Whereas the name of Nehor brings to mind popular priests supported by money from the deceived masses (see Alma 1:3–6), Melchizedek "did preach repentance unto his people" and "did establish peace in the land in his days; therefore he was called the prince of peace, for he was the king of Salem" (Alma 13:18).

Melchizedek, whose name likely means "my king of righteousness," is an intriguing model for Alma to employ as an illustration of entering the rest of God. History and legends abound from Jewish and Christian sources presenting a conflicting and enigmatic portrait of Melchizedek.[59] Modern revelation, however, strongly supports Alma's invoking his name as an illustration of powerful faith and righteousness (see Genesis 14:25–40 JST; Hebrews 5:7–8 JST; D&C 107:3–4). In light of what has been restored through the Joseph Smith Translation, Alma was not exaggerating when he claimed: "Now, there were many before him, and also there were many afterwards, but none were greater" (Alma 13:19).

Most intriguing is the way Alma employed Melchizedek as a model for "receiv[ing] the office of the high priesthood according to the holy order of God" and righteously using this power and authority to "preach repentance" and to "establish peace," with the purpose of helping his fellow Saints "enter into the rest of the Lord" (Alma 13:18, 16). The temple themes to which Alma has been alluding seem to be almost personified by Melchizedek's example. Other sources have connected Melchizedek with the temple and its sacred ordinances. For example, Josephus wrote that Melchizedek was the first to build a temple in Jerusalem.[60] Ancient scripture and modern revelation identify him as a "king" and a "priest of the most high God" (Genesis 14:18; Genesis 14:17 JST; Hebrews 7:1).[61] The Prophet Joseph Smith declared that Melchizedek "had power and authority over that of Abraham, holding the key and the power of endless life."[62] Because Melchizedek was such a great high priest, and "out of respect or reverence to the name of the Supreme Being, to avoid the too frequent repetition of his name," the priesthood was ultimately named after Melchizedek (D&C 107:4).

Melchizedek: A Type of Christ

As with all prophets before and after the meridian of time, Melchizedek is a type of Jesus Christ.[63] He was called "the prince of peace" (Alma 13:18) as a type of *the* Prince of Peace. As righteous as Melchizedek was—and, as Alma declared, "none were greater" (Alma 13:19)—Jesus Christ, not Melchizedek, is the righteous one. Alma made it clear through his teaching that while Melchizedek was an excellent example, those who enter into the holy order are "washed white through the blood of the Lamb" (Alma 13:11). The ordinances of the holy order were given in such a manner "that thereby the people might look forward on the Son of God" (Alma 13:16).

This is in complete contrast to the counterfeit order of Nehor, whose entire existence and scheme was part of "a very subtle plan, as to the subtlety of the devil, for to lie and to deceive this people" (Alma 12:4). To Zeezrom, Alma declared, Satan "hath exercised his power in thee" (Alma 12:5). To all of Ammonihah, Alma gave the warning that Satan had laid a snare "to catch this people, that he might bring you into subjection unto him, that he might encircle you about with his chains, that he might chain you down to everlasting destruction, according to the power of his captivity" (Alma 12:6). Alma admonished that unless they repented "they shall be chained down to an everlasting destruction, according to the power and captivity of Satan, he having subjected them according to his will" (Alma 12:17).

Life or Death

As Alma prophesied, "utter destruction . . . according to the fierce anger of the Lord" was the end result of the order of Nehor in Ammonihah (Alma 9:18; see Alma 16:3, 9). Prior to the final Lamanite invasion that completely destroyed the city, the wicked had turned against even their own blood by "cast[ing] into the fire" their innocent wives and children who had "believed or had been taught to believe in the word of God" (Alma 14:8). The consequences of following the order of Nehor were that "every living soul of the Ammonihahites was destroyed, and also their great city, which they said God could not destroy, because of its greatness" (Alma 16:9). As was later decreed in the Book of Mormon concerning another antichrist, "thus we see the end of him who perverteth the ways of the Lord; and thus we see that the devil will not support his children at the last day, but doth speedily drag them down to hell" (Alma 30:60). In contrast, those who did repent and did not harden their hearts against the word of God were fully supported and sustained by the Lord. The records make clear that Amulek, Zeezrom, and others who repented and followed Jesus Christ and his holy order went on to lead wonderful lives of gospel learning, obedience, service, and joy (see Alma 15:4–12; 16:13; 31:5–6, 32; 34; Helaman 5:10, 41).

Conclusion

The conflict in Ammonihah between the holy order of the Son of God and the order of Nehor serves as a reminder that a constant war rages for the hearts, minds, and souls of men. Though impossible on the grand scale, Satan continues to strive to frustrate God's plan for each of his children through the use of lies and deception (see Moses 4:6). Prophets of our own time have warned of Satan's tactics. President Harold B. Lee warned that Satan "is the master of deceit, adulteration, and counterfeit."[64] President Spencer W. Kimball added, "he has devised and concocted every plan imaginable to deceive and fetter man. He is clever. He is experienced. He is brainy. He seeks to nullify all the works of the Savior. He is the arch deceiver."[65]

The rise of the order of Nehor and its institutional entrenchment in Ammonihah provides an excellent case study for the effects of priestcraft on a community. Consumed with a passion for riches and power, most of the leading lawyers and judges of Ammonihah rejected the true priesthood, doctrines, and ordinances of the gospel of Jesus Christ. Blinded by pride and false belief and having lost the light and the Spirit they once had, these practitioners of priestcraft stooped to bribery, lying, mockery, corruption, persecution, and murder. Their own ultimate fate was destruction, both physically and spiritually.

Contrast the actions and consequences of this imitative order with that of Alma and the high priesthood. Bound by sacred temple covenants, Alma resigned a powerful government position in order to more effectively consecrate his time and efforts to teaching the gospel of Jesus Christ and building the church. Alma and his companion Amulek gave up comfort and family in order to preach to the hard-hearted who ridiculed and rejected their every invitation to repent and return to the Lord, whom they had forgotten. Called with a holy calling, Alma and those of the holy order sacrificed their all that they might help others enter into the rest of the Lord. In this they were following the pattern of him after whom they were called and ordained.

The conflict between these two orders also provided insight into Nephite temple worship and understanding during this period. Alma and many of his contemporaries held and honored the higher priesthood; they worshiped in holy temples where they received the ordinances and covenants of the Melchizedek Priesthood, thereby learning the mysteries of the kingdom and growing in their knowledge of God. These Nephites patterned their lives after the Savior's life and employed Melchizedek as a model of righteousness. By repenting, humbling themselves, obeying, and serving, they sought to receive the blessings of entering into the rest of God.

Alma's very presence in Ammonihah attests to his desire to help those who once were enlightened to return to the path of eternal life. He taught that the way of salvation is only "according to the power and deliverance of Jesus Christ" (Alma 9:28), who "shall come into the world to redeem his people;

and he shall take upon him the transgressions of those who believe on his name; and these are they that shall have eternal life, and salvation cometh to none else" (Alma 11:40). The teachings of Alma and Amulek to these apostates are permeated with evidence of a knowledge of holy temples containing the highest ordinances, covenants, and theology. All the ordinances are patterned in such a way as to look forward to the Son for redemption (see Alma 13:2; Moses 5:8). An undeviating call for men to "repent, and harden not [their] hearts" against the true mysteries of God and to rely upon the mercy "through mine Only Begotten Son" (Alma 12:33) fills these chapters.

Notes

1. Excellent studies have been published that examine many of these issues. See, for example, Robert L. Millet, "The Holy Order of God," in *The Book of Mormon: Alma, the Testimony of the Word*, ed. Monte S. Nyman and Charles D. Tate Jr. (Provo, Utah: BYU Religious Studies Center, 1992), 61–88; and John W. Welch, "The Melchizedek Material in Alma 13:13–19," in *By Study and Also by Faith: Essays in Honor of Hugh W. Nibley*, ed. John M. Lundquist and Stephen D. Ricks (Salt Lake City: Deseret Book and FARMS, 1990), 2:238–72.

2. See, for example, Millet, "The Holy Order of God," 61–63; Bruce R. McConkie, *A New Witness for the Articles of Faith* (Salt Lake City: Deseret Book, 1985), 311; Bruce R. McConkie, *The Promised Messiah: The First Coming of Christ* (Salt Lake City: Deseret Book, 1978), 427; Joseph Fielding Smith, *Doctrines of Salvation* (Salt Lake City: Bookcraft, 1956), 3:84, 104; Joseph Fielding Smith, *Answers to Gospel Questions* (Salt Lake City: Deseret Book, 1957–66), 1:123–26; *Teachings of the Prophet Joseph Smith*, comp. Joseph Fielding Smith (Salt Lake City: Deseret Book, 1976), 180–81. See also Doctrine and Covenants 84:23–26; 107:1–4; 2 Nephi 6:2; Alma 4:20; 13:1, 6; 43:1–2; and 49:30.

3. In *Teachings of the Prophet Joseph Smith*, 335, Joseph Smith taught that the Levitical Priesthood does not have power to confer the Holy Ghost.

4. Smith, *Answers to Gospel Questions*, 1:125; see Alma 13:1; 43:1–2; and Doctrine and Covenants 107:1–4.

5. McConkie, *A New Witness*, 311; see also McConkie, *The Promised Messiah*, 427.

6. *Teachings of the Prophet Joseph Smith*, 322–23.

7. Ibid., 172.

8. Ibid., 337.

9. Ibid., 308.

10. Ezra Taft Benson, "What I Hope You Teach Your Children about the Temple," *Ensign*, August 1985, 8.

11. Leibel Reznick, *The Holy Temple Revisited* (New Jersey: Aronson, 1990), xi.

12. Menahem Haran, *Temples and Temple-Service in Ancient Israel* (Winona Lake, Ind.: Eisenbrauns, 1985), 1.

13. Hugh W. Nibley, "Temples: Meaning and Functions of Temples," in *Encyclopedia of Mormonism*, 4:1459.

14. Hugh W. Nibley, "Return to the Temple," in *Temple and Cosmos* (Salt Lake City: Deseret Book and FARMS, 1992), 49.

15. Joshua Berman, *The Temple: Its Symbolism and Meaning Then and Now* (Northvale, N.J.: Aronson, 1995), xx.

16. Stephen D. Ricks, "Temples through the Ages," in *Encyclopedia of Mormonism*, 4:1463.

17. Nibley, "Temples: Meaning and Functions of Temples," 4:1462.

18. John W. Welch, "The Temple in the Book of Mormon," in *Temples of the Ancient World: Ritual and Symbolism*, ed. Donald W. Parry (Salt Lake City: Deseret Book and FARMS, 1994), 298.

19. McConkie, in *The Promised Messiah*, 427, tentatively wrote: "We suppose their sacrifices were those that antedated the ministry of Moses. . . . There is, at least, no intimation in the Book of Mormon that the Nephites offered the daily sacrifices required by the law or that they held the various feasts that were part of the religious life of their Old World kinsmen." Welch, "The

Temple in the Book of Mormon," 302–9, argues that the Nephites performed the ordinances, including sacrifices and offerings, of the law of Moses until the end of such requirements was announced in 3 Nephi 9. For the ties between coronation, kingship, and Book of Mormon temples, see ibid., 326–36. For the connection of ancient Israelite festivals and temples in the Book of Mormon, see ibid., 338–39, 352–61; see also John A. Tvedtnes, "King Benjamin and the Feast of Tabernacles," in *By Study and Also by Faith*, 2:197–221; Hugh W. Nibley, "Tenting, Toll, and Taxing," in *The Ancient State* (Salt Lake City: Deseret Book and FARMS, 1991), 33–98; Hugh W. Nibley, "Old World Ritual in the New World," in *An Approach to the Book of Mormon*, 3rd ed. (Salt Lake City: Deseret Book and FARMS, 1988), 295–310; and Terrence L. Szink and John W. Welch, "King Benjamin's Speech in the Context of Ancient Israelite Festivals," in *King Benjamin's Speech: "That Ye May Learn Wisdom"* (Provo, Utah: FARMS, 1998), 147–223.

20. Welch, "The Temple in the Book of Mormon," 300, refers to these as temple texts, which he defines as writings "that [contain] the most sacred teachings of the plan of salvation that are not to be shared indiscriminately, and that [ordain] or otherwise [convey] divine powers through ceremonial or symbolic means, together with commandments received by sacred oaths that allow the recipient to stand ritually in the presence of God."

21. See McConkie, *The Promised Messiah*, 427; and Smith, *Answers to Gospel Questions*, 121–26.

22. Robert L. Millet, *The Power of the Word* (Salt Lake City: Deseret Book, 1994), 132.

23. John L. Sorenson, *An Ancient American Setting for the Book of Mormon* (Salt Lake City: Deseret Book and FARMS, 1985), 143.

24. Welch, "The Temple in the Book of Mormon," 323.

25. Ibid., 311.

26. See Nibley, *Temple and Cosmos*, 61–66, for an interesting discussion on secrecy and the temple. For further discussion of the Garden of Eden and the eternal plan of God in ways similar to known temple liturgy, see ibid., 70–77; 306–9; Stephen D. Ricks, "Liturgy and Cosmogony: The Ritual Use of Creation Accounts

in the Ancient Near East," in *Temples of the Ancient World,* 118–25; and Donald W. Parry, "Garden of Eden: Prototype Sanctuary," in *Temples of the Ancient World,* 126–51.

27. See Noah Webster, *American Dictionary of the English Language,* 1828 ed., s.v. "forward."

28. See Nibley, *Temple and Cosmos,* 49–54; see also *Teachings of the Prophet Joseph Smith,* 305.

29. McConkie, *The Promised Messiah,* 448.

30. Welch, "The Temple in the Book of Mormon," 365–66.

31. *Teachings of the Prophet Joseph Smith,* 227.

32. Ibid., 365.

33. McConkie, *A New Witness,* 340.

34. Joseph F. Smith, *Gospel Doctrine* (1919; reprint, Salt Lake City: Bookcraft, 1998), 376.

35. Nehor's name may derive from the Hebrew root NḤR, which means "to snort," suggesting the idea of anger or contentiousness.

36. Webster, *American Dictionary,* 1828 ed., s.v. "priestcraft."

37. Ibid., s.v. "priesthood."

38. See *History of the Church,* 6:314–15.

39. Hugh W. Nibley, *Since Cumorah,* 2nd ed. (Salt Lake City: Deseret Book and FARMS, 1988), 245: "A like fate was suffered centuries later by the traitor Zemnarihah. This goes back to a very old tradition indeed, that of the first false preachers, Harut and Marut (fallen angels), who first corrupted the word of God and as a result hang to this day between heaven and earth confessing their sin. Their counterpart in Jewish tradition is the angel Shamhozai, who 'repented, and by way of penance hung himself up between heaven and earth.'"

40. *Teachings of the Prophet Joseph Smith,* 67.

41. Recalled by Daniel Tyler in *Juvenile Instructor* 27/16, 15 August 1892, 492.

42. Several studies have been published concerning the reason for the detailed description in Alma 11 of the monetary system of Ammonihah. See "Weights and Measures in the Time of Mosiah II" (Provo, Utah: FARMS, 1983); John W. Welch, "Weighing and

Measuring in the Worlds of the Book of Mormon," *Journal of Book of Mormon Studies* 8/2 (1999): 36–46; Paul R. Jesclard, "A Comparison of the Nephite Monetary System with the Egyptian System of Measuring Grain," *Society for Early Historic Archaeology Newsletter* 134 (October 1973): 1–7; and Richard P. Smith, "The Nephite Monetary System," *Improvement Era*, May 1954, 316–17.

43. See Gordon C. Thomasson, "What's in a Name? Book of Mormon Language, Names, and [Metonymic] Naming," *Journal of Book of Mormon Studies* 3/1 (1994): 1–27.

44. See the discussion by Hugh W. Nibley, "Man's Dominion, or Subduing the Earth," in *Brother Brigham Challenges the Saints* (Salt Lake City: Deseret Book and FARMS, 1994), 13–16.

45. See Welch, "The Temple in the Book of Mormon," 366–67.

46. If Antionah is questioning the possibility of eternal life, this might be a departure from Nehor's original dogma that "in the end, all men should have eternal life" (Alma 1:4). If Antionah and the order of Nehor at Ammonihah did not have the doctrine of eternal life among them, then this may be an example of Alma's teaching that "he that will harden his heart, the same receiveth the lesser portion of the word" (Alma 12:10). Perhaps the idea of eternal life still existed in the false order of Nehor, but the concept devolved to the more secular view of living on through one's fame or fortune.

47. See M. Catherine Thomas, "Benjamin and the Mysteries of God," in *King Benjamin's Speech*, 277–94.

48. See Clark D. Webb, "Mysteries of God," in *Encyclopedia of Mormonism*, 2:977–78.

49. See Welch, "The Temple in the Book of Mormon," 364.

50. James Strong, *The New Strong's Exhaustive Concordance of the Bible* (Nashville: Nelson, 1990), #3466.

51. William E. Vine and John R. Kohlenberger III, eds., *The Expanded Vine's Expository Dictionary of New Testament Words* (Minneapolis: Bethany House, 1984), 769; see also Gerhard Kittel, ed., *Theological Dictionary of the New Testament*, trans. Geoffrey W. Bromiley (Grand Rapids, Mich.: Eerdmans, 1967), 4:803–28.

52. Kittel, *Theological Dictionary of the New Testament*, 4:803–6, as quoted in Welch, "The Temple in the Book of Mormon," 364.

53. Noah Webster, *American Dictionary*, 1828 ed., s.v. "mystery."

54. Ezra Taft Benson, *Come unto Christ* (Salt Lake City: Deseret Book, 1983), 19.

55. *Teachings of the Prophet Joseph Smith*, 358.

56. See Bruce C. Hafen, *The Broken Heart: Applying the Atonement to Life's Experiences* (Salt Lake City: Deseret Book, 1989), 156–57; McConkie, *The Promised Messiah*, 317–19; Welch, "The Melchizedek Material in Alma 13:13–19," 2:238–72; Robert L. Millet, *The Power of the Word: Saving Doctrines from the Book of Mormon* (Salt Lake City: Deseret Book, 1994), 138–53; and Millet, "The Holy Order of God," 61–86.

57. See Smith, *Gospel Doctrine*, 58.

58. Millet, "The Holy Order of God," 75.

59. See Welch, "The Melchizedek Material in Alma 13:13–19," 238–72.

60. See Josephus, *Wars* 6.10.1.

61. See *Teachings of the Prophet Joseph Smith*, 322.

62. Ibid.

63. See Joseph F. McConkie and Donald W. Parry, *A Guide to Scriptural Symbols* (Salt Lake City: Bookcraft, 1990), 82.

64. Harold B. Lee, *Decisions for Successful Living* (Salt Lake City: Deseret Book, 1973), 155.

65. *The Teachings of Spencer W. Kimball*, ed. Edward L. Kimball (Salt Lake City: Bookcraft, 1982), 34.

CHAPTER 9

THE KEEPER OF THE GATE

John Gee

The term *mystic* is currently applied to one who "seeks by contemplation and self-surrender to obtain union with or absorption into the Deity" and thereby obtains a "spiritual apprehension of truths that are inaccessible to the understanding."[1] Originally, however, it referred to "one initiated" into the mysteries.[2] Several major changes have occurred in the history of this word and its usage, not the least of which is the adoption of Neoplatonic philosophy in most mystical traditions.[3] The nature of some of these changes can perhaps best be seen in the examination of the possible origins of one phenomenon in one branch of mysticism, the Jewish Merkavah mystic.

Most of what we know about the Merkavah mystics derives from the *hekhalot* literature. The hekhalot literature[4] is a category of Jewish literature "that deals with the *hekhalot,* the heavenly 'palaces' or 'halls' through which the mystic passes to reach the divine throne. It is no coincidence that the term *hekhal* is taken from the architecture of the temple, where it is used precisely for the entrance hall to the holiest of holies."[5] The goal of the Merkavah mystic is to "descend"[6] to the chariot *(merkavah)*, which is then used to ascend to the throne of God.[7]

One of the earlier rabbinic commentaries on the Mishnah,[8] the Tosefta, contains a story, referred to as the Pardes episode, that has important implications for the hekhalot literature. (Pardes is the Greek word *paradeisos* loaned into Aramaic; the word, also loaned into English as "paradise," is ultimately of Persian origin: *paradayadam,* meaning "pleasant retreat.")[9] In the Pardes episode, Rabbi Ishmael warns the Merkavah mystic to guard his tongue in the sixth heaven,[10] since "the guards of the sixth *hekhal* would ruin those who descend the *merkhavah* without authority."[11]

The Pardes episode runs as follows:

> Four entered into Paradise, Ben Azzai, Ben Zoma, Aher and Rabbi Aqiva. One looked and died; one looked and was injured; one looked and cut down young shoots; one ascended in peace and descended in peace. Ben Azzai looked and died; about him scripture says: Precious in the sight of the Lord is the death of his saints [Psalm 116:15]. Ben Zoma looked and was injured; about him scripture says: Hast thou found honey? eat so much as is sufficient for thee, etc. ["lest thou be filled therewith, and vomit it," Proverbs 25:16].[12] Elishua [Aher] looked and cut down young shoots; about him scripture says: Suffer not thy mouth to cause thy flesh to sin; etc. ["neither say thou before the angel, that it was an error: wherefore should God be angry at thy voice, and destroy the work of thine hands?" Ecclesiastes 5:6]. Rabbi Aqiva ascended in peace and descended in peace; about him scripture says: Draw me, we will run, etc. ["after thee: the king hath brought me into his chambers," Song of Solomon 1:4].[13]

The Pardes episode suggests that Ben Azzai was a saint and therefore died; Ben Zoma saw more than was sufficient

for him and so was injured; Aher spoke about things that
he should not and damaged others thereby; and Aqiva was
drawn into the chambers of the king. In telling this story,
the Babylonian Talmud adds the following after the first
sentence: "Rabbi Aqiva said to them: When you arrive at
the stone of pure alabaster, say not, Water, water!"[14] The
Sitz im Leben of the hekhalot literature itself is wanting,[15]
and this forms a major impediment to understanding the
literature. The earliest manuscripts of the hekhalot literature, however, come from Egypt,[16] and there are at least
superficial parallels between Egyptian texts and hekhalot
literature. Each is "an outstanding example of an extremely
fluid corpus of texts which has reached, very late and in a
variety of ways, a stage of redaction which permits us to
recognize defined works" although "the boundaries between the different texts . . . seem very unstable."[17] At least
one of the major themes in hekhalot literature—getting
past the gatekeeper—has a long history in Egypt, and an
investigation of the context of those statements might open
the door to new avenues of research.

The Pyramid Texts

The earliest large literary corpus, the Pyramid Texts,[18]
was first carved into the walls of the pyramid of the Fifth
Dynasty King Unas (2356–2323 B.C.)[19]—though both royalty
and commoners may have used certain of the texts at an
earlier date.[20] These Pyramid Texts give a conception of the
universe where the heavens spread out like a vault not only
above but below the earth.[21] "On each side [of the expanse
of heaven] is a doorway that keeps out commoners and foreigners but through which the gods and the king can gain
access to the sky."[22] Since the eternal abode of the dead was
in the northern sky, "the path along which the deceased

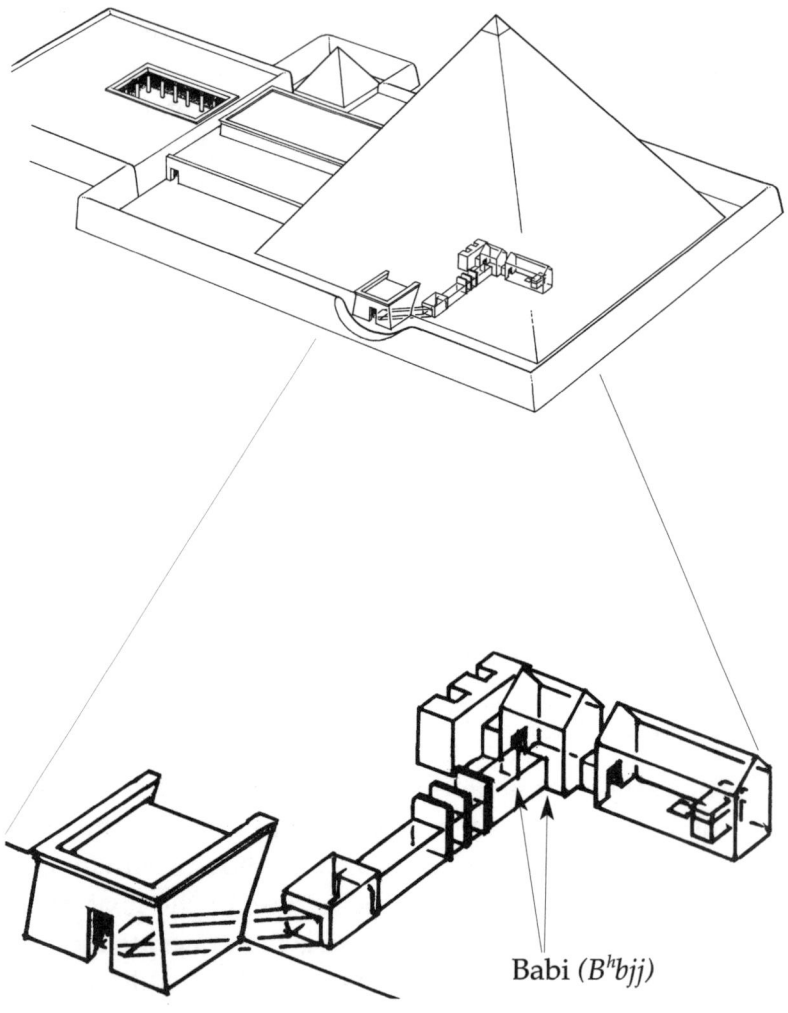

Figure 8. Babi, the gatekeeper, appears on either side of the door leading out of the pyramid complex of Unas.

must travel in order to reach this place is almost entirely restricted to the idea of ascending the heavens and to the manifold ways of mastering both the ascent and the crossing of the sky."[23] The universe described in the Pyramid Texts is also reflected in the architecture of the pyramid: the sarcophagus chamber is called the $d(w)^h t$, the underworld, while the antechamber is known as the $^h ht$, the dawn sky.[24] As the b^h (spirit) of the deceased king follows the texts leading out of the pyramid, "the final lines in the antechamber speak of opening 'the door of the $^h ht$ for the emergence of the day-bark.'"[25] In the corridor that leads out of the antechamber, the first text encountered deals with the doorkeeper, Babi $(B^h bjj)$—whose name seems to be a substantivized *nisbe* adjective[26] from the Semitic word *bab*, "door" or "gate,"[27] thus meaning "he of the gate." In the text, the king is instructed: "Pull back the doorbolt of Babi. Open the doors of heaven."[28] After passing through the gate, "King Unas is Babi, master of the mysteries."[29] With one exception,[30] Babi appears in the pyramids only at entryways.[31] Our purpose is not to look at all the doorway passages in the Pyramid Texts, but merely to show that the idea of having to pass the gatekeeper on the way to the sky extends back as far as we have any records of ascension to heaven.

The Coffin Texts

By the end of the Old Kingdom,[32] the Pyramid Texts also appear on coffins of those who could afford them.[33] Just as no two pyramids contain the same collection of texts, the texts on the coffins also vary; they are sometimes adopted in a straightforward manner, and sometimes adapted and changed, thus producing the collection of texts we know as the Coffin Texts.[34]

> The main purpose of this new genre of funerary litera-
> ture is to "equip" the dead with the necessary knowl-
> edge . . . describing . . . the 2 ways, the 7 gates, the 21 por-
> tals, . . . the door-keepers and heralds. . . . The deceased
> must not only know the names of all these entities and
> every detail concerning their nature, he must also have
> full command of the words needed to face each and
> everyone of them.[35]

We would be mistaken, however, to think that the Coffin
Texts are simply funerary texts.[36] Walter Federn showed
that many of the Coffin Texts do not deal with anything funerary; rather, "many, if not all, of the Coffin Texts were
primarily used in *this* life" and seem "to reflect a ceremony
of admitting, after due initiation, a person into a 'secret society,' in which gods or at least superhuman beings were
impersonated by humans."[37] Mordechai Gilula demonstrated conclusively the use of Coffin Texts by the living.[38]

In the Coffin Texts we also encounter the gatekeeper.
Though Babi generally has moved on to other occupations,[39]
he is still connected with the gatekeepers.[40] Of the several
passages in the Coffin Texts dealing with passing the gates,[41]
we will concentrate here on only one selection of texts that
are grouped together.[42] The texts list the keepers of the gate
from the outer gate to the fourth gate.[43] Rituals are performed on a specified day to cause the gatekeepers to cower
and let the individual through.[44] After passage, the individual breaks into a joyful acclamation because he or she can
join the sun in the solar bark in opening up the darkness.[45]
Another grouping of texts concerning the three "gates of
darkness" follows these texts in some coffins.[46] Here again
each keeper of the gate is named, but in this case passage is
granted because the individual is in the presence of the sun
god whom the individual praises with anthems. At the end

we find out that these texts belong to the divine shrine.[47] Thus the gatekeeper sections of the Coffin Texts seem also to belong to the initiation portions of the Coffin Texts.

The Book of the Dead

The successor to the Coffin Texts is known as the Book of the Dead (hereafter BD).[48] Some of the chapters contain elements taken from the Litany of the Sun and the Book of Caverns as well as the Coffin Texts and the Pyramid Texts.[49] Among the Coffin Texts taken over into the Book of the Dead were many of the gatekeeper spells.[50] Here we will examine two groups of spells, BD 125 and BD 144–47.

BD 125—perhaps the most famous chapter of the Book of the Dead, known both as the "Negative Confession" and the "Judgment of the Dead"—can be outlined as follows: (1) The chapter is said to be used when one reaches the "hall of the Two Truths."[51] (2) The individual announces himself, acknowledging his situation and detailing his purity on this august occasion.[52] (3) The individual addresses the forty-two divine judges and reviews his obedience to a different commandment with each of the judges.[53] (4) The individual offers a prayer summarizing his passing the test and requesting to be rescued from Babi.[54] (5) The individual answers questions about his ritual preparations.[55] (6) The individual confronts various gatekeepers in the form of parts of the door and to pass them must mention each by name.[56] (7) Ritual instructions for the use of the document are given.[57]

BD 144–47 involve the passage of either seven, fourteen, eighteen, or twenty-one gates; in tombs they are often written around the tomb's false door.[58] In BD 144 there is a list of the seven keepers of the seven gates whose names are identical to those from the Coffin Texts examined, though the order is different; other recited material is similar but has also been adapted. At the end of the chapter, a list of instructions specifies the offerings to be made at each of the gates and even the time of day of performing the text, as well as an admonition to secrecy.[59] This text is placed adjacent to the false door in the tomb of Senenmut.[60] BD 145, also found next to the false door in the tomb of Senenmut,[61] developed over the years, becoming more explicit with time. Whereas in the Eighteenth Dynasty only the words of address to the various gatekeepers were included, by the Nineteenth Dynasty the interrogation at each gate was also included, particularly a specification that the individual must identify the oil with which he or she has been anointed, the type of garment he or she wears, and the type of staff or scepter in the hand. The number of gates increased from fourteen in the Eighteenth Dynasty to eighteen in the Nineteenth Dynasty to twenty-one in the Twenty-first Dynasty. By the Twenty-first Dynasty, an epilogue detailing the individual's cultic activities is also appended.[62] BD 146 gives the names of the keepers of the twenty-one gates followed by a long declaration of the individual's qualifications in connection with the gates just passed through; at the end the individual declares his initiation into the mysteries on the day of the festival.[63] This text is found not only leading to the false door in the tomb of Senenmut,[64] but astride the northern doorway of the hall of the Osireion at Abydos.[65] In BD 147, the gates number only seven, but each has a keeper of the gate *(iry ꜥḥ)*, a guardian *(sꜣw)*, and an announcer *(smyw)*, all depicted in the accompanying vignettes.[66] Many of the names of the gatekeepers are the same as those of BD 144 and the Coffin Texts. The words the individual is to say at each gate are also entailed. Some manuscripts add that the purpose of the chapter is to allow the individual to enter the presence of the god and be among the blessed. A recent exposition summarizes these passages:

> The gate is a most pregnant symbol of transition. In the 145th and 146th chapters of the Book of the Dead, this idea finds itself systematically elaborated into a sequence of 21 gates which the deceased must pass in order to reach the "one, whom they conceal," the "weary one," i.e. Osiris. The gates are guarded by demons or better, as of late more correctly differentiated, by apotropaic gods. Their iconography, characterized by animal masks and knives, identifies them as dangerous and terrifying beings. The deceased wards off their threat by calling them by name, but also by knowing the names of the gates; he secures unhindered passage by showing proof of his purity. He knows the mythical significance of the water, in which he has bathed, and wears the appropriate clothing. The nature of the doorkeepers (and of the "apotropaic gods" in general) is ambiguous: the terror they embody is meant to ward off evil, the conceptual manifestations of which are ignorance, impurity and violence. The gates and their keepers build a 21-, 14-(15) or 7-fold (the number as such not being all that important) protective enclosure around the "weary one," namely the dead Osiris, who lives on as a deceased god within the concealment of these walls. The wish of the deceased human being is to identify his fate with that of Osiris. Only within the innermost enclosure of this most secluded and therefore holiest of all cosmic spheres will he also live as Osiris. The terrifying creatures at the gates will then be his own guards, protecting him from all evil.[67]

The inaccuracy of calling this work the "Book of the Dead" is increasingly recognized. The Egyptians called it the *rʰw nw prt m hrw*, "the chapters of *prt* (going forth, ascending) by day."[68] While many call BD 125 the "Judgment of the Dead,"[69] insisting that the entire Book of the Dead "reflects ritual acts performed during and after the burial,"[70] evidence from the text itself argues against this interpretation, for in this chapter, unlike any other in the Book of the Dead save one,[71] a specific date is mentioned—the last day of the second month of Peret (probably mid-January).[72] Since Egyptian mummification takes place within seventy days following death[73] (in which case the burial dates would be spread throughout the year), the ritual described in Book of the Dead 125 cannot be a *funerary* rite. The last day of the second month of Peret, however, does have temple significance: It is the day of groundbreaking for new temples,[74] the day on which priestly associations *(snt)*[75] end their year,[76] and the day before the festival of entering the holy of holies.[77] "Siegfried Morenz expressed the view that a central aspect of Ancient Egyptian burial ceremonies lay in a sort of priestly initiation to the realm of the dead. Twenty years later, his former student R. Grieshammer was able to substantiate this general hypothesis by capitalizing on one crucial element, the 'Negative Confession' in 'The Judgement of the Dead,' thereby elevating it to the realm of fact. . . . Grieshammer's conclusions, however, lead to the inversely formulated premise that the initiation rites, and not vice versa, furnished the prototypes of Egyptian funerary religion: a view which has so far been treated with great reserve."[78] This was demonstrated convincingly by a later papyrus from Egypt, in Greek, which shows that BD 125 is part of the induction ritual of the priests.[79] The initiation texts from the Coffin Texts were only intensified in the Book of the Dead.[80] Thus "before entering the hall of judgement . . . , the deceased must again be able to transpose the individual parts of the gate onto a specific mythical plane; similarly, in the so-called spells for the 'deification of the limbs,' his body is sacramentally interpreted by equating each part of his body with a deity. . . . It thus seems justified to consider whether a dramatic initiatory interrogation, rather than the mere philological need for commentary, underlies these spells."[81] So the questions in BD 125 "refer to a mystical knowledge, and more precisely yet to knowledge from the Osiris mysteries."[82]

The 125th chapter of the Book of the Dead is not the only chapter that has the connection with initiation:

> The knowledge and the passage of the gates (Book of the Dead 144–147) undoubtedly display features recalling initiation rituals. . . . Initiation ideas do not represent an autonomous field in Egyptian religion; on the contrary, there are clear correlations between them and the temple rituals. This emerges in the clearest form in the case of the admittance liturgies which were recited by the priests at the beginning of their daily service or upon entering the temple.[83]

Jan Assmann describes BD 144–47 in the following way:

> This sequence of seven gates also seems to have been an important principle in temple architecture, especially in the Late Period. . . . The underworld is imagined as a temple, in the innermost and holiest part of which Osiris sits enthroned. The path of the deceased to Osiris corresponds to the path of the priest on his way to the innermost sanctuary of the god. The path of the priest is furthermore sacramentally explained as an ascent to the heavens. He "opens the door-wings of the sky in Karnak" and "sees the mysteries of the horizon." . . . Egyptian "funerary mythology" in no way represents an autonomous field of religious speculation, but is actually deeply interwoven with the ideas and concepts of the earthly cult of the gods.[84]

The Book of the Dead had a long life. Manuscripts survive from the Eighteenth Dynasty (1550–1307 b.c.)[85] to the

Roman period (A.D. 63).[86] Sections of BD 125 were incorporated into the Books of Breathings dating to the centuries
surrounding the turn of the era,[87] and, as previously mentioned, the Book of the Dead was still used in priestly initiations in the second century A.D.[88]

The Anastasi Priestly Archive

With the conquest of Alexander the Great, Egypt came
under Hellenic hegemony. Though the Ptolemies allowed
demotic to be used in Egyptian courts, they preferred Greek
to be used in business documents and royal decrees[89] and
undertook the translation of documents into Greek.[90] The
Romans, apparently during the reign of Tiberius, prohibited the Egyptians from using their language for any legal
document, thus putting demotic on the decline.[91] The
Egyptians, who never had any aversion to adopting foreign cults and deities,[92] adopted the Greek ones as well and
syncretized them into their pantheon.[93] The Greeks also
adopted Egyptian gods,[94] for "religion was the one sphere
of life in which the Greeks, and especially the Greek-
speaking rulers, hesitated to dismiss the local tradition."[95]
The mixture that resulted produced Greek, hieratic, and
demotic texts dealing with religious themes.[96] When these
multilingual texts were first discovered in the early nineteenth century, scholars thought they were bilingual translations and that the Greek would be helpful in deciphering
Egyptian.[97] To some extent they were, but the elation soon
turned to revulsion when it was discovered that the first
three columns were "devoted to magic ceremonies" [sont
consacrées à des cérémonies magiques]; in fact, the whole
papyrus "consisted of formulas for superstitious practices
and theurgy that almost all the gnostics and philosophers
of the first centuries of our era tried to imitate" [consiste

entièrement en formules pour les pratiques superstitieuses, pour la théurgie, que presque toutes les sectes gnostiques et philosophiques des premiers siècles de notre ère pratiquaient à l'envi].[98] After that the scholars "only caught wind of the 'gnostic cheese' in the Christian era magical documents" [in allen magischen Dokumenten der nachchristlichen Zeit nur den 'fromage gnostique' rochen].[99] After acquiring the label *magic*, they remained for years a curious oddity, interesting only those scholars dealing in ancient sorceries.[100] They were collected by the papyrologist Karl Preisendanz[101] under the title *Papyri Graecae Magicae* "Greek Magical Papyri," although the documents are neither Greek[102] nor magical,[103] and not even necessarily papyri. Nonetheless, they have recently begun to receive significant attention.[104] Though the manuscripts themselves are generally dated paleographically to the late third and early fourth centuries A.D.,[105] some of the texts were in use by the late second century.[106]

The Anastasi priestly archive contains texts on many topics ranging from memory spells[107] to instructions for constructing seal rings,[108] to calling down divine messengers and revelations,[109] to initiations,[110] to prayers to the sun god,[111] all of which appear in the hekhalot texts. In the Egyptian documents in the Anastasi priestly archive, the gatekeepers appear within the initiation texts. We will look briefly at two: the wrongly labeled "Mithras Liturgy" and the so-called "Eighth Book of Moses,"[112] both of which are now viewed as reflecting Egyptian culture.[113]

The so-called Mithras Liturgy contains written records of the proceedings of the "mysteries . . . which the great god Helios Mithras commanded me by his archangel to pass down so that I alone, a supplicant, may enter heaven and view everything."[114] Later the initiate addresses deity by giving twenty-one epithets and names followed by the command, "Open to me!" accompanied by *nomina barbara*[115] and entreaties.[116] "Say all these things completing the first with fire and spirit; then begin the second likewise until thou hast completed the seven immortal gods of the world."[117] Later in the ritual, "thou shalt see the doors opening and seven virgins in white linen wearing serpent masks coming out of the depths. They are called the fates of heaven and grasp golden wands. When thou seest these things, greet them thus: 'Hail, O seven fates of heaven, revered and good virgins, holy and communal of Min who is in the temple,[118] most holy guardians of the four pillars.'"[119] Each is then greeted by name.[120] Then "another seven gods wearing black bull masks and girt about with linen come forth grasping seven golden diadems."[121] They are the "possessors of the pole star *(polokratores),*" a distinctively Egyptian touch.[122] These seven "guardians of the pivot *(knodakophylakes)*" must also be named in order for the initiate to see the god.[123] Instructions for the specific time (the new moon in Leo) and other purifications are also provided.[124]

In the "Eighth Book of Moses," the initiate, after performing the rite, is required by the instructions to say "the account of the hour-gods which is in the key and which compels them and those appointed over the weeks, and thou [i.e., the initiate] shalt be initiated into them. Then for the general calling down *(systasei),* have a natron square in which thou hast written the great name of the seven vowels."[125] The initiation was intended to be kept secret: "I order thee, child, and the uses of the holy book which all the sophists initiate from this holy and blessed book, as I adjured thee, child, in the temple which is in Jerusalem, after being filled with the wisdom of God, to make the book unfindable."[126] Again both the time (the last day of the month in Aries) and the specific purifications are detailed.[127]

Egyptian Christian Texts

By the fourth century, the Egyptians had adopted some Christian beliefs and practices,[128] though it is not entirely clear if many of the Egyptians who became Christians ever entirely gave up their Egyptian practices.[129]

In the *Apocalypse of Paul* from the Nag Hammadi library, Paul is taken on a trip through the heavens. The first three heavens are skipped over (probably because of a reading of 2 Corinthians 12). In the fourth heaven, Paul witnesses the judgment of a soul by the gatekeeper of the fourth heaven. Paul then proceeds through the gate to the fifth heaven where one angel had an iron rod and three others carried whips to punish evildoers. Paul proceeds through these gates following his paralemptor. In the sixth heaven a light and voice from above instruct the gatekeeper to let Paul and his paralemptor through. In the seventh heaven, Paul sees a man seated upon a throne who proceeds to question him. Paul passes to the eighth heaven by means of a sign that he carries. There he ascends with his fellow apostles through the ninth unto the tenth heaven.[130]

The fragmentary *First Book of Jeu*[131]—a compilation where "similar or related 'documents' are either grouped together or placed one following another in sequence"[132]—is relevant here. The account concerns the great and hidden mysteries: The resurrected Jesus appears to his apostles and gives them instructions in the mysteries that will let them know the will of God. After a break in the text, Jesus instructs the apostles that they will have access to the true God by going through several treasuries *(thesauros)* defended by three guards *(phylax)* accompanied by twelve spears *(proboloue)*[133] at the gates *(pyle)*, all of which have names. After an overview of twenty-eight of these store-houses, the text breaks off. It resumes in the midst of an ec-static hymn praising God for his creation of at least thirteen aeons and gives the name of each; after thirteen aeons the text breaks off again. When it resumes, Jesus is leading his apostles through the fifty-fourth of sixty storehouses, ex-plaining how to gain access. The following is an example of the procedure:

> Hearken now to the layout of this treasury to which you come. Seal yourselves with this seal *(sphragis)*[134] which is [a picture is drawn here]. This is its name: *Zoxaezoz.* Say it only once while this number (or stone, *psephos*) is in your hand: 600515; and say this name three times: *ooieezazamaza* and the guards and the orders and the veils will always withdraw themselves until you enter the place of their father and he will give you the mystery un-til you enter the mystery. This is the layout of this treas-ury and all of those who pertain to it.[135]

After this grand tour, Jesus, at the entreaty of his disci-ples, gives them one seal, number, and procedure that will unlock all the gates to all the treasuries. Inside the seventh innermost treasury Jesus forms a circle with his disciples and, standing in the middle, sings a hymn of praise to God with the disciples antiphonally chanting "amen, amen, amen." There the book ends.

Many of these things were already found in early Christianity. Jesus had promised to give his apostles secret keys to get past the gates of Hades.[136] Early Christians also looked forward to receiving a stone *(psephos)* with a secret name engraven on it, allowing them to rule over many na-tions and even sit on the throne of God.[137] They also had a long tradition of secrecy,[138] including secret ceremonies[139] with antiphonal chanting,[140] as well as a secret knowledge of "the celestial things, the arrangement of the angels, and the calling down (*systaseis*)[141] of the archangels (*archontes*), both seen and unseen."[142] But among the "unorthodox" Egyptian Christian documents it is difficult to separate the Egyptian elements from the Christian.

The Hekhalot Literature

At the time of the exile, some groups of Jews moved to Egypt to avoid Babylonian domination.[143] By the Persian period, a large Jewish colony flourished at Elephantine[144] to the extent that they even founded a Jewish temple there.[145] Jews also served as mercenaries in the garrisons at Migdol, Taphanes, Memphis, and Hermopolis with other Aramaic-speaking Semites.[146] The myriad of prisoners brought in by Ptolemy I Soter reinforced their presence.[147] Inscriptional remains attest Aramaic-speaking people in Egypt having adopted some of the Egyptian religious practices,[148] including being initiated into the Osirian mysteries.[149] Whether others borrowed from the Jews or the Jews borrowed from the Egyptians, Aramaic speakers were soon mixing the two religions.[150] Not all Jews adopted pagan practices; enough Jews resisted this syncretism that they became hated.[151]

Despite religious or ethnic tensions, the Egyptians themselves borrowed from Jewish religion. Thus the syncretistic Greco-Egyptian texts of the fourth century A.D. import several biblical figures, including Isaac[152] and Solomon.[153] The name Eve was used whenever the female ancestor was unknown.[154] They also contain copies of an entire prayer attributed to Jacob[155] and more than one book attributed to Moses.[156] One of the few names to appear on both demotic and Greek papyri of this sort is Abraham.[157] But the most common divine name in the papyri is Iao, the Greek version of the tetragrammaton.[158] "The influence worked both ways. Hebrew elements, taken over at some early time by the Greek syncretists, returned in their new Hellenized forms into the circles of Aramaic speaking Jewish esotericists."[159] Other scholars view the matter slightly differently: "Just as a number of gnostic elements found their way into Merkavah mysticism so did also certain Merkavah elements find their way into gnosticism."[160] (As we have seen above, Scholem's magicians and Gruenwald's gnostics are not isolated from each other.)

> The degree of receptivity which some Jewish circles showed to ideas originating from pagan sources is still one of the most bewildering problems which the student of the Judaism of the Talmudic period faces. It will in no way ease the problem if we assume that some Jewish circles timidly and carelessly collected whatever they found in the international market of religions. But it seems equally true to maintain that once foreign ideas had found their way into Judaism they were not—or even could not be—easily swept under the carpet. . . . In most cases, however, the impression one gets is that those people were attracted by complex pictures even when these pictures were composed of the most heterogeneous elements. The artificial combination of various and sometimes even conflicting religious elements was the fashion of the day, and if this was believed to enrich one's religious experience, the question of the cost was not raised.[161]

It may be significant that the earliest manuscripts of the hekhalot literature come from Egypt.[162] "It is probably through the influence of these magical performances that we find in some hekhalot texts the idea that certain practices are useful only for bringing about certain experiences at specific dates."[163] Prayers to the sun with strings of epithets, some of which are clearly Egyptian, also clearly derive from this common milieu.[164] Others have enumerated additional examples of materials that reflect the Egyptian background of the *PGM* borrowed into the hekhalot literature;[165] our interest lies in the gatekeeper passages of the hekhalot literature.

The seventeenth chapter of the *Hekhalot Rabbati*[166] (which appears in the manuscripts for the most part as a single unit),[167] like much of the hekhalot literature itself,[168] was concerned with heavenly ascensions. During the heavenly ascension the mystic had to pass by various gates and their keepers. Perhaps the most conspicuous feature of the text is the use of the seals to get past the keepers of the heavenly gates. The seals have special names attached to them, the one for the guard on the right side being compounded with the divine name, while the one for the guard on the left side is compounded with the *Sar ha-Panim*. It is tempting to speculate that the common element in two of these, ṬWṬRWSY'Y-YWY and ṬWṬRBY'L-YWY, might stand for the Egyptian God Thoth (*Ḏḥwty-rsy=i* "Thoth is my guard"[169] and *Ḏḥwty* RBY 'L "Thoth my master is god").[170] Though incantations might accompany the seals, they are nowhere described.[171] The parallels from Coptic texts mentioned above prove nothing as it may be that the Jewish sources influence the Christian. Since it is specifically the use of the seals that connects the hekhalot literature to magic,[172] we have the ironic situation that whereas in the Bible what was classified as magic was that practiced by outsiders,[173] what is labeled as magic here may be originally a Jewish feature.

Table 1. Phenomena Associated with the Gatekeeper

	PT	CT 1100–1106	CT 1107–15	BD 125	BD 144	BD 145	BD 146	BD 147	Mithras Liturgy	8th Book of Moses	Apocalypse of Paul	1st Jeu	Hekhalot Rabbati
no. of gates	1	4	3	1	7	14–21	21	7	1	2	10	60	7
gatekeepers per gate	1	1	1	42/12	1	1	1	3	7	7	1	15	2
interview	no	no	no	yes	no	no	no	no	no	yes	yes	no	no
name	no	yes	yes	yes	yes	yes	yes	yes	yes	yes	no	yes	yes
seal	no	no	no	no	no	no	no	no	no	no	yes	yes	yes
prayer	no	yes	yes	yes	yes	yes	no	yes	yes	yes	no	yes	no
hymn	no	yes	yes	no	no	no	yes	no	yes	no	no	yes	no

Temporary Conclusions

The summary of the phenomena associated with the gatekeeper appears in table 1, from which it can be seen that the *Hekhalot Rabbati* passage belongs to the same sort of complex as the passages in Egyptian and Christian tradition. This is not the same thing as a history of the tradition. "It is almost impossible to write a history of ideas, traditions, and motifs, which in any case cannot consist of isolated quotations loosely linked" [Eine Geschichte von Ideen, von Traditionen, von Motiven zu schreiben, wird nahezu unmöglich und kann jedenfalls nicht darin bestehen, isolierte Zitate herauszupikken und aneinanderzureihen].[174] Yet that is all that has been done here; the preceding has merely run roughshod over several texts not normally associated, suggesting a common tradition,[175] though not proving it. Some historical background has been included to show that it is reasonable to suggest that the Egyptian traditions might have influenced both Jewish and Christian traditions,[176] though the differences are well worth noting; we are suggesting adaptation, not plagiarism. The presence of the gatekeepers, stronger in some texts than in others, indicates a temple initiation in the Egyptian texts and therefore suggests an initiation in the Jewish and Christian texts. This is all suggestion and not proof. It can "only be provisional, since a comparison of motifs presupposes in the last resort a comparison of systems."[177] To say that the system represented in the texts was some form of "magic" seems dubious and problematic. At this point we might finally be able to ask whether the *Sitz im Leben* of certain passages in the hekhalot literature might be connected in some way with some Jewish initiation. Such questions I leave to the experts in hekhalot literature who can subject this complex to the requisite inner analysis.[178]

Notes

I would like to thank Robert Ritner for some insightful discussions and for reminding me of an important piece of information and Peter Schäfer for some useful comments; I exculpate them from any mistakes either in method or in fact in this chapter.

1. *Oxford English Dictionary*, 2nd ed., s.v. "mystic."

2. Henry G. Liddell and Robert Scott, *A Greek-English Lexicon*, 9th ed. (Oxford: Clarendon, 1968), 1156, s.v. "mystes" and "mystikos." See Walter Burkert, *Ancient Mystery Cults* (Cambridge, Mass.: Harvard University Press, 1987), 9–10.

3. See the discussions in William J. Hamblin, "'Everything Is Everything': Was Joseph Smith Influenced by the Kabbalah?" *FARMS Review of Books* 8/2 (1996): 262–64; William J. Hamblin, "Temple Motifs in Jewish Mysticism," in *Temples of the Ancient World: Ritual and Symbolism*, ed. Donald W. Parry (Salt Lake City: Deseret Book and FARMS, 1994), 461–62. The earliest Christian with tendencies toward mysticism was Origen (see Johannes Quasten, *Patrology* [Utrecht, Netherlands: Spectrum, 1950], 2:94–100), a student of Ammonius Saccas "the Socrates of Neoplatonism," who also taught the Neoplatonist philosopher Plotinus; Erik R. Dodds, "Ammonius Saccas," in *The Oxford Classical Dictionary*, ed. N. G. L. Hammond and H. H. Scullard, 2nd ed. (Oxford: Clarendon, 1970), 53. Origen, like other early Christian mystics—Ammonas (see Quasten, *Patrology*, 3:153–54) and Macarius (see ibid., 3:162–63)—was Egyptian. Evagarius of Pontus, though not Egyptian, was a student of both Origen and Macarius and spent the last seventeen years of his life in Egypt (see ibid., 3:169–76).

4. For an overview of hekhalot literature, see Peter Schäfer, *The Hidden and Manifest God: Some Major Themes in Early Jewish Mysticism*, trans. Aubrey Pomerance (Albany, N.Y.: State University of New York, 1992).

5. Ibid., 2; see Menahem Haran, *Temples and Temple-Service in Ancient Israel* (Oxford: Clarendon, 1978), 14, 355.

6. There has always been something strange about using the verb *yārad*, "to descend," for entering the chariot. Biblical usage is different. When Sisera descends from the chariot (*yēred mēʿal hammerkābāh*, Judges 4:15), he is getting off. The normal verb used for mounting a chariot is *ʿālāh: yaʿălēhû ʿal-hammerkābāh*, "they got on the chariot" (1 Kings 20:33, author's translation). Elijah is said to ascend (*yaʿal*) with the chariot (see 2 Kings 2:11).

7. See Schäfer, *Hidden and Manifest God*, 2.

8. See Jacob Neusner, *Invitation to the Talmud*, rev. ed. (San Francisco: Harper and Row, 1984), 70–71; Kathleen Kuiper, ed., *Merriam-Webster's Encyclopedia of Literature*, s.v. "Tosefta."

9. Originally meaning "that which is beyond or behind the wall"; Roland G. Kent, *Old Persian: Grammar, Texts, Lexicon*, 2nd ed. (New Haven, Conn.: American Oriental Society, 1953), 195.

10. See TB Ḥagigah 14b and Peter Schäfer, ed., *Synopse zur Hekhalot-Literatur* (Tübingen: Mohr, 1981), 146–47, §§339, 345.

11. Schäfer, *Synopse zur Hekhalot-Literatur*, 96–97, §224.

12. Typical of rabbinic literature, the reason for using a particular passage as a proof text is often obscure. Here, the first phrase of the verse is cited and the reader is expected to know the entire verse since the crucial phrase comes in the uncited portion of the verse. Scriptures have been harmonized to the King James Version for ease of reference.

13. Tosefta Ḥagigah 2, 3–4.

14. TB Ḥagigah 14b; Schäfer, *Synopse zur Hekhalot-Literatur*, 146–47, §§339, 345.

15. For cautions about hastily "reconstructing ephemeral historical contexts," see Peter Schäfer, "Merkavah Mysticism and Rabbinic Judaism," *Journal of the American Oriental Society* 104/3 (1984): 541. The most ambitious effort to supply such has been David J. Halperin, *The Faces of the Chariot: Early Jewish Responses to Ezekiel's Vision* (Tübingen: Mohr, 1988); see also David J. Halperin, "A New Edition of the Hekhalot Literature," *Journal of the American Oriental Society* 104/3 (1984): 551.

16. See Peter Schäfer, ed., *Geniza-Fragmente zur Hekhalot-Literatur*

(Tübingen: Mohr, 1984), 10–11. These include the earliest manuscripts containing portions of *3 Enoch* and the *Hekhalot Rabbati*, though none in the same form in which they are presently generally known. To me, it makes more sense to see the Geniza fragments as based on the larger works rather than the later works as expansions and adaptations of the shorter ones. It is also worth noting that of the other books of Enoch, the manuscripts for the Greek version come from Egypt (see Campbell Bonner, *The Last Chapters of Enoch in Greek* [London: Christophers, 1937], 3–4), and the Slavonic is thought to have originated in Judea (see James H. Charlesworth, ed., *The Old Testament Pseudepigrapha* [hereafter *OTP*] [Garden City, N.Y.: Doubleday, 1983], 1:95–97), as is the Ethiopic (see *OTP*, 1:7–8), which was brought to Ethiopia via a Greek version in Egypt (see R. H. Charles, trans., *The Book of Enoch* [London: Oxford University Press, 1913], xvii). This suggests a locus around Judea and the Nile Delta for the production of the Enoch literature.

17. Schäfer, "Merkavah Mysticism," 538. Schäfer, of course, refers only to the hekhalot literature.

18. See Jan Assmann, "Death and Initiation in the Funerary Religion of Ancient Egypt," in *Religion and Philosophy in Ancient Egypt* (New Haven, Conn.: Yale Egyptological Seminar, 1989), 136: "These 'Pyramid Texts' represent the oldest substantial corpus of religious texts known to mankind" (compare ibid., 143).

19. Dating for Egypt in general follows John Baines and Jaromír Málek, *Atlas of Ancient Egypt* (New York: Facts on File, 1980). Unas's dates are found on pp. 34 and 36.

20. One of the evidences that the rituals from the Pyramid Texts were used by commoners is the presence of model kits for the opening of the mouth (see PT 37–57); examples include MFA 13.3144, 13.3252, 13.3257, 13.3263, 13.3265–66, 13.3269, and 28.1148, in Ann M. Roth, "Model Equipment with a *peshesh-kef*," in *Mummies and Magic: The Funerary Arts of Ancient Egypt*, ed. Sue D'Auria, Peter Lacovara, and Catharine H. Roehrig (Boston: Museum of Fine Arts, 1988), 80–81; MMA 07.228.117, in William C. Hayes, *The Scepter of Egypt: A Background for the Study of the*

Egyptian Antiquities in the Metropolitan Museum of Art (New York: The Metropolitan Museum of Art, 1953), 1:118. Other evidences include oil tablets; see MFA 24.599, in Nigel Strudwick, "Oil Tablet," in *Mummies and Magic*, 81–82; BM 6123, in Stephen Quirke, *Ancient Egyptian Religion* (London: British Museum, 1992), 149. One can also compare the offering lists from the Pyramid Texts with those from private mastabas. See Eberhard Otto, *Das ägyptische Mundöffnungsritual* (Wiesbaden: Harrassowitz, 1960), 2:1–2; Hartwig Altenmüller, *Die Texte zum Begräbnisritual in den Pyramiden des Alten Reiches* (Wiesbaden: Harrassowitz, 1972), 273–79.

21. See PT 215 §149, in Kurt Sethe, *Die altaegyptischen Pyramidentexte* (Leipzig: Hinrichs, 1908), 1:85.

22. James P. Allen, "The Cosmology of the Pyramid Texts," in *Religion and Philosophy in Ancient Egypt*, 5; compare 5 n. 30: "All four doorways are mentioned in 1252c–f. For the doorways barring *(ḥsf)* commoners *(rḥwt)* and foreigners *(ṯḥnw, fnḫw)*, see 876b, 1726a–b. *1916a, *1949b, N 1055+33. . . . For the king and gods passing through these doors, see 659a, 981–85, 1408–11, *1929a–b, N 1055+44 = Nt 692. Besides the ubiquitous term *ꜥ/ꜥwj pt*, the doors are also called *sbʰ(w) pt* (799a, 1156, 1252c–f, 1720a) and *ꜥwj shdw* (727a, 1474c)."

23. Assmann, "Death and Initiation," 143.

24. See Allen, "Cosmology of the Pyramid Texts," 17–26; and Quirke, *Ancient Egyptian Religion*, 152–55.

25. Allen, "Cosmology of the Pyramid Texts," 25, citing PT 311 §496. Because the verb *prj* means both "go forth" (see James P. Allen, *The Inflection of the Verb in the Pyramid Texts* [Malibu: Undena, 1984], 569) and "ascend" (PT 215 §149), we might translate this as "for the ascension of the day-bark."

26. For this form, see Alan H. Gardiner, *Egyptian Grammar*, 3rd ed. (Oxford: Griffith Institute, 1957), 61–63, §§ 79, 81.

27. Attested in Akkadian (*bābu*, see *Chicago Assyrian Dictionary*, 2:14–26), Aramaic *(bab, baba')*, and Arabic *(bab)*. In literary Late Egyptian (all examples are Eighteenth Dynasty), *bʰbʰw* means "hole." See Raymond O. Faulkner, *A Concise Dictionary of Middle Egyptian* (Oxford: Griffith Institute, 1962), 77; "hole" fits

the context of b^hb^h in P. Anastasi IV.1b.12, in Alan H. Gardiner, *Late-Egyptian Miscellanies* (Brussels: Fondation Égyptologique Reine Élisabeth, 1937), 35; the definition in Leonard H. Lesko and Barbara S. Lesko, eds., *A Dictionary of Late Egyptian* (Providence, R.I.: B.C. Scribe, 1982), 1:146, is in error.

28. PT 313 §502; compare Allen, "Cosmology of the Pyramid Texts," 25. I have bowdlerized the translation to make it comprehensible to the nonspecialist.

29. PT 320 §516.

30. See PT 278 §419, which is located in the southeast corner of the east wall of the antechamber to the right of the door to the *serdab* (room in a mastaba tomb where statues of the deceased were usually placed) in the pyramid of Unas; see Sethe, *Die altaegyptischen Pyramidentexte,* 3:119.

31. See PT 313 §502 (Pyramid of Unas, west wall entrance from antechamber 3:120), 320 §§515–16 (Pyramid of Unas, east wall entrance from antechamber 3:120), 539 §1310 (Pyramid of Pepi II south wall of the "Wartesaal" on the right of door leading toward the antechamber 3:133), 549 §1349 (Pyramid of Pepi II south wall of the "Wartesaal" on the left of the door leading to the antechamber 3:133).

32. See David P. Silverman, "Divinity and Deities in Ancient Egypt," in *Religion in Ancient Egypt: Gods, Myths, and Personal Practice,* ed. Byron E. Shafer (Ithaca: Cornell University Press, 1991), 72–73, esp. n. 86.

33. For a discussion on the fallacies of the common assumption that this means that the funerary cults were a sign of democratization, see Ragnhild B. Finnestad, "The Pharaoh and the 'Democratization' of Post-Mortem Life," in *The Religion of the Ancient Egyptians: Cognitive Structures and Popular Expressions,* ed. Gertie Englund (Uppsala: Academiae Ubsaliensis, 1989), 89–93; Jørgen P. Sørensen, "Divine Access: The So-Called Democratization of Egyptian Funerary Literature as a Socio-Cultural Process," in ibid., 109–25.

34. See Silverman, "Divinity and Deities," 47–48; T. G. H. James, *Ancient Egypt: The Land and Its Legacy* (Austin: University

of Texas Press, 1988), 92; see also David P. Silverman, "Textual Criticism in the Coffin Texts," in *Religion and Philosophy in Ancient Egypt*, 30–34; the process is described in Stephen E. Thompson, "The Origin of the Pyramid Texts found on Middle Kingdom Saqqâra Coffins," *Journal of Egyptian Archaeology* 76 (1990): 17–20.

35. Assmann, "Death and Initiation," 143.

36. "No death of Osiris is mentioned in . . . the Coffin Texts, but his resurrection is constantly referred to." Silverman, "Divinity and Deities," 29.

37. Walter Federn, "The 'Transformations' in the Coffin Texts: A New Approach," *Journal of Near Eastern Studies* 19/4 (1960): 250.

38. See Mordechai Gilula, "Hirtengeschichte 17–22 = CT VII 36 m-r," *Göttinger Miszellen* 29 (1978): 21–22.

39. See, for example, CT 576, in *The Egyptian Coffin Texts*, ed. Adriaan de Buck (Chicago: University of Chicago Press, 1956), 6:191.

40. See CT 668, in ibid., 6:296; compare CT 1101, in ibid., 7:420.

41. See CT 901, 1001, 1060–63, 1079, 1081, 1100–1113, 1165, 1169, 1180–81, in ibid., 7:107–8, 218–19, 317–22, 348–51, 354, 415–45, 508, 511–12, 518–19.

42. See CT 1100–1106, in de Buck, *Egyptian Coffin Texts*, 7:416–35.

43. See CT 1100–1106, in ibid. Coffin B3C is unusual because the names of the gatekeepers are listed separately from the rest of the text at the very beginning of the section. This indicates that CT 1100–1106 are seen as a unit.

44. See CT 1100, in de Buck, *Egyptian Coffin Texts*, 7:418–19.

45. See CT 1104–6, in ibid., 7:430–35.

46. CT 1107–15, in ibid., 7:436–46. The break in the placement on the coffins seems to be after 1115 not 1113.

47. See CT 1115, in ibid., 7:446.

48. First established in Richard Lepsius, *Älteste Texte des Todtenbuchs nach Sarkophagen des altaegyptischen Reichs im Berliner Museum* (Berlin: Hertz, 1867).

49. See Thomas G. Allen, trans., *The Book of the Dead, or Going*

Forth by Day (Chicago: University of Chicago Press, 1974), 3. The chapters connected with the Litany of the Sun are Book of the Dead (hereafter BD) 42, 127, 180, 181; BD 168 seems to be derived from the Book of Caverns. For the Litany of the Sun, see Edouard Naville, *La Litanie du soleil: Inscriptions recueillies dans les tombeaux des rois à Thèbes* (Leipzig: Engelmann, 1875); James H. Breasted, *De hymnis in solem sub rege Amenophide IV conceptis* (Berlin: Paul, 1894).

50. See de Buck, *Egyptian Coffin Texts*, 4:xiii; 7:xii–xiii; Allen, *Book of the Dead*, 235–36. These gatekeeper spells also have affinities to the Book of Gates, for which see Erik Hornung, *Die Unterweltsbücher der Ägypter* (Zürich: Artemis, 1992), 195–308. The gates of the netherworld are another common motif that will not be explored here.

51. BD 125 d P, in Allen, *Book of the Dead*, 97.

52. See BD 125 a S 1–3, in Allen, *Book of the Dead*, 97. Similar lists of purity can be found on Shurpu tablet II where the problem is to purify someone who has committed one of these transgressions. See tablet II in Erica Reiner, *Šurpu: A Collection of Sumerian and Akkadian Incantations* (Graz: Weidner, 1958), 13–18; compare tablet IV, in ibid., 25–29; tablet VIII, lines 41–90, in ibid., 41–44.

53. See BD 125 b S 1–42, in Allen, *Book of the Dead*, 98–99.

54. See BD 125 c S 1–2, in Allen, *Book of the Dead*, 99.

55. See BD 125 c S 3–6, in Allen, *Book of the Dead*, 99–100.

56. See BD 125 c S 7–8, in Allen, *Book of the Dead*, 100.

57. See BD 125 c T 1–5, in Allen, *Book of the Dead*, 100–101.

58. See Peter F. Dorman, *The Tombs of Senenmut: The Architecture and Decoration of Tombs 71 and 353* (New York: Metropolitan Museum of Art, 1991), plates 57–59, 64–79.

59. See Allen, *Book of the Dead*, 120–22.

60. See Dorman, *Tombs of Senenmut*, plates 57–59, 70–79.

61. See ibid., plates 57, 59, 68–69.

62. The various versions may be found in Allen, *Book of the Dead*, 123–33.

63. "She has served as an initiate before Osiris at his Beautiful

festival of assuming the White Crown." Allen, *Book of the Dead*, 137. See Richard Lepsius, *Das Todtenbuch der Ägypter nach dem hieroglyphischen Papyrus in Turin* (Leipzig: Wigand, 1842), plate LXVII, which has *iw ir.n=f ʰḥw iqr m-bʰḥ Wsir m ḥb=f nfrt nt ḫmn m ḫḏt*.

64. See Dorman, *Tombs of Senenmut*, 119–20, plates 58–59, 66–69.

65. See Margaret A. Murray, *The Osireion at Abydos* (1903; reprint, London: Histories and Mysteries of Man, 1989), 20, and plate XI.

66. See Allen, *Book of the Dead*, 137–39.

67. Assmann, "Death and Initiation," 147–48; compare 148–49:

> This idea was even adapted into a board game with the characteristic name "passage." It requires two players. The object of the game is to find oneself in a passage through 30 fields of salutary or evil nature until one arrives in the vicinity of the god, who then grants sustenance (bread and water) and justification. It was, without any doubt, also played in lifetime for the sole purpose of "enjoyment" (*sḥmḫ jb*, Egyptian for "enjoyment," lit.: "to cause the heart to forget"), but has almost exclusively come to us from the funerary context. Particularly informative in this matter is the evidence from the tomb of Sennedjem: here, the scene is found above a door, thus already imparting the sense of "passage" through its very location. Furthermore, near the game-board, a table covered with food offerings figuratively conveys the purpose and goal of the "passage": securing access to and availability of eternal sustenance.

68. Allen, *Book of the Dead*, 1.

69. Miriam Lichtheim, *Ancient Egyptian Literature: A Book of Readings* (Berkeley: University of California Press, 1976), 2:119, 124.

70. Ibid., 2:119. This was emphatically denied in the earliest

publication of the Book of the Dead; see Lepsius, *Todtenbuch der Ägypter*, 3–4.

71. See BD 140. Significantly, the same date is mentioned in both places.

72. See Gardiner, *Egyptian Grammar*, 205.

73. See P. Setna I 4/24–25, in Wilhelm Spiegelberg, *Die demotischen Denkmäler* (Strassburg: Fischbach, 1906), 2.2: Tafel XLV; F. Ll. Griffith, *Stories of the High Priests of Memphis: The Sethon of Herodotus and the Demotic Tales of Khamuas* (Oxford: Clarendon, 1900), 114–17; Lichtheim, *Ancient Egyptian Literature*, 3:132; Herodotus, *Historiae* 2.86.5; A. J. Spencer, *Death in Ancient Egypt* (Harmondsworth, England: Penguin, 1982), 112.

74. See CG 34012, in Kurt Sethe, *Urkunden der 18. Dynastie*, Urkunden des ägyptischen Altertums, vol. 4, part 3 (Leipzig: Hinrichs, 1907), 835–36; Paul Barguet, *Le temple d'Amon-Rê à Karnak: Essai d'exégèse* (Cairo: L'institut français d'archéologie orientale, 1962), 33, 296–97; compare Claude Traunecker, *Coptos: Hommes et dieux sur le parvis de Geb* (Leuven: Peeters, 1992), 253.

75. For the reading of this word, see George R. Hughes, "The Sixth Day of the Lunar Month and the Demotic Word for 'Cult Guild,'" *Mitteilungen des deutschen archäologischen Instituts zu Kairo* 16 (1958): 147–60.

76. See P. Lille no. 29, 4, in Françoise de Cenival, *Les associations religieuses en Égypte d'après les documents démotiques* (Cairo: L'institut français d'archéologie orientale, 1972), 3.

77. See P. Berlin 13603 4/24, in Wolja Erichsen and Siegfried Schott, *Fragmente memphitischer Theologie in demotischer Schrift (Pap. demot. Berlin 13603)* (Mainz: Akademie der Wissenschaften und der Literatur, 1954), 21, Tafel VI: p^h ḥb ꜥyq ḥryw p.t "the festival of entering the upper part of heaven." For the upper part of heaven as a designation for the holy of holies, see Jean-Marie Kruchten, *Les annales des prêtres de Karnak (XXI-XXIIImes dynasties) et autres textes contemporains relatifs à l'initiation des prêtres d'Amon* (Leuven: Departement Oriëntalistiek, 1989), 59, 62, 67, 245–51, 286; Jaroslav Černy, "Note on $^{dˁ}wy-pt$ 'Shrine,'" *Journal of Egyptian Archaeology* 34 (1948): 120; compare Siegfried Morenz, *Egyptian*

Religion, trans. Ann E. Keep (Ithaca: Cornell University Press, 1973), 88.

78. Assmann, "Death and Initiation," 135, 136.

79. The papyrus derives from Oxyrhynchus and dates to the second century A.D. The first recognition of the connection with BD 125 was in Reinhold Merkelbach, "Ein ägyptischer Priestereid," *Zeitschrift für Papyrologie und Epigraphik* 2 (1968): 7–30; compare Reinhold Merkelbach, "Nachträge zu Band 1 und 2," *Zeitschrift für Papyrologie und Epigraphik* 3 (1968): 136; Reinhold Merkelbach, "Ein griechisch-ägyptischer Priestereid und das Totenbuch," in *Religions en Égypte hellénistique et romaine* (Paris: Presses Universitaires de France, 1969), 69–73. A more popular exposition of this text noting its connection to Roman literature may be found in Reinhold Merkelbach, *Die Unschuldserklärungen und Beichten im ägyptischen Totenbuch, in der römischen Elegie und im antiken Roman* (Gießen: Universitätsbibliothek Gießen, 1987), 5–34.

80. See Federn, "'Transformations' in the Coffin Texts," 253–55.

81. Assmann, "Death and Initiation," 145.

82. Ibid., 150.

83. L. Kákosy, review of *Religion and Philosophy in Ancient Egypt, Bibliotheca Orientalis* 48/5–6 (1991): 773.

84. Assmann, "Death and Initiation," 149.

85. The manuscripts (at least 47) listed in Erik Hornung, *Das Totenbuch der Ägypter* (Zürich: Artemis, 1990), 525–28, all date from the New Kingdom (1550–1070 B.C.). Another list of manuscripts from a wider date may be found in Allen, *Book of the Dead,* 242–47. The Eighteenth Dynasty manuscripts in the Cairo Museum have now been edited in Irmtraut Munro, *Die Totenbuch-Handschriften der 18. Dynastie im Ägyptischen Museum Cairo,* 2 vols. (Wiesbaden: Harrassowitz, 1994). The fullest listing of Eighteenth-Dynasty manuscripts with discussion is Irmtraut Munro, *Untersuchungen zu den Totenbuch-Papyri der 18. Dynastie* (London: Kegan Paul, 1988).

86. The latest manuscript of the Book of the Dead is Bibliothèque Nationale E 140, published in Franz Lexa, *Das demotische Totenbuch der Pariser Nationalbibliothek (Papyrus des Pamonthes)*

(Leipzig: Hinrichs, 1910). The papyrus dates to the tenth year of Nero (3/29–30) = A.D. 63.

87. See P.-J. de Horrack, "Le livre des respirations d'après les manuscrits du Musée du Louvre," *Bibliotheque Egyptologique* 17 (1907): plate vii, lines 9–14.

88. See Merkelbach, "Ein ägyptischer Priestereid," 7–30; compare Merkelbach, "Nachträge," 136; Merkelbach, "Ein griechisch-ägyptischer Priestereid," 69–73; Merkelbach, *Die Unschulds-erklärungen und Beichten*, 5–34.

89. See Stephen Quirke and Carol Andrews, *The Rosetta Stone* (New York: Abrams, 1989), 6. Contra Dorothy J. Thompson, *Memphis under the Ptolemies* (Princeton: Princeton University Press, 1988), 103, Greek was not a "prestige language" in ancient Egypt. If Greek women kept legal records in demotic because that meant they could use the Egyptian courts, where they actually had rights, how is Greek prestigious? See also Robert K. Ritner, "Implicit Models of Cross-Cultural Interaction: A Question of Noses, Soap, and Prejudice," in *Life in a Multi-Cultural Society: Egypt from Cambyses to Constantine and Beyond*, ed. Janet H. Johnson (Chicago: Oriental Institute of the University of Chicago, 1992), 289.

90. See Pseudo-Aristeas, in *OTP*, 2:12–34.

91. See Naphtali Lewis, "The Demise of the Demotic Document: When and Why," *Journal of Egyptian Archaeology* 79 (1993): 276–81.

92. See PT 280–81 §421–22, in Sethe, *Die altaegyptischen Pyramidentexte*, 1:219; Thomas Schneider, "Mag.pHarris XII, 1–5: Eine kanaanäische Beschwörung für die Löwenjagd?" *Göttinger Miszellen* 112 (1989): 53–63; François Lexa, *La magie dans l'Égypte antique* (Paris: Geuthner, 1925), 1:61 nn. 1–2; Quirke, *Ancient Egyptian Religion*, 46–47, 114, 173.

93. See Thompson, *Memphis under the Ptolemies*, 90, 99, 104.

94. See the dedication of a Greek gymnasium to the Egyptian crocodile god Sobek (now in Trinity College, Dublin), in Edwyn Bevan, *A History of Egypt under the Ptolemaic Dynasty* (London: Methuen, 1927), 332–33; Ritner, "A Question of Noses," 284.

95. Quirke and Andrews, *Rosetta Stone*, 6.

96. See Janet H. Johnson, "The Demotic Magical Spells of Leiden I 384," *Oudheidkundige mededeelingen uit het Rijksmuseum van Oudheden te Leiden* 56 (1975): 47–53.

97. See C. J. C. Reuvens, *Lettres à M. Letronne . . . sur les papyrus bilingues et grecs, et sur quelques autres monumens gréco-égyptiens du Musée d'antiquités de l'Université de Leide* (Leiden: Luchtmans, 1850), 4: "Together with other accounts, it could well facilitate explication of the hieratic writing and the hieroglyphs" [il pourra même peut-être, sous plusieurs autre rapports, faciliter l'explication de l'écriture hiératique et hiéroglyphique].

98. Ibid., 7, 10.

99. Karl Preisendanz, ed., *Papyri Graecae Magicae: Die griechischen Zauberpapyri* (Leipzig: Teubner, 1928), 1:v.

100. They were "examples of gross superstition that did not even approach 'literature'" [Erzeugnissen krassen Aberglaubens, denen der Name "Literatur" nicht zukam]. Preisendanz, *Papyri Graecae Magicae*, 1:v.

101. In Preisendanz, *Papyri Graecae Magicae;* this has now been supplemented by Robert W. Daniel and Franco Maltomini, eds., *Supplementum Magicum,* vol. 1 (Opladen: Westdeutscher Verlag, 1990). "The texts included in Suppl. Mag. . . . are all of Egyptian provenance" (ibid., ix.); as, we might add, are the overwhelming majority of the texts in Preisendanz, *Papyri Graecae Magicae.*

102. See John Gee, "Abracadabra, Isaac and Jacob," review of "The Use of Egyptian Magical Papyri to Authenticate the Book of Abraham: A Critical Review," by Edward H. Ashment, *Review of Books on the Book of Mormon* 7/1 (1995): 35–46, 75–76; Robert K. Ritner, "Egyptian Magical Practice under the Roman Empire: The Demotic Spells and Their Religious Context," in *Aufstieg und Niedergang der römischen Welt* (Berlin: de Gruyter, 1995), II.18.5:3333–79.

103. The problem is in defining *magic;* see Gee, "Abracadabra, Isaac and Jacob," 46–71; Marvin Meyer and Richard Smith, "Introduction," in *Ancient Christian Magic: Coptic Texts of Ritual Power* (San Francisco: HarperSanFrancisco, 1994), 1–8 (although

it is not certain that the label *ritual power* has any particular meaning either).

104. Most of the attention has been misguided or seriously flawed by bad assumptions or methodology, particularly the assumption that the papyri are Greek and not Egyptian. Two prominent flawed publications are Hans D. Betz, "The Delphic Maxim 'Know Yourself' in the Greek Magical Papyri," *History of Religions* 21/2 (1981): 156–71; and Morton Smith, *Jesus the Magician* (San Francisco: Harper and Row, 1978). Unfortunately, portions of this have also permeated some of the translations and much of the commentary in Hans D. Betz, ed., *The Greek Magical Papyri in Translation including the Demotic Spells* (Chicago: University of Chicago Press, 1986).

105. See Betz, *Greek Magical Papyri in Translation*, xxiii–xxviii. Paleography is not the firmest basis on which to date a document, especially a literary document. These dates are accepted with the caveat that they might be very wrong.

106. See Origen, *Contra Celsum* 1.22.

107. See Preisendanz, *Papyri Graecae Magicae* (hereafter *PGM*), *PGM* I.232–47; III.410–78.

108. See *PGM* V.447–58; VII.628–42; XII.201–350; *PDM* (demotic portions of *PGM*) xii.6–20; compare *PGM* IV.2125–39.

109. See *PGM* I.1–195; II.1–183; III.165–262, 633–731; IV.1–25, 52–85, 154–285, 850–1114; V.54–69, 370–446; Va.1–3; VII.222–59, 319–69, 505–28, 540–78, 664–85, 703–55, 795–861, 1009–16; VIII.64–110; XII.1–95, 144–60, 190–92; XXIIb.27–35; XXIVa.1–25; LVII.1–37; LXII.24–51; LXXVII.1–24; *PDM* xii.21–49; xiv.1–308, 395–427, 459–553, 627–35, 695–705, 750–71, 805–85, 1078–89, 1110–29, 1141–54, 1163–79, 1199–1205; lxi.1–30, 63–78, Louvre E 3229, 5/15–22, 6/1–19, in Janet H. Johnson, "Louvre E 3229: A Demotic Magical Text," *Enchoria* 7 (1977): 63–64, 71–73.

110. See *PGM* IV.26–51, 475–829; XIII.1–734.

111. See *PGM* III.494–611; IV.88–93; VI.1–47; VII.727–39; XXXVI.211–30.

112. The Mithras Liturgy is a modern designation while the

"Eighth Book of Moses" is an ancient one (see *PGM* XIII.3, 343–44).

113. See Reinhold Merkelbach, *Abrasax: Ausgewählte Papyri religiösen und magischen Inhalts* (Opladen: Westdeutscher, 1992).

114. *PGM* IV.476, 482–85. I have tampered with the grammar here as the antecedent of "which" is not "mysteries" but I do not think I have violated the original intent.

115. These so-called *nomina barbara* or *voces magicae* are often Greek transcriptions of a foreign language; see Adolf Erman, "Die ägyptischen Beschwörungen des grossen Pariser Zauberpapyrus," *Zeitschrift für ägyptische Sprache und Altertumskunde* 21 (1883): 89–109; Jürgen Osing, *Der spätägyptische Papyrus BM 10808* (Wiesbaden: Harrassowitz, 1976); Ritner, "Egyptian Magical Practice," 3361–64; Gee, "Abracadabra, Isaac and Jacob," 75–76; Heinz J. Thissen, "Ägyptologische Beiträge zu den griechischen Magischen Papyri," in *Religion und Philosophie im alten Ägypten,* ed. Ursula Verhoeven and Erhart Graefe (Leuven: Peeters, 1991), 293–302; Terence DuQuesne, "The Raw and the Half-Baked: Approaches to Egyptian Religion," *Discussions in Egyptology* 30 (1994): 34.

116. See *PGM* IV.587–616.

117. *PGM* IV.617–20.

118. Taking Μινιμιρροφορ as Late Egyptian *Mnw imy r^h–pr.* Demotic *Mn mr rpi* "Min overseer of the temple" is also possible.

119. *PGM* IV.661–69.

120. See *PGM* IV.670–73.

121. *PGM* IV.673–76.

122. The Egyptian constellation of Ursa Major *(ms ḫtyw)* was represented as a bull's leg, or even a bull; see O. Neugebauer and Richard A. Parker, *Egyptian Astronomical Texts* (London: Brown University Press, 1960, 1969), 1: plate 8, and 3: plate 24. By contrast, the Greeks thought of Ursa Major as a bear or a wagon (Homer, *Iliad* 18.487; *Odyssey* 5.273); the Romans conceived it as a Bear *(ursa);* the Mesopotamians conceived it as a long wagon (mar-gíd-da, *ereqqu*).

123. *PGM* IV.678.

124. See *PGM* IV.750–87.

125. *PGM* XIII.35–39.

126. *PGM* XIII.231–34.

127. See *PGM* XIII.343–60.

128. See *PGM* IV.1227–64, 3019–20.

129. For example, see *The Gospel of the Egyptians,* translated by Bentley Layton as *The Holy Book of the Great Invisible Spirit,* in *The Gnostic Scriptures* (Garden City, N.Y.: Doubleday, 1987), 105–20, which contains many of the same elements of the *PGM.* For an interesting view of the attraction of Christians to Egyptian religion, see *Clementine Recognitions* 1.5, in *Patrologiae Cursus Completus . . . Series Graecae* (hereafter *PG*), ed. Jacque-Paul Migne (Paris: Garnier, 1857), 1:1209.

130. See *Apocalypse of Paul* V 17.19–24.9, in James M. Robinson, ed., *The Nag Hammadi Library in English,* 3rd ed. (San Francisco: HarperCollins, 1988), 257–59.

131. Also called by itself *The Book of the Knowledge of the Unseen God* and *The Book of the Great Account of the Mysteries.* The most recent publication of the text is *The Books of Jeu and the Untitled Text in the Bruce Codex,* ed. Carl Schmidt, trans. Violet MacDermot (Leiden: Brill, 1978). The citations refer to the pages in Schmidt's edition (located on the top of the page). MacDermot has done a great service by making the Coptic text available again.

132. Ibid., xiii.

133. The singular is *probole.* It is common to translate this term as "emanation," as though it belonged to the Neoplatonism of Plotinus. A more literal translation seems appropriate here—"guard"; see Liddell and Scott, *Greek-English Lexicon,* 1472.

134. The seal also plays a significant part in nonnormative Coptic beliefs classified as "magic." These Coptic "magical texts present, on the whole, a coherent picture of the existing world" where four cherubim carry "the seat of God the Father, a combination of throne and chariot. Under him there are seven heavens and fourteen firmaments supported by four columns apparently placed on the earth" (Werner Vycichl, "Magic," in *The Coptic Encyclopedia,* ed. Aziz S. Atiya [New York: Macmillan, 1991],

5:1499). These texts "show the magician as the successor of the Egyptian priest. He not only invokes the old divinities under Christian and even under Islamic rule but he must also be 'pure' like an Egyptian priest and wear a white linen garment" (ibid., 1500; compare Pierre du Bourguet, "Magical Objects," in Atiya, *Coptic Encyclopedia*, 1509–10). "Coptic magical spells are full of senseless names and deformations" (Vycichl, "Magic," 1501). Egyptian, Greek, Jewish, and Christian divine beings are all invoked with varied frequency (see ibid., 1501–3), and "elements of different creeds—Egyptian, Greek, Jewish, Christian, Gnostic —may be found together in the same text" (ibid., 1503). Sometimes the ceremonies involve the priest reciting prayers while a group of "seven boys who have not yet reached the age of puberty . . . begin to circle him seven times" (ibid., 1507; compare the circling of the priest before he recites his Sumerian incantation; "I am a pure man" [ğe$_{26}$-e lú-kù-ga me-en] is also attested in Mesopotamia; see Reiner, *Šurpu*, 11; compare tablet V–VI, lines 173–86, in ibid., 35) while the client holds a "seal in his right hand during the whole ceremony" (Vycichl, "Magic," 1508), a seal (Arabic *khatm*) "written on white unlined paper" consisting of a square around which are written "the names of the four angels" and in which is written a short prayer (ibid., 1507). Since no gatekeeper is mentioned, this example did not merit discussion in the text.

135. *1 Jeu,* in Schmidt, *Books of Jeu,* 84.

136. See Matthew 16:18–20.

137. See Revelation 2:17, 26–28; 3:21.

138. See Matthew 13:11, 14–16; 19:11; Mark 4:2, 33; Luke 18:34; 22:67; John 1:5; 3:12; 6:60–61; 8:43; 10:27; 16:12, 18, 25; 20:9; Acts 10:41; 16:6; 1 Corinthians 3:1–2; 2 Corinthians 12:4; Ephesians 3:3–5; Colossians 1:26; Hebrews 5:11; 2 John 1:12.

139. See Pliny the Elder, *Epistulae* 10.96.7; Clement of Alexandria, *Epistle to Theodore,* in Morton Smith, *Clement of Alexandria and a Secret Gospel of Mark* (Cambridge: Harvard University Press, 1973), 446–53.

140. See Pliny the Elder, *Epistulae* 10.96.7.

141. This can also mean "communication," "introduction," "guardianship," "political constitution" (Liddell and Scott, *Greek-English Lexicon*, 1734–35), but in the *PGM*, it is used as the equivalent of Egyptian *pḥ-nṯr* "arrival of the god"; see Robert K. Ritner, "Gleanings from Magical Texts," *Enchoria* 14 (1986): 95; Johnson, "Louvre E 3229," 90–91.

142. Ignatius, *Epistula ad Trallianos* 5.1–2. Ignatius, the second of the Apostolic Fathers, is considered strictly orthodox, though note Joseph B. Lightfoot, *The Apostolic Fathers: Clement, Ignatius, and Polycarp* (1889; reprint, Peabody, Mass.: Hendrickson, 1989), 2.1:30–31, citing Socrates, *Historiae Ecclesiasticae* VI.8.

143. See Jeremiah 42–43.

144. On the community, see Herbert Donner, "Elemente ägyptischen Totenglaubens bei den Aramäern Ägyptens," in *Religions en Égypte hellénistique et romaine*, 36–37.

145. See James B. Pritchard, ed., *Ancient Near Eastern Texts Relating to the Old Testament*, 3rd ed. (Princeton: Princeton University Press, 1969), 492.

146. See Thompson, *Memphis under the Ptolemies*, 85; compare 98–99.

147. See ibid., 85–86.

148. See Donner, "Elemente ägyptischen Totenglaubens," 40–42, citing Herbert Donner and W. Röllig, *Kanaanäische und aramäische Inschriften*, 4th ed. (Wiesbaden: Harrassowitz, 1979), no. 267.

149. See Donner, "Elemente ägyptischen Totenglaubens," 43, citing Donner and Röllig, *Kanaanäische und aramäische Inschriften*, no. 269, and read in the light of Merkelbach, "Ein griechisch-ägyptischer Priestereid," 69–73.

150. See the mixed oath by Yaho and Khnum, in Pritchard, *Ancient Near Eastern Texts*, 491; compare Thompson, *Memphis under the Ptolemies*, 98–99.

151. See Thompson, *Memphis under the Ptolemies*, 99, 104.

152. See, for example, *PGM* XII.817, XXIIb.1.

153. For notes on Egyptian usage of Hebrew names, see Origen, *Series Veteris Interpretationis Commentariorum Origenis in Matthaeum* 110, in *PG*, 13:1757.

154. See P. Köln 5514, in Robert W. Daniel, "It Started with Eve," *Zeitschrift für Papyrologie und Epigraphik* 74 (1988): 249–51.

155. See *PGM* XXIIb.1–26; see also *OTP*, 2:715–23.

156. See *PGM* XIII.1–734. Compare *PGM* XIII.734–1077; *PDM* xiv.131; Johnson, "Louvre E 3229," 94. There is a new edition of *PGM* XIII in *Two Greek Magical Papyri in the National Museum of Antiquities in Leiden: A Photographic Edition of J 384 and J 395 (=PGM XII and XIII)*, ed. Robert W. Daniel (Opladen: Westdeutscher, 1991), 32–81. For a discussion of the versions of the text, see Morton Smith, "The Eighth Book of Moses and How It Grew (PLeid. J 395)," in *Atti del XVII Congresso internazionale di papirologia* (Naples: Centro Internazionale per lo studio di papiri ercolanesi, 1984), 683–93, summarized in Betz, *Greek Magical Papyri in Translation*, 181–82.

157. See Johnson, "Louvre E 3229," 94–96. Compare A. Delatte and Philippe Derchain, *Les intailles magiques gréco-égyptiennes* (Paris: Bibliothèque Nationale, 1964), nos. 26, 396, 507, 513, 516.

158. See Betz, *Greek Magical Papyri in Translation*, 335; F. Ll. Griffith and Herbert Thompson, *The Demotic Magical Papyrus of London and Leiden* (London: Grevel, 1909), 3:142 no. 253; and Preisendanz, *Papyri Graecae Magicae*, 3:223–24.

159. Gershom G. Scholem, *Jewish Gnosticism, Merkabah Mysticism, and Talmudic Tradition* (New York: Jewish Theological Seminary of America, 1960), 76. Some of Scholem's arguments remain unconvincing (see ibid., 65–74), such as his assertion that ʾAzbogah = ogdoas; furthermore, Lilith is much more likely to go back to the Akkadian Lamaštu demon; see Walter Farber, "Lamastu," in *Reallexikon der Assyriologie und Vorderasiatischen Archäologie*, ed. Erich Ebeling et al. (Berlin: de Gruyter, 1983), 6:439–46.

160. Ithamar Gruenwald, *Apocalyptic and Merkavah Mysticism* (Leiden: Brill, 1980), 118; compare *OTP*, 1:236–38.

161. Gruenwald, *Apocalyptic and Merkavah Mysticism*, 118.

162. See n. 16 above.

163. Gruenwald, *Apocalyptic and Merkavah Mysticism*, 102. "Thus we find special practices for mystical experiences and revelations

which are to be accomplished on the Feast of Shavuʿot, on New Year['s] Day, at the beginning of every month, etc." (ibid.).

164. It is standard to compare *Sepher Ha-Razim* 4:61–72 to *PGM* IV.1596–715, but perhaps *PDM* xiv.856–75 should be considered as well.

165. Among other things, Gruenwald, *Apocalyptic and Merkhavah Mysticism*, 231–32; Judah Goldin, "The Magic of Magic and Superstition," in *Aspects of Religious Propaganda in Judaism and Early Christianity*, ed. Elisabeth Schüssler Fiorenza (Notre Dame, Ind.: University of Notre Dame Press, 1976), 132–36.

166. For more on the problems associated with this text, see Peter Schäfer, *Hekhalot-Studien* (Tübingen: Mohr, 1988), 63–74.

167. See ibid., 69.

168. For a description of the hekhalot literature in general, see Gruenwald, *Apocalyptic and Merkavah Mysticism*, 98–99. It is questionable whether we can even talk about individual works of hekhalot literature, but rather manuscripts reflecting various traditions, for "even a cursory comparison of the writing shows that the hekhalot literature inscriptions are in a very corrupt state" [schon ein flüchtiger Vergleich der Handschriften zeigt, daß die Textüberlieferung der *Hekhalot*-Literatur in einem extrem korrupten Zustand ist]; Schäfer, *Synopse zur Hekhalot-Literatur*, p. v; compare Schäfer, *Hekhalot-Studien*, 8–16.

169. For parallels, see Hermann Ranke, *Die ägyptischen Personennamen* (Glückstadt: Augustin, 1935–77) 1:305.1. Other possibilities are *Ḏḥwty-rḫ* "Thoth knows" (ibid., 1:408.11), and, less likely, *ttj-rs.w* (ibid., 1:385.5). P. Alexander (see *OTP*, 1:272 n. n) sees this name as derived from Greek *tetras;* the presence of the *wāw* would militate against the last two interpretations. The names are problematic as can be seen when comparing Saul Lieberman, "Metatron, the Meaning of His Name and His Functions," in Gruenwald, *Apocalyptic and Merkavah Mysticism*, 235–41, with *OTP*, 1:228.

170. For other examples from the *PGM* of names combining both Hebrew and Egyptian elements, see Thissen, "Ägyptolo-

gisiche Beiträge," 297–98. See also Gruenwald, *Apocalyptic and Merkavah Mysticism*, 107:

> Much work has still to be devoted to the deciphering of the names of the seals and of the spells scattered in the literature of the period. As a matter of fact, only the combined efforts of scholars from different branches and fields of knowledge can bring about the desired progress in the study of the magico-theurgic practices found in the magical papyri, in the amulets and bowls, in the writings of gnosticism, and in Jewish mysticism and magic. Only a comprehensive and comparative study of all this vast material will enable us to understand the technique of creating these names and spells, and this notwithstanding the fact that in several cases the names were obscured on purpose, so as to prevent people from using or misusing them. In addition, it should be noticed that errors and confusion were often introduced by careless and ignorant copyists.

171. See Gruenwald, *Apocalyptic and Merkavah Mysticism*, 106–7.
172. See ibid., 99, 102–3.
173. See Stephen D. Ricks, "The Magician as Outsider: The Evidence of the Hebrew Bible," in *New Perspectives on Ancient Judaism*, ed. Paul V. M. Flesher (Lanham, Md.: University Press of America, 1990), 5:125–34.
174. Schäfer, *Hekhalot-Studien*, 65.
175. If it seems strange to connect the Egyptian religious texts with Merkabah mysticism, it has been suggested before on a more tenuous basis; see Hugh Nibley, *The Message of the Joseph Smith Papyri: An Egyptian Endowment* (Salt Lake City: Deseret Book, 1975), 123.
176. "When we consider Merkabah mysticism in the light of these non-Jewish religious world views of late antiquity we can see how completely it fits into the religious climate of its time" (*OTP*, 1:238).
177. Schäfer, *Hekhalot-Studien*, 249.
178. See ibid.

CHAPTER 10

THE GREAT MOSQUE AND ITS KAʿBA AS AN ISLAMIC TEMPLE COMPLEX IN LIGHT OF LUNDQUIST'S TYPOLOGY OF ANCIENT NEAR EASTERN TEMPLES

Gaye Strathearn and Brian M. Hauglid

Ancient Near Eastern civilizations, such as Sumeria, Babylon, Assyria, Egypt, and Israel, were diverse cultural entities that have each made a unique contribution to the development of Western civilization. Yet along with their diversity and uniqueness, we find significant points of cultural contact and overlap. One such element is the importance each placed on its temple complexes. These complexes provided both religious and social structure for the surrounding communities. Although each temple complex incorporated singular features, John Lundquist has listed nineteen features shared by temples throughout the ancient Near East.[1] Lundquist's typology highlights "extraordinary cultural, historical and religious continuity" in areas that are otherwise plagued by "extraordinary cultural disruptions."[2] This methodology has its limitations, especially when we consider that the typology represents an academic construction rather than any single reality. Even if one acknowledges the limitations, such a typology has considerable value, especially given the comparatively few archaeological and textual remains of temples from the ancient world. The typology provides a standard by which we can evaluate the available material. Using it as a measuring stick, we can then see parallels between ancient Near Eastern temple complexes and other institutions that might otherwise have been overlooked.

One such possible parallel occurs with the Great Mosque of Mecca and its Ka'ba, although the same comparisons cannot be drawn for all Islamic mosques. The Ka'ba, as we shall see, sets the Great Mosque apart from other mosques. Even in pre-Islamic times the Ka'ba was a sacred site and was considered to be "the sacred House of Allāh."[3] With the rise of Islam, the Ka'ba continued to make its surrounding area sacred, especially since Muhammad cleansed it of what he considered pagan idols (with the exception of the images of Jesus and Mary). Since that time the Ka'ba has played a central role in the religious life of Muslims around the world. As such, scholars have compared its functional similarities to the Jewish temple in Jerusalem.[4] In at least one tradition Solomon compares his temple to the Ka'ba when he prays, "My God and Master, thou hast clad me with the garments of prophethood and hast given me great dominion. I ask thee to give me in building thy holy house what thou gavest Abraham thy friend in building the Kaaba."[5]

Heribert Busse believes that three main similarities exist between the Jewish temple and the Ka'ba. First, the temple and the Ka'ba have a common foundation in Semitic religion. Second, after the destruction of the Jewish temple in Jerusalem, two successors arose: the Christian Church of the Holy Sepulchre and the Muslim Ḥaram al-Sharīf (which occupies the site previously occupied by the temple). Busse further argues that "Jewish traditions concerning the Temple were transferred to the Ḥaram al-

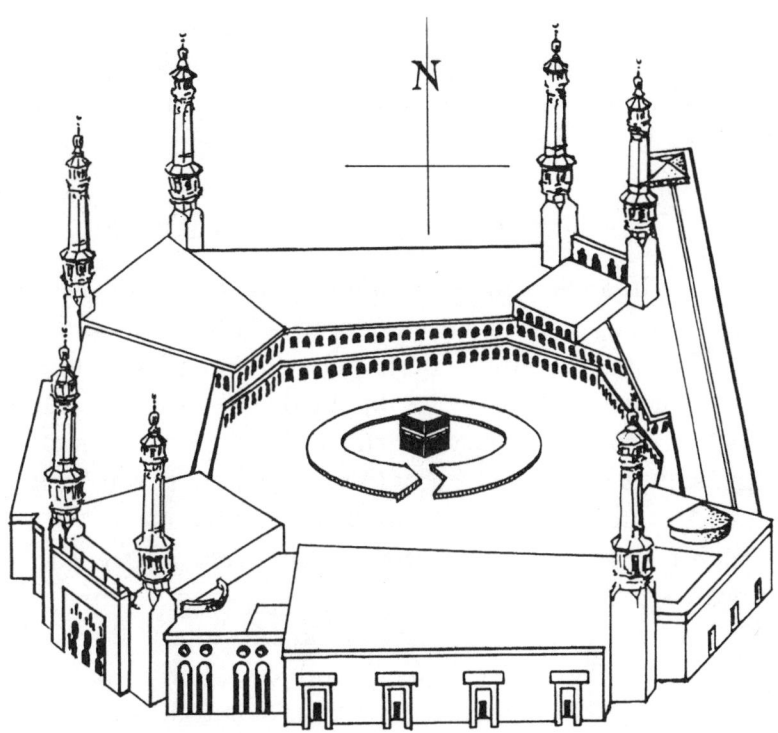

N

Figure 9. Every year during the month of pilgrimage to the Great Mosque of Mecca, tens of millions of devout Muslims circumambulate the Kaʿba counterclockwise in a ritual that emphasizes its central importance to their faith.

Sharīf: part of them came directly from the Temple, part of them via the Church of the Holy Sepulchre."[6] Third, a transfer of traditions occurred "from the Temple to the [Kaʿba] via [the] Ḥaram al-Sharīf (or the Church of the Holy Sepulchre) in order to make the [Kaʿba] a sanctuary equal to the Temple or even superior to it."[7] In his article Busse concentrates on his second and third points, but we will, through Lundquist's typology, focus more on Busse's first point: that the temple and the Kaʿba have a common

Semitic origin. We will first give a brief overview and description of the Great Mosque and its Kaʿba and will then show, on a point-by-point basis, how those structures parallel typologically the temple complexes of the ancient Near East.

The Great Mosque and Its Kaʿba

The Great Mosque stands today as the holy center of Islam (see fig. 9). Ever since the prophet Muhammad delivered God's command, "From whatsoever place thou issuest, turn thy face towards the Holy Mosque" (sura 2:144),[8] untold millions from all continents have prostrated themselves five times a day toward this magnetic center. The Mosque is also known as *Bait Allah* (House of God),[9] which is synonymous in the ancient Near East with the word *temple*.

The central edifice of the Great Mosque is the Kaʿba (see fig. 10). The word *kaʿba* is Arabic for "any square [or cubic] house, or chamber, or the like,"[10] and thus the Kaʿba derives its name from the appearance of the building. A. J. Wensinck described it as being

> built of layers of the grey stone produced by the hills surrounding Mecca. It stands on a marble base 10 inches high. . . . The four walls of the Kaʿba are covered with a black curtain *(kiswa)* which reaches to the ground and is fastened there with copper rings. . . . At two-thirds of its height a gold embroidered band *(ḥizām)* runs round, which is covered with verses from the Ḳurʾān in fine calligraphy.[11]

Zahra Freeth and H. Winstone refer to the Kaʿba as "Islam's holy of holies."[12] Of central importance to the Kaʿba is the Black Stone *(al-Ḥajar al-Aswad)* embedded in the eastern corner; this the pilgrims touch as they participate in

Figure 10. This fifteenth-century tourist map depicts the most important elements of the Great Mosque; the square outer walls enclose the courtyard where the black rectangular KaꜤba stands in the center, with the black stone in its eastern corner at the lower left and near the small door. Unlike most temples, the corners, rather than the sides, are oriented to the compass directions.

their ritual circumambulations (*ṭawāf*) of the KaꜤba. Among the traditions associated with this stone is one that says it was originally an angel whose duty it was to prevent Adam from partaking of the forbidden fruit, but "at the crucial moment, the angel had not paid attention, not thinking that Adam would ever really sin."[13] As punishment for his lapse of concentration, the angel was changed "into a white stone, [which was] destined to be placed in the wall of the Kaʿba at Mecca until Judgment Day."[14] Although the stone was originally white, over time it has turned black "because it rubs off the impurities from the souls of the pilgrims when they simply touch it."[15] A similar tradition says that the stone represents "'the right hand of God upon earth,' [which during the resurrection] will have two eyes to see, and a tongue to speak and give testimony on behalf of those who have kissed it in the sincerity of their hearts."[16] The stone is thus one of the important elements that contributes to the sacredness of the Kaʿba. Other elements will be identified as we work through the typology.

The Great Mosque, Its Kaʿba, and Lundquist's Typology

Our research identifies at least thirteen points of correlation between the Great Mosque, the Kaʿba, and Lundquist's typology.[17] While each of these points individually may be passed off as coincidence, collectively they illuminate a significant pattern. The Great Mosque and its Kaʿba are steeped in symbols and traditions intimately connected with ancient Near Eastern temple complexes. Just as those temple complexes provided a centralized unifying force for their communities, so too the Great Mosque provides a similar function for an ever-growing international community of Muslims. In order to highlight the temple function of the Great Mosque and its Kaʿba, we will identify the thirteen points of correspondence with Lundquist's typology and discuss each in terms of Islamic tradition.

1. "The temple is the architectural embodiment of the cosmic mountain."[18]

Throughout the ancient Near East, mountains were associated with sacred space. The cosmic mountain can be either a natural mountain, as was the case with Mount Sinai,[19] or a symbolic representation, as was the case with the pyramids of Egypt and the ziggurats of Mesopotamia (see fig. 12, p. 307). In the Qurʾān the House or the sacred precinct is associated with a mountain:

> By the Mount[20]
> and a Book inscribed
> in a parchment unrolled,
> by the House inhabited
> and the roof uplifted
> and the sea swarming,
> surely thy Lord's chastisement is about to fall;
> there is none to avert it. (sura 52:1–8)

Mecca is situated between two mountains and is considered to be inseparably connected to them.[21] In addition, three aspects of the Kaʿba are associated with mountain symbolism. First, Islamic tradition identifies the place where Abraham built the Kaʿba as either a "small, brown hill" or a "round, red hill."[22] An account from eastern Turkey records that before the flood "Gabriel raised up the Well-appointed House and gave it a place in the fourth sphere of heaven." In its place Gabriel "brought a mountain of the same dimensions as that house and set it down in the place of the Well-appointed House" where it remained until the time of Abraham. When Abraham was commanded to build the Kaʿba "the mountain moved from its place and Gabriel said: 'Build it there!'"[23]

Second, tradition has Abraham building the Kaʿba from rocks taken from five mountains: "Mount Sinai, the Mount of Olives, Mount Ḥirā, Mount Libanon and Mount Jūdī."[24] Third, tradition places the Kaʿba opposite the polar star, which is the highest point in the heavens. Al-Kisāʾī writes the following: "Tradition says: the polestar proves that the Kaʿba is the highest situated territory; for it lies over against the centre of heaven."[25] The Kaʿba, therefore, in Islamic tradition has important ties to the cosmic mountain of Lundquist's typology.

2. "The cosmic mountain represents the primordial hillock, the place which first emerged from the waters that covered the earth during the creative process."[26]

Wensinck explains that Islamic tradition initially associated the primordial hillock with Jerusalem.[27] However, the site of the primordial hillock was transferred to Mecca when the Jewish tribes of Medina rejected Muhammad, and the *qibla* (direction of prayer) was changed from Jerusalem to Mecca. Thus Mecca becomes the first land to appear out of the waters of chaos. The creation began by stretching out the earth around this center. "The first land to appear upon the face of the water was Mecca. Then God unfolded the earth out from under it."[28] In a more detailed description, Yāqūt writes, "The first land which God created on the earth is the place of Mecca. Then God unrolled the land from under the earth. [This place] is the navel of the earth, the middle of the world and the mother of cities, for it has the Kaʿba. A wall surrounds Mecca, and Mecca is surrounded by the sacred precinct, and the sacred precinct is surrounded by the world."[29] Thus the Qurʾān refers to Mecca as the "Mother of Cities" (sura 42:7), and Muslims view Mecca and its Kaʿba as the center of the world, with all things radiating from them.[30]

3. "The temple is often associated with the waters of life which flow forth from a spring within the building itself."[31]

Ṭabarī taught that before heaven and earth were created, the Kaʿba was upon the waters.[32] Today the waters of life flow from a sacred well in the southeast of the Kaʿba in the Great Mosque known as the Zamzam or the "Well of Ishmael." The shaft of the well is approximately "130 feet in depth" and "possesses the miraculous property that its level will never fall,"[33] regardless of how much water the pilgrims to the Kaʿba use. Islamic tradition associates this well with the biblical story of Abraham and Hagar. When Hagar and her son Ishmael were cast out by Abraham, they became desperate for water after their small supply was spent. Hagar went in search of water. After going back and forth between Safa and Marwa seven times, the Zamzam well miraculously appeared. One tradition says that water gushed out after Ishmael dug the earth with his finger,[34] while another tradition indicates that Gabriel uncovered the water source.[35] Ignaz Goldziher says that long before the advent of Islam, the Persians "claim to have made pilgrimages to this holy spring in honour of Abraham."[36] Today, pilgrims to the area view the water as having special health-giving powers. They drink the water and "take it home with them to give to the sick."[37]

4. "The temple is built on separate, sacral, set-apart space."[38]

Islamic traditions emphasize the sacred nature of both the origin and the earthly location of the Kaʿba. There are two traditions about its origin—according to one tradition the Kaʿba originated in heaven; after Adam's expulsion God caused "the House in Mecca to descend."[39] In yet another tradition God commanded Adam "to build a house to resemble the Visited House."[40] Likewise, after the flood[41] Abraham was commanded to rebuild the Kaʿba. It is the latter of these two traditions that is important for this point in Lundquist's typology.

Steven Holloway says that "in the ancient Near East, when God commands a human being to construct a building, that building is a temple."[42] These traditions about Adam and Abraham certainly meet Holloway's criteria.

Furthermore, Mircea Eliade makes it clear that humans do not choose sacred ground. Rather, it is transformed from the profane through either "a dazzling hierophany, or the principles of cosmology . . . or by a 'sign' expressing a hierophany."[43] There are a number of traditions where this principle is observed in God's command to Abraham to build the Kaʿba. We have noted above the removal of a mountain to provide a place for the building. Other traditions say that when given the command to build, Abraham was stymied because he did not know the dimensions. God, therefore, provided a visible sign to give Abraham the needed dimensions. One version says that God "sent a cloud the size of the Kaaba and told him to dig foundations not to exceed the size of the cloud,"[44] while another says that "a snake came and curled up on the spot" and that "Abraham built the Kaʿba according to the dimensions of the snake."[45] Thus the Kaʿba qualifies as sacred ground because its location was determined by a "dramatic irruption of the sacred."[46]

5. "The temple is oriented toward the four world regions or cardinal directions, and to various celestial bodies such as the polar star."[47]

We have already noted one detail relevant to this point: the tradition that places the Kaʿba opposite the polar star.

The oblong nature of the present Kaʿba means that it is much more difficult to establish that it is oriented toward the four world regions or cardinal directions. A. J. Wensinck argues that "four lines drawn from the centre through the four corners . . . would roughly indicate the four points of the compass."[48] Perhaps more definitive evidence for this point of the typology is that earlier structures were much more closely aligned to the cardinal directions. For example, although the front of the present Kaʿba with the door in it faces the northeast, one *ḥadīth* relates Muhammad as saying, "Were your nation not close to the Pre-Islāmic Period of Ignorance, I would have had the Kaʿba demolished and would have included in it the portion which had been left, and would have made it at a level with the ground and *would have made two doors for it, one towards the east and the other towards the west, and then by doing this it would have been built on the foundations laid by Abraham.*"[49] According to this *ḥadīth*, the foundations of Abraham were much more closely aligned to the cardinal directions than the present Kaʿba indicates. Thaʿlabī also taught that the Kaʿba that God brought down from heaven for Adam had two doors, one on the east and another on the west.[50]

Lundquist points out that the cosmic orientation can thus be used as "an astronomical observatory, the main purpose of which is to assist the temple priests in regulating the ritual calendar."[51] The Islamic calendar follows a lunar cycle. The time of the yearly *ḥajj* (the major pilgrimage to the Kaʿba) is determined by the phases of the moon and rotates throughout the seasons of the year.[52] In addition, this cosmic orientation reflects the idea that the earthly temple is a copy or counterpart of a heavenly model. F. E. Peters confirms the traditional Islamic claims that God built the original Kaʿba for Adam on the plan of his own residence in heaven.[53] We shall return to this concept in point seven.

6. "Temples, in their architectonic orientation, express the idea of a successive ascension toward heaven."[54]

The Mesopotamian ziggurat is probably the best example of a structure with an architectonic orientation portraying the idea of successive ascension to heaven. It was constructed with varying numbers of levels—usually three, five, or seven. The upper level was reached by a monumental staircase. The worshipers ascended the staircase, and deity descended from heaven to meet them.[55] The place of the meeting between the two realms was a place of great sacredness.

Although the Great Mosque's architecture is not as clear in its successive orientation as that of the ziggurats, different levels are still suggested. The Kaʿba is surrounded by a roadway on which the pilgrims make their ritual circumambulations. The roadway lies below the level of both the floor of the Kaʿba and the courtyard of the mosque.[56] In addition, the door to the Kaʿba is about seven feet above the ground. It is reached by a wooden staircase that runs on wheels and is pushed up to the door.[57] The symbolism of this design as a meeting place between the immortal and mortal realms is reinforced by the experience of Muhammad's night journey and ascension (*al-miʿrāj*) into heaven. The Qurʾān explicitly states that Muhammad was taken from the "Holy Mosque" (*al-masjid al-ḥarām;* sura 17:1)[58] to Jerusalem, from where he ascended up to heaven.[59]

7. "The plan and measurements of the temple are revealed by God to the king, and the plan must be carefully carried out."[60]

The temple structure represents the earthly replica of a heavenly counterpart. It is therefore necessary that the earthly design and measurements be accurate. Adam was commanded to build the Kaᶜba so that it resembled the Visited House.[61] Islamic traditions describe the heavenly mosque as the place in the seventh heaven where angels worship. Jan Knappert records that "God creates seventy thousand new angels . . . every morning" specifically so that they can worship him and that each morning the "angel Jibril [Gabriel] calls the faithful to prayer from the minaret that was created out of pure diamond."[62] Given the prominence of the angel Jibril in the heavenly mosque, it is therefore not surprising that he also plays an important role in some traditions concerning the establishment of its earthly counterpart. "He [i.e., Gabriel] also told [Adam] that God commanded him to build there [i.e., in Mecca] His House, which is the Kaaba, which he should circumambulate and in which he should offer prayer as he had seen the angels do at the Visited House."[63] We have already noted the supernatural direction given to Abraham to ensure the correct dimensions of the Kaᶜba. Thus the building of the earthly Kaᶜba was under the control and supervision of the divine realm.

8. Temples are associated with initiation "into the presence of deity."[64]

Each year when the Israelite high priest entered the holy of holies on the Day of Atonement, he symbolically entered the presence of God. Similarly, during the three Israelite pilgrim festivals of the Passover, the Feast of Weeks, and the Feast of Tabernacles, all Israelite men were required to go to the temple and appear before the Lord (see Exodus 23:14–17). For Muslims, their visit to the Kaʿba represents a similar concept.[65] Thaʿlabī taught that when God brought down the Kaʿba for Adam he told him to "circumambulate it just as you circumambulate the throne [of God]. Come to it just as you come to the throne."[66] Therefore, as pilgrims enter the area made sacred by the Kaʿba, they purify themselves in anticipation of coming into the presence of God. One pilgrim described the emotions he felt when he prayed at the Kaʿba: "Truly we were at that hour in another world: we were in the house of God and in God's immediate presence."[67]

Upon entering the Great Mosque, the pilgrims, as part of the ritual, circumambulate the Kaʿba seven times. This is symbolic of the actions performed by the angels in heaven as they circle the throne of God.[68] Hence, each pilgrim symbolically enters the presence of God and encircles his throne. When the pilgrims return home they are entitled to add the epithet *ḥājj* or *ḥājji* (male) or *ḥājja* (female) (i.e., one who has performed the pilgrimage) to their name. They "will be met with joy and respect, possibly in a festive and ceremonial manner. In general, [their] prestige in the community will be increased and, in the outlying regions of the Muslim world, [they] will become a center of religious fervor and missionary activity."[69]

9. "The temple is associated with the realm of the dead, the underworld, the afterlife, the grave."[70]

Lundquist argues that the "rites and worship of ancestors" serve as the connecting link to the realm of the dead, the underworld, the afterlife, and the grave.[71] Among the Egyptians, the Babylonians, and the Hittites, tombs and temples were integrally joined. The temple was viewed as the "link between this world and the next."[72]

The Kaʿba serves a similar function in Islam. On one level, the pilgrimage to Mecca—required of each Muslim who is financially able—represents death. Ali Shariati taught that

> Before departing to perform the Hajj, all of your debts should be paid. Your hates and angers toward relatives or friends must disappear. A will must be drawn. All of these gestures are an exercise in the preparation for death (which will overtake everyone some day). . . .
> Now you are free to join eternity.[73]

On another level, tradition places the graves of over seventy prophets beneath *al-Ḥijr* (the screen or the partition) in the Great Mosque. These include Adam, Eve,[74] Hagar,[75] and Ishmael.[76] In fact, "Every prophet, after his people had perished, would establish himself at [Mecca]; there he and his followers with him used to perform worship till he died."[77] Some traditions even place the grave of Muhammad in Mecca despite the traditional site in Medina. They argue that Muhammad and all prophets belong to Mecca because "this is his essential starting point and termination of his career." Thus, they argue, "Mecca is his real grave."[78] Muslims around the world reflect their desire to be associated with the Kaʿba at death by being oriented in their graves to face the Kaʿba.[79]

This connection with the rites of ancestors is further reinforced by Muhammad's pronouncement that it is acceptable for people to perform the *ḥajj* on behalf of elderly relatives. One *ḥadīth* says, "Hazrat Ibn Abbas relates: A woman asked the Holy Prophet: 'O messenger of Allah, the pilgrimage has been made obligatory duty by Allah on his servants at a time when my father has reached old age and has not strength to ride an animal. Can I perform the pilgrimage on his behalf?' He answered, 'Yes!'"[80] Today Muslims have extended this injunction to include deceased family relatives.[81] The vicarious pilgrim uses money from the deceased's estate to cover the costs of the journey to Mecca. However, the pilgrim himself receives no personal religious benefit from such a pilgrimage.[82]

10. "God's word is revealed in the temple."[83]

Temple sanctuaries have often been the site of divine revelation. Isaiah received his prophetic call while in the temple, and Moses received revelation on Mount Sinai.[84] In the Great Mosque, during the early Islamic period, revelation of God's will usually came "in the course of an incubation, that is, sleeping in a sacred place."[85] We have already noted Muhammad's night journey and ascension into heaven, which began at the Kaʿba, but tradition also records others who received revelation while in the Great Mosque. Uri Rubin records a number of those traditions:

> It is related that Kināna heard a voice while sleeping in Ḥijr, telling him about his future. Al-Naḍr b. Kināna dreamt in the same place that a cosmic luminous tree was emerging from his loins which symbolized his noble descendants, and especially Muḥammad. ʿAbd al Muṭṭalib dreamt in the Ḥijr that a cosmic chain grew out of his body and turned into a green tree. He also dreamt there that he was dressed in a beautiful robe which meant that it was time for him to marry. In the same place, ʿAbd al Muṭṭalib was also inspired by a series of dreams to dig Zamzam. Āmina, Muḥammad's mother, dreamt in the Ḥijr that she was about to give birth to "Aḥmad," the lord of mankind.[86]

These revelations underscore the sacred nature of the Great Mosque and its importance as a conduit linking the earthly and heavenly spheres.

11. "The temple and its ritual are enshrouded in secrecy."[87]

Lundquist points out that "secrecy relates to the sacredness of the temple precinct and the strict division in ancient times between sacred and profane space."[88] At Herod's Temple, signs were posted forbidding gentiles to enter.[89] When Muhammad returned in triumph to Mecca from Medina, he cleansed the Ka'ba of its pagan deities and dedicated it to the worship of God. Muhammad subsequently received a revelation restricting Mecca and its environs to Muslims:

> O believers, the idolaters are indeed unclean; so let them not come near the Holy Mosque after this year of theirs. (sura 9:28)

Since that revelation, a sacred zone *(haram)* has encompassed Mecca. The profane zone is clearly delineated from the sacred by checkpoints on all roads leading into Mecca. It is forbidden for non-Muslims to pass these points, and those Muslims entering the city to take part in either of the two pilgrimages must be in a state of ritual purity *(ihrām)*.[90] This purification is accomplished by performing ablutions, putting on a ritual garment (also known as *ihrām)*, making a declaration of intention, and offering prayers.[91]

12. "The temple is a place of sacrifice."[92]

It is said that in pre-Islamic times animal sacrifice was performed at the Ka'ba and that the blood was smeared on the Black Stone.[93] In fact, one tradition says that Abraham's father Terah made sacrifice at the Ka'ba.[94] Islam is, in principle, opposed to blood sacrifice. As the Qurᵓān reveals, "The flesh of them [i.e., that of sacrificial animals] shall not reach God, neither their blood, but godliness from you shall reach Him" (sura 22:37). However, earlier in the same revelation, sacrifice is associated with the Kaᶜba: "There are things therein profitable to you unto a stated term; thereafter their lawful place of sacrifice is by the Ancient House" (sura 22:33).[95] We have at least one *ḥadīth* that describes Muhammad sacrificing camels during the rite of standing.[96] Another *ḥadīth* describes Muhammad offering sacrifice at the end of the *ḥajj* between Safa and Marwa,[97] a practice that has continued into modern times. However, while the sacrifices do not actually occur at the Kaᶜba, Burton noted that the animals' faces are turned toward it before they are killed.[98]

In addition to the blood sacrifices, it should be noted that the *ḥajj* itself is a form of sacrifice for many of the pilgrims. Usually people save for many years to make the trip.[99] Ali Shariati indicates that at Mina the pilgrim acts as Abraham who "brought his son [Ishmael] to sacrifice." He suggests that for modern pilgrims the Ishmael that they sacrifice could be any one of a number of worldly possessions. Then he says,

> Whoever and whatever, you should have brought it with you to sacrifice here. I cannot tell you which one, but I can give you some clues to help—whatever weakens your faith, whatever stops you from "going", whatever distracts you from accepting responsibilities, whatever causes you to be self-centered, whatever makes you unable to hear the message and confess the truth, whatever forces you to "escape", whatever causes you to rationalize for the sake of convenience, whatever makes you blind and deaf. . . . You are in the position of Ibrahim whose weakness was in his love for [Ishmael] (his son).

He was teased by Satan. Imagine yourself at the peak of honor, full of pride and there is only ONE THING for which you can give up everything and sacrifice any other love for its love. THAT IS YOUR [ISHMAEL]! Your [Ishmael] can be a person, an object, a rank, a position or even a "weakness"![100]

Thus, in both ancient and modern times, pilgrimage to the Kaʿba was closely tied to sacrifice.

13. "The temple is the central, organizing, unifying institution" and "plays a legitimizing political role in the ancient Near East."[101]

In this section we have chosen to combine two of Lundquist's points because they are closely associated. The idea of transferring the pilgrimage to Islam appears to have developed while Muhammad was in Medina. Although the *umma* (Islamic community) was growing with converts from the local Arab tribes, Muhammad sought to unify all the Arab tribes under the banner of Islam. Paul Wheatley suggests that the Kaʿba enabled Muhammad to make "the transformation from a kin-based society to a rudimentary state organization."[102] In doing so, he was able to unify numerous tribal factions into a single unified group: the Kaʿba became a unifying force for Muhammad.

As a result, ever since Muhammad took control of Mecca and cleansed the Kaʿba during the seventh century, Muslims from around the world have turned their eyes, hearts, and thoughts five times a day to the Kaʿba in Mecca. The idea of *qibla* (direction of prayer) is a dramatic symbol of the unity of the Islamic *umma* worldwide. It has become a "powerful implosion of religious energy"[103] and brings about a feeling of intense unity among Muslims. Frederick Denny informs us: "When the Muslim performs the salat [ritual prayer], he or she is in a sense participating in the heavenly journey of the Prophet Muhammad; a little personal *miʿrāj* is made."[104]

The Kaʿba is also the central focus of the *ḥajj*. The pilgrims focus on the Kaʿba a number of times during the *ḥajj*. They perform the *ṭawāf* (circumambulations) three times: at the beginning of the *ḥajj*, after they return from Arafat, and at its conclusion. Thus, the *ḥajj* is also a powerful example of the unifying effect that the Kaʿba provides for Islam.

Conclusion

The central importance of the temple and its associated institutions in the ancient world has long been noted by scholars. The temple was the source of religious, political, and economic stability for the ancient temple states. The temple and its rituals enabled the ancients to make sense of the vicissitudes of life and to set their lives in order according to the will of the gods. In this paper we have used Muslim sources to show how Mecca, with its Great Mosque and Kaʿba, fits into that ancient temple typology. In at least thirteen aspects it relates to other ancient Near Eastern temples. Further research is needed to establish the extent to which the remaining points might also be associated with the Great Mosque, but there is sufficient evidence in the foregoing discussion to posit a substantial connection with ancient temple ideology and practices, even though Muslims do not specifically view the Great Mosque as a temple. By viewing the Great Mosque from a temple perspective, we can see that at least one aspect of Islam's development was not an isolated phenomenon but was intimately connected with a long and illustrious history of temple-ordered societies.

Notes

1. See John M. Lundquist, "The Common Temple Ideology of the Ancient Near East," in *The Temple in Antiquity: Ancient Records and Modern Perspectives*, ed. Truman G. Madsen (Provo, Utah: BYU Religious Studies Center, 1984), 53–75. This article expands on two earlier articles: "The Legitimizing Role of the Temple in the Origin of the State," in *Society of Biblical Literature: 1982 Seminar Papers*, ed. Kent H. Richards (Chico, Calif.: Scholars Press, 1982), 271–97, and "What Is a Temple? A Preliminary Typology," in *The Quest for the Kingdom of God: Studies in Honor of George E. Mendenhall*, ed. H. B. Huffmon, F. A. Spina, and A. R. W. Green (Winona Lake, Ind.: Eisenbrauns, 1983), 205–19.

2. Lundquist, "What Is a Temple?" 206.

3. Uri Rubin, "The KAʿBA: Aspects of Its Ritual Functions and Position in Pre-Islamic and Early Islamic Times," *Jerusalem Studies in Arabic and Islam* 8 (1986): 105.

4. For examples, see Gustave E. von Grunebaum, *Muhammadan Festivals* (New York: Schuman, 1951), 20, and Heribert Busse, "Jerusalem and Mecca, the Temple and the Kaaba: An Account of Their Interrelation in Islamic Times," in *The Holy Land in History and Thought*, ed. Moshe Sharon (Leiden: Brill, 1988), 236–46.

5. W. M. Thackston Jr., trans., *The Tales of the Prophets of al-Kisaʾi* (Boston: Twayne, 1978), 305.

6. Busse, "Jerusalem and Mecca," 237.

7. Ibid.

8. All quotations from the Qurʾān are taken from Arthur J. Arberry, *The Koran Interpreted* (New York: Macmillan, 1955).

9. See F. E. Peters, *Jerusalem and Mecca: The Typology of the Holy City in the Near East* (New York: New York University Press, 1986), 7.

10. Edward W. Lane, *An Arabic-English Lexicon* (Beirut: Librairie du Liban, 1980), 2010.

11. A. J. Wensinck, "Kaʿba," in *The First Encyclopaedia of Islam, 1913–1936*, ed. M. Th. Houtsma et al. (Leiden: Brill, 1987), 4:584–85. See the lavish color photographs by Peter Sanders in

Greg Noakes, "The Servants of God's House," *Aramco World* (January–February 1999): 48–67.

12. Zahra Freeth and H. V. F. Winstone, *Explorers of Arabia: From the Renaissance to the End of the Victorian Era* (London: Allen and Unwin, 1978), 101.

13. Jan Knappert, *Islamic Legends: Histories of the Heroes, Saints, and Prophets of Islam* (Leiden: Brill, 1985), 1:81.

14. Ibid.

15. Ibid.

16. S. M. Zwemer, "The Palladium of Islam," *Muslim World* 23 (April 1933): 111.

17. The remaining five points in Lundquist's typology (see "The Common Temple Typology," 57, 59) are that "the temple is associated with the tree of life," "sacral, communal meals are carried out in connection with temple ritual, often at the conclusion of or during a covenant ceremony," "the tablets of destiny (or tablets of the decrees) are consulted in the cosmic sense by the gods," "there is a close interrelationship between the temple and law in the ancient Near East," and "the temple and its cult are central to the economic structure of ancient Near Eastern society."

18. Lundquist, "What Is a Temple?" 207.

19. For an excellent discussion on Mount Sinai as a temple, see Donald W. Parry, "Sinai as Sanctuary and Mountain of God," in *By Study and Also by Faith: Essays in Honor of Hugh W. Nibley,* ed. John M. Lundquist and Stephen D. Ricks (Salt Lake City: Deseret Book and FARMS, 1990), 482–500.

20. This mount refers to the place where Muhammad received his revelation.

21. See A. J. Wensinck, *The Ideas of the Western Semites concerning the Navel of the Earth* (Amsterdam: Muller, 1916), 11, 13.

22. Gordon D. Newby, *The Making of the Last Prophet: A Reconstruction of the Earliest Biography of Muhammad* (Columbia: University of South Carolina Press, 1989), 74. See also Bukhārī, *Ṣaḥīḥ,* trans. Muhammad M. Khan (New Delhi: Kitāb Bhavan,

1984), 4:378–79; Ṭabarī, *Jāmiʿ al-bayān ʿan taʾwīl al-Qurʾān* (Cairo: Muṣṭafā al-Bābī al-Ḥalabī, 1968), 1:547–48.

23. Al-Rabghūzī, *The Stories of the Prophets: Qiṣaṣ al-Anbiyāʾ: An Eastern Turkish Version*, trans. H. E. Boeschoten, J. O'Kane, and M. Vandamme (Leiden: Brill, 1995), 2:129.

24. Ibid.; see also Thaʿlabī, *Kitāb ʿArāʾis al-majālis fī qiṣaṣ al-anbiyāʾ* (Egypt: Muṣṭafā al-Bābī al-Ḥalabī, 1340), 61–62; Ṭabarī, *Jāmiʿ al-bayān*, 1:546; Yāqūt, *Muʿjam al-buldān* (Beirut, 1955–57), 4:465.

25. Translation and original Arabic script in Wensink, *Navel of the Earth*, 15.

26. Lundquist, "What Is a Temple?" 208.

27. See Wensinck, *Navel of the Earth*, 18.

28. Thaʿlabī, *Qiṣaṣ*, 3–4; translation by Brian Hauglid; see also A. J. Wensinck, "The Semitic New Year and the Origin of Eschatology," *Acta Orientalia* 1 (1922): 175.

29. Yāqūt, *Muʿjam al-buldān*, 4:463; translation by Brian Hauglid.

30. "Thus the first village to be built was Mecca and the first house was the Glorious Kaaba." Thackston, trans., *Tales of the Prophets of al-Kisaʾi*, 62.

31. Lundquist, "What Is a Temple?" 208.

32. See Ṭabarī, *Jāmiʿ al-bayān*, 1:547–48.

33. Von Grunebaum, *Mohammadan Festivals*, 24.

34. See Thackston, trans., *Tales of the Prophets of al-Kisaʾi*, 152; Newby, *The Making of the Last Prophet*, 74; see also Grant Alexander, "The Story of the Kaʿba," *Moslem World* 28 (1938): 45; Robin Bidwell, *Travellers in Arabia* (London: Hamlyn, 1976), 31.

35. See A. Guillaume, trans., *The Life of Muhammad: A Translation of Isḥāq's Sīrat Rasūl Allāh* (Oxford: Oxford University Press, 1955), 45; Al-Rabghūzī, *Stories of the Prophets*, 119.

36. Ignaz Goldziher, *Muslim Studies* (Albany: State University of New York Press, 1966–77), 1:136.

37. B. Carra de Vaux, "Zamzam," in *The First Encyclopaedia of Islam*, 8:1212.

38. Lundquist, "What Is a Temple?" 209.

39. M. J. Kister, "Legends in tafsīr and ḥadīth Literature," in

Approaches to the History of the Interpretation of the Qurʾān, ed. Andrew Rippin (Oxford: Clarendon, 1988), 107. See also Abd-al-Razzāq, *Al-Muṣannaf* (Gujarat, India: Majlis Ilmi, 1972), 94; Thaʿlabī, *Qiṣaṣ,* 60.

40. Thackston, trans., *Tales of the Prophets of al-Kisaʾi,* 62. The "Visited House" refers to the "heavenly prototype of the Kaaba." Ibid., 339 n. 14.

41. There are two main traditions about what happened to the Kaʿba during the flood. One tradition maintains that it was taken into "the fourth sphere of heaven" (Al-Rabghūzī, *Stories of the Prophets,* 129; Thaʿlabī, *Qiṣaṣ,* 61; see also Thackston, trans., *Tales of the Prophets of al-Kisaʾi,* 102). Another reports that "the waters of the Deluge did not reach the Kaʿba, but that they surrounded it" and that the "Kaʿba itself remained free in the air" (*Khamis* 1:92:21; original Arabic script and translation in Wensinck, *Navel of the Earth,* 15; see also Ṭabarī, *Jāmiʿ al-bayān,* 1:546).

42. Steven Holloway, "What Ship Goes There? The Flood Narratives in the Gilgamesh Epic and Genesis Considered in Light of Ancient Near Eastern Temple Ideology" (unpublished paper), 9.

43. Mircea Eliade, *Patterns in Comparative Religion* (New York: New American Library, 1958), 369.

44. Thackston, trans., *Tales of the Prophets of al-Kisaʾi,* 154. See also Al-Rabghūzī, *Stories of the Prophets,* 129; Newby, *The Making of the Last Prophet,* 73.

45. Al-Rabghūzī, *Stories of the Prophets,* 129.

46. Mircea Eliade, "The Prestige of the Cosmogonic Myth," *Diogenes* 23 (fall 1958): 2.

47. Lundquist, "What Is a Temple?" 210.

48. Wensinck, "Kaʿba," 4:584. Compare F. E. Peters, *The Hajj: The Muslim Pilgrimage to Mecca and the Holy Places* (Princeton: Princeton University Press, 1994), 13.

49. Bukhārī, *Ṣaḥīḥ,* 2:383–84, emphasis added.

50. See Thaʿlabī, *Qiṣaṣ,* 25.

51. Lundquist, "The Common Temple Ideology," 57.

52. See Richard C. Martin, "Pilgrimage: Muslim Pilgrimage,"

in *The Encyclopedia of Religion,* ed. Mircea Eliade (New York: Macmillan, 1987), 11:339.

53. See Peters, *Jerusalem and Mecca,* 10.

54. Lundquist, "What Is a Temple?" 211.

55. See Lundquist, "The Common Temple Ideology," 57–58.

56. See Maurice Gaudefroy-Demombynes, *Muslim Institutions* (London: Allen and Unwin, 1954), 85.

57. See Wensinck, "Kaʿba," 4:585.

58. Al-Hasan reportedly heard Muhammad say that Gabriel came to him while he "was sleeping in the [Ḥijr]." Guillaume, *The Life of Muhammad,* 182. One commentary, in a footnote to *masjid,* says, "here it refers to the Kaʿba at [Mecca]." Abdullah Yusuf ʿAli, *The Holy Qurʾān: English Translation of the Meanings and Commentary* (Medina, Saudi Arabia: Islamic Researches, 1413 hijrī [1992/3 C.E.]), 774. These two apparent contradictions may be reconciled by U. Rubin's argument that the pre-Qurayshī Ḥijr "was an integral part of the sanctuary, so that both the Ḥijr and the Kaʿba formed one unit, being a sacred ring-like enclosure, made of loose stones and covered with the *kiswa.*" Rubin, "The KAʿBA," 101. This situation probably gives rise to the following *ḥadīth:* "I asked the Prophet whether the round wall (near Kaʿba) [i.e., the Ḥijr] was part of the Kaʿba. The Prophet replied in the affirmative. I further said, 'What is wrong with them, why have they not included it in the building of the Kaʿba?' He said, 'Don't you see that your people (Quraysh) ran short of money (so they could not include it inside the building of the Kaʿba)?'" Bukhārī, *Ṣaḥīḥ,* 2:382–83.

59. Busse argues that "there is ample evidence that the localisation of these events in Jerusalem was preceded by their localisation in Mecca. This is attested by traditions on the Ascension in which Jerusalem is not mentioned at all, which means that *isrāʾ* [Muhammad's night journey] was at first understood as Muhammad's Ascension to heaven from the [Kaʿba]. . . . This was possible because the Arabs believed already in pre-Islamic times that the [Kaʿba] had a heavenly counterpart." Busse, "Jerusalem and Mecca," 242.

60. Lundquist, "What Is a Temple?" 211.

61. See Thackston, trans., *Tales of the Prophets of al-Kisaʾi*, 62.

62. Knappert, *Islamic Legends*, 1:28–29.

63. Thackston, trans., *Tales of the Prophets of al-Kisaʾi*, 61; see also Newby, *The Making of the Last Prophet*, 74–75; Ṭabarī, *Jāmiʿ al-bayān*, 1:546, 548.

64. Lundquist, "What Is a Temple?" 212–13.

65. For a good description of the pilgrimage *(ḥajj)*, see Ali Shariati, *Hajj*, trans. Ali A. Behzadnia and Najla Denny (Houston, Tex.: Free Islamic Literatures, 1978).

66. Thaʿlabī, *Qiṣaṣ*, 60; translation by Brian Hauglid.

67. As quoted by Wensinck, "Kaʿba," 4:588.

68. See Thackston, trans., *Tales of the Prophets of al-Kisaʾi*, 61; and Ahmad Kamal, *The Sacred Journey, Being Pilgrimage to Makkah* (New York: Van Rees, 1961), 43.

69. Von Grunebaum, *Mohammadan Festivals*, 41.

70. Lundquist, "What Is a Temple?" 215.

71. Ibid.

72. Ibid.

73. Shariati, *Hajj*, 6.

74. "They laid him [i.e., Adam] in a grave, his head at the site of the Kaaba and his feet stretched out," and Eve was buried along side of him. Thackston, trans., *Tales of the Prophets of al-Kisaʾi*, 84–85.

75. See Newby, *The Making of the Last Prophet*, 74.

76. See Thackston, trans., *Tales of the Prophets of al-Kisaʾi*, 154; Wensinck, "Kaʿba," 4:585.

77. Wensinck, *Navel of the Earth*, 28.

78. Al-Ḥalabī, 1:197, as cited in Wensinck, "Kaʿba," 4:590.

79. See Martin, "Pilgrimage: Muslim Pilgrimage," 11:338.

80. Number 1279, in *Riyadh-Us-Saleheen: English Translation with Arabic Text*, comp. Yahya B. S. An-Nawawi, trans. S. M. Madni Abbasi (Karachi: Dar Ahya Us-Sunnah Al Nabawiya, n.d.), 2:616.

81. See Mahmoud M. Ayoub, *The House of ʿImrān*, The Qurʾan and Its Interpreters, vol. 2 (Albany, N.Y.: State University of New

York Press, 1992), 266; Martin, "Pilgrimage: Muslim Pilgrimage,"
11:340; see also James A. Toronto, "Islam," in *Religions of the
World: A Latter-day Saint View,* rev. and enl. (Provo, Utah: Brigham
Young University, 1997), 230.

82. See von Grunebaum, *Mohammadan Festivals,* 16.

83. Lundquist, "The Common Temple Ideology," 59.

84. Spencer W. Kimball received the revelation that extended
the blessings of the priesthood to all worthy male members of the
Church "after extended meditation and prayer in the sacred
rooms of the holy temple" (Official Declaration—2).

85. Peters, *The Hajj,* 16.

86. Rubin, "The KAʿBA," 112–13.

87. Lundquist, "What Is a Temple?" 218.

88. Ibid.

89. Josephus records that "When you go through these [first]
cloisters, unto the second [court of the] temple, there was a partition made of stone all round, whose height was three cubits: its
construction was very elegant; upon it stood pillars, at equal dis-
tances from one another, declaring the law of purity, some in
Greek, and some in Roman letters, that 'no foreigner should go
within that sanctuary;' for that second [court of the] temple was
called 'the Sanctuary,'" *Wars* 5.2. In 1871 one of these warnings
was discovered by Clermont-Ganneau. It reads: "No man of another nation to enter within the fence and enclosure round the
temple. And whoever is caught will have himself to blame that
his death ensues." Cited in C. K. Barrett, ed., *The New Testament
Background: Writings from Ancient Greece and the Roman Empire
That Illuminate Christian Origins,* rev. ed. (San Francisco: Harper
& Row, 1989), 53.

90. See Bidwell, *Travellers in Arabia,* 116.

91. See Shariati, *Hajj,* 8–16; Kamal, *The Sacred Journey,* 21–23.

92. Lundquist, "What Is a Temple?" 217.

93. See Wensinck, "Kaʿba," 4:591, and Rubin, "The KAʿBA,"
105–7.

94. See Thackston, trans., *Tales of the Prophets of al-Kisaʾi,* 136.

95. F. E. Peters notes the following, "At the time of this verse

the place of sacrifice was apparently still near the Kaʿba, as it had been throughout Islamic times." It was only "during the Farewell Pilgrimage [that] the Prophet limited sacrifice to the 'slaughtering place' at Mina." Peters, *The Hajj,* 368 n. 139.

96. See Bukhārī, *Ṣaḥīḥ,* 2:362.

97. See ibid., 2:376.

98. See Richard F. Burton, *The Guidebook: A Pictorial Pilgrimage to Mecca and Medina* (London: Clowes and Sons, 1865), 38.

99. See Frederick M. Denny, *An Introduction to Islam,* 2nd ed. (New York: Macmillan, 1994), 130.

100. Shariati, *Hajj,* 84.

101. Lundquist, "The Common Temple Ideology," 58–59.

102. Paul Wheatley, *The Pivot of the Four Quarters: A Preliminary Enquiry into the Origins and Character of the Ancient Chinese City* (Chicago: Aldine, 1971), 288.

103. Denny, *An Introduction to Islam,* 120.

104. Ibid.

CHAPTER 11

INSIDE A SUMERIAN TEMPLE: THE EKISHNUGAL AT UR

E. Jan Wilson

Introduction

In *Temples of the Ancient World,* frequent reference was made to the temple built by Gudea, an ancient Sumerian king in southern Mesopotamia (who began his reign in 2143 B.C.).[1] This was quite appropriate since the oldest known temples in the world were those of the Sumerians, a rather enigmatic ethnic group that inhabited southern Mesopotamia even before the beginning of the First Dynasty in Egypt. It was the Sumerians who developed the first writing system (ca. 3000 B.C.) and also constructed some of the earliest temples.

The first temple, according to Sumerian tradition, was in Eridu on the edge of the Persian Gulf. According to Sumerian legends, it was there that civilization began and there that the first temple was built to Enki (or Ea), the god of underground fresh water. Enki, as the god of wisdom, remained very important in the Sumerian pantheon for many centuries and was "consulted" whenever the Sumerians undertook the construction or reparation of a temple, perhaps also because of his connection with the earliest temple.

Other gods of the ancient Sumerians included An (the "father" god), Enlil (a son of An, but eventually chief god of the Sumerian pantheon), Inanna (a goddess of war who also had unclear connections to prostitution), Utu (the sun-god), and Nanna (the moon-god). I shall bring up Nanna again when I discuss the great temple in Ur, which was his main cultic site.

Sumerian temples were very central to urban life because each city had its chief god who was thought to be the patron and protector of that city. If calamities befell the city, it was assumed that the local god had deserted his temple and hence his people. Elaborate rituals were then performed to coax the god to return to his temple and reestablish peace and tranquility in the city and its environs.

In the early periods of Mesopotamian history, the temple was more important to the city than the palace.[2] Indeed, kingship was not even a permanent institution in the earliest Sumerian periods. The secular leader of a particular community (as opposed to the chief priest, or en) was simply the "big man" (lú-gal), who was elected by the citizens for a period of one year. Thus the temple, with its established economic base and respected priestly castes, was permanent, but the lay leader of the community was only temporary. That eventually changed, however, when the growing problem of constant interurban warfare produced the practical necessity of maintaining a strong leader in office for longer periods in order to provide stability and experienced leadership during perilous times. In the course of time, strong men were able to make their office permanent, and the Sumerian word lú-gal came to mean "king" in the sense in which we usually understand it. That finally led to a shift in power and influence from the temple to the royal house, as was most apparent in the empires of the Akkadians and their heirs (the Babylonians and Assyrians) after they had supplanted the Sumerians as the dominant culture in Mesopotamia.

The Sumerian temples, in their most developed phase, showed structural similarities to later Israelite temples. In fact, at least two of the temples excavated in Israel (Nahariya and Tell Beit Mirsim) seem to be based on Sumerian floor plans.[3] This relationship is significant because it is one of the few physical attestations of a movement from southern Mesopotamia westward toward Syria-Palestine (most scholars have thought only in terms of emigration eastward from Syria into Mesopotamia) during a historical period in which the Abraham stories in Genesis and the Book of Abraham report such a journey for Abraham and his family.[4] For that reason, a closer look at Sumerian temples in general, and the main temple at Ur in particular, will provide valuable additional insights into the subject of temples in antiquity.

General Features of Sumerian Temples

Temples and Towers

The earliest temples in southern Mesopotamia consisted of small, one-room structures, but already during the Early Dynastic Period we see the development of a temple type consisting of an artificial terrace on which a rectangular building (up to 12.5 by 24 meters in size) contains an elongated central cult room and two side tracts of rooms. The similarity of the floor plan of one of these temples to the later Temple of Solomon can be seen in figure 11.

It appears that a transition in function is reflected in the gradually changing architecture of Mesopotamian temples

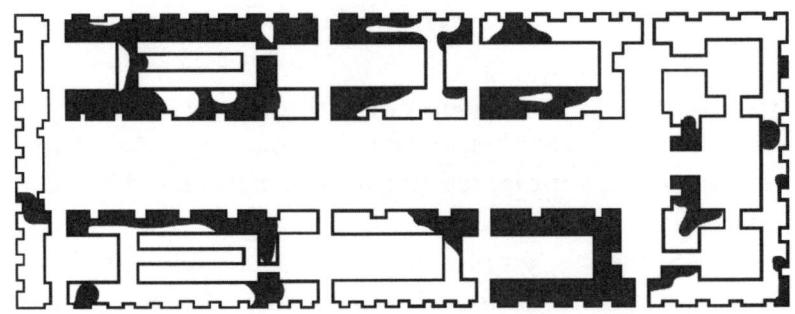

Figure 11. Floor plan of a temple from ancient Uruk (above) and Solomon's Temple (below).

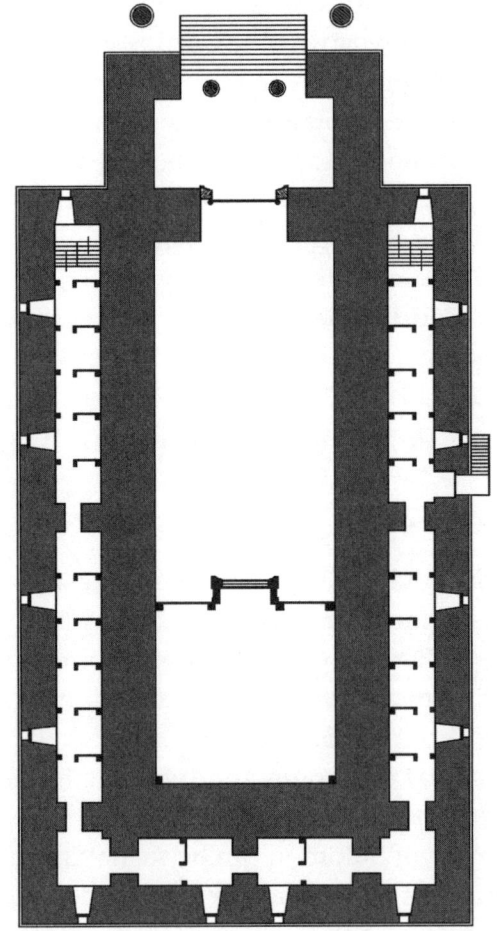

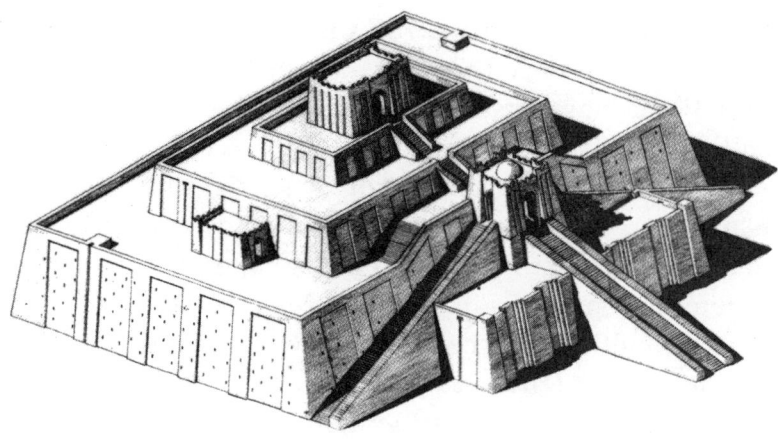

Figure 12. The Ziggurat of Ur Nammu, restored.

during the prehistoric and early historical periods. In the earliest times, the temples were apparently open to everyone, and the altar was located inside the one-room structure. Later, however, there was no longer room for the masses except in the exterior courtyards, and the altar was moved outside.[5] As population growth continued (and the state became more formally organized), the public had access to the administrative areas, but not to the temple rooms proper—corresponding to the exclusion of the public from the king's inner chambers, but also mirroring the situation in heaven.[6] In any case, temple architecture gradually became more complex.

The ziggurat, one of the new major features, was a tower-like structure erected adjacent to a normal temple building. It was sometimes referred to as a "stepped pyramid," but it was not a pyramid in either form or function. Rather than having flat sides angled toward the pinnacle, the ziggurat consisted of three to five levels of ever-decreasing size; instead of culminating in a pointed pinnacle, the top was a flat surface with a shrine.[7] While the pyramids of Egypt may have been used for burials (though this too is disputed), the ziggurats of Mesopotamia were clearly sites of cultic worship.

It would have been one of these ziggurats that was featured in the book of Genesis as the Tower of Babel. Indeed, the fact that the ziggurats were integral components of temple complexes in southern Mesopotamia and were used for cultic rituals corresponds well with the comment by Herodotus (*Histories* 1.181) that the Tower of Babel was actually a temple. Furthermore, it is worth noting that there were no ziggurats in Mesopotamia prior to the Neo-Sumerian period (ca. 2200–2000 B.C.).[8] This is significant because, if we date Abraham to approximately 2000 B.C. or slightly before (Ur was destroyed by the Elamites and their confederates in 2003 B.C.), then we have an indication that a significant chronological gap between the tower story in Genesis 10 and the beginning of the Abraham narrative immediately thereafter in Genesis 11 does not exist. The two events may indeed have followed each other in close succession, with the tower episode even occurring during the twenty-second century B.C. (at the earliest) and Abraham coming on the scene within decades of that event.

If we consider that the tower in the Genesis story could not have been the ziggurat at Babylon (because Babylon, or "Babel," was still a small town with no ziggurat), then the ziggurat of that story might even have been the ziggurat at Ur, which was put into its final form by Ur-Nammu, who was king between 2111 and 2094 B.C.[9] The ziggurat in Ur is, in fact, the earliest example of the multistaged form of ziggurat.[10]

The purpose of these towers (in accord with the account in Genesis) is expressed in a Sumerian hymn describing the ziggurat of the temple in Eridu: "Eunir [name of the ziggurat], which has grown high, (uniting) heaven and earth."[11]

Sacred Areas: Approaching Deity

Within the temples in Sumer were three special features, which, taken together, constituted the *sine qua non* of sacred edifices. These were the adytum (called ki-ku$_3$ or "holy place" as well as ki-nam-ti-la or "place of life"),[12] the abzu (which was also called "holy sanctuary"; Sumerian eš$_3$-ku$_3$), and the *duku* (du$_6$-ku$_3$) or "holy mound."[13]

The adytum was the place where the statue of the god was placed. Elaborate meals were prepared there for the chief deity in any temple, and it was assumed, when the food was placed on a table before the statue, that the god himself somehow partook of the meal (it should be noted here that the Sumerians never thought that the statue itself was the god; it was a representation and simultaneously a physical structure that the god might inhabit during those times when he was pleased with the inhabitants of a city). In order to approach the adytum, there were appropriate purification rituals to be observed first.

The abzu and the *duku* are more mysterious areas of the temple, both in terms of function and in terms of their exact locations. The abzu derived its name from the term for the underground sources of fresh water, which were the abode of the god of wisdom, Enki.[14] Just what form the abzu took in Sumerian temples is still debated, but it appears likely that it was some body of water, such as a pool or cistern,[15] and that this body of water represented a communication with the subterranean water and hence with Enki. It also appears from one of the temple hymns that the hand-washing ceremony (šu-luḫ) was performed in the same room as the abzu, or perhaps even in the abzu itself.[16] If the latter turns out to be the case, then we might be dealing with a form of total washing (perhaps even immersion) in which case the term šu-luḫ ("hand-washing") is actually a synecdoche (i.e., the part representing the whole). This, however, cannot be confirmed from the existing sources.

The *duku* has some special but unclear relationship to the abzu. Its name means "holy mound" or "holy hill." From what we know about temples in general, it would be tempting to assume that perhaps the *duku* is the primeval hillock that emerges from the waters during creation, but this cannot be confirmed from currently available texts. What we can say with certainty about the *duku* is that two functions are associated with it. The first (and best-known) function of the *duku* is as a place of divine judgment. This is demonstrated in a bilingual text known as VR50+51:

> Incantation. Shamash, when you come out of the great mountain,
> When you come out of the great mountain,
> the mountain of the springs (of water),
> When you come out of the *duku* where fates are determined,
> When you come out of the (place) where heaven and earth are connected,
> from the foundation of heaven, to (this) place,
> The great gods will present themselves before you for judgment;
> The Anunnaki will present themselves to you for decisions.[17]

The important points to be noted here are that (1) Shamash (the sun-god) was the god of judgment and therefore presided over the divine court; (2) the *duku* is called "a great mountain"; and (3) even the other gods are subjected to judgment there.

A lesser-known function of the *duku* is that of the location of some sort of cultic meal. In one temple hymn it is called the "House, holy mound, where pure food is eaten."[18] What is unclear here is the connection between the cultic meal and judgment. It is conceivable that the meal was spread out in the *duku* room to invite and entice Shamash to be present so that the human supplicants could then submit their requests.

Priestly Castes and Administration

The priestly personnel in Mesopotamian temples were essentially in three categories: cultic, divination, and incantation priests. The first two categories included women as well as men. In fact, the "chief" priest (Sumerian en) was male if the deity at the shrine in question was female, but if the deity at that temple was male (as in the case of the moon-god, Nanna, in Ur), then the en was female.

Since this was the highest, most prestigious priestly office in any given city, it was also subject to becoming a political gift. In Ur that office was traditionally the prerogative of sisters and daughters of the reigning monarch (beginning at least with the installation of Enḫeduanna, daughter of Sargon of Akkad shortly after 2350 b.c.) and continued so throughout Babylonian records. If inscriptions from Neo-Babylonian times can be considered indicative of much earlier practices, then it seems apparent that as part of the installation ceremonies of the en-priestess in Ur, the candidate received a new name. Of the eighteen names of en-priestesses at Ur that were known to Nabonidus,[19] at least fourteen of them contained the theophoric element "an" (the name of the supreme Sumerian god).

The en-priestesses were not supposed to marry (except for the en-priestess in Nippur), but they nonetheless had children from time to time. J. Renger thinks such offspring may have been the result of the annual *hieros gamos*, in which the king would ritually marry the en-priestess in a cultic ceremony that was supposed to guarantee fertility and abundant produce at harvest time.[20]

The en-priests and priestesses were associated only with the major gods. They functioned as the appointed spouse of the main deity of a given city, performed sacrifices, and performed purification rites (e.g., šu-luḫ ceremonies). They lived in a building on the temple grounds known as the gipar.

Another high-ranking priest was the *sanga*-priest. This office combined cultic and administrative responsibilities. The education required was that of a scribe, and it appears that the *sanga*-priest also functioned as a member of a panel of judges. The office was not hereditary, but rather was appointed by the king. In fact, there were kings who were also *sanga*-priests.[21]

One type of priest is the *gudu*-priest (Sumerian gudu₄), one who made bloodless offerings, took care of offerings for the dead, and also had musical chores. Of particular interest to Latter-day Saints is the fact that the Akkadian designation for this type of priest was *pašīšu*, which means "anointed" and is probably the origin of the Hebrew word *passim* in the expression *kutonet passim*—the garment associated with Joseph in the Genesis account and translated in the KJV as "coat of many colors." If *passim* is from the Akkadian word *pašīšu*, then the "coat of many colors" becomes the "garment of anointing," which is more acceptable both linguistically and theologically. Interestingly, the *gudu*-priest also had special clothing associated with his office.

The issue of special clothing for certain priestly offices appears in many texts, but one may generalize that all those who participated in the presentation of temple rituals (the MES) had to wear special garments. The garment in question was known as the *ma* (Sumerian túg-ma$_6$) and was apparently made of linen.[22]

Other types of priests, which will not be discussed here, included singers, exorcists, and those who practiced extispicy (examining entrails).

Economic Organization

The Sumerian temples were, perhaps first and foremost, economic centers in their respective communities. Any temple of even moderate size had to maintain a full-time staff. This required regular and reliable sources of income. There were, of course, the offerings of animals and other substances made by worshipers, but the temple economies did not rely on offerings alone. Temples of any significant size also controlled lands (varying in extent during different time periods) that produced crops. These lands might be leased out to tenant farmers, who would pay a percentage of the increase to the temple as a form of rent on the land.

These economic activities required a system of bookkeeping, and the ancient Sumerians developed a rather impressive system of accounting. Many inscriptions recovered from the Ur III period (ca. 2100–2000 B.C.) are actually economic texts listing transactions involving animals, produce from farmland, and even banking records of deposits and withdrawals from "silver" accounts.[23]

Sumerian Temples and Creation

Of the various rituals that took place in Mesopotamian temples, perhaps the best-known was the creation ritual associated with the beginning of the new year. In later times, the Babylonians would recite a creation myth known by its incipit as the *Enuma Elish*.[24] But it is very likely that something of the sort already existed in Sumerian times. Creation motifs appear in numerous texts that may have been associated with temple rituals.[25] For example, the Sumerian story of Enki and Ninmaḫ deals with the creation of mankind. In it, the goddess Nammu asks her son, Enki, to create man to do the work of the gods, who are complaining of their work loads (the usual reason for creating man, according to Mesopotamian tradition). Enki instructs Nammu on how to pinch off clay above the abzu and create man. During a feast that ensues, Ninmaḫ (Nammu's assistant) gets drunk and tries to create men, but since she is drunk, all her creations are defective. The account then lists the various defects.

In any case, the Mesopotamian creation accounts differ from the biblical account in the relationship of man to deity. In Mesopotamia man is the slave of the gods, not the offspring of deity as in our own tradition. One notable exception to that is a bilingual story of the creation by the chief Babylonian god, Marduk, in which man is the offspring of the gods. Because of this unusual twist, it is worth reproducing here in toto.[26]

CT 13, PLATES 35–37
1. Incantation: a holy house, a house of Gods, in a holy place was not yet made.
2. No reed had sprung up, no tree had been created.
3. No brick had been laid, no brick structure had been built.

4. A house had not been made, a city had not been built.
5. A city had not been made, people (or settlement) had not been established.
6. Nippur had not been made, Ekur had not been built.
7. Uruk had not been made, Eanna had not been built.
8. The ocean (the *apsu*) had not been made, Eridu had not been built.
9. A holy house, a house of Gods their habitation had not been made.
10. All lands were sea.
11. When in the midst of the sea there was a channel.[27]
12. Then (one day) Eridu was made and Esagil was built.
13. Esagil whose foundation Lugaldulkuga laid in the midst of the *apsu*
14. The city of Babylon was made, and Esagil was completed.
15. The gods, the Anunnaki he created together.
16. The holy city, the dwelling of their heart's delight, they proclaimed supreme.
17. Marduk constructed a raft upon the face of the water.
18. He formed the dust and poured it out with the raft.
19. In order to settle the gods in the dwelling of their heart's delight
20. He formed mankind.
21. The goddess Aruru together with him created the seed of mankind.
22. The beasts in the field and the living creatures in the steppe he formed.
23. The Tigris and the Euphrates he created, he set them in place.
24. Their names he named well.
25. The grass, the rush of the marsh, the reed, and the forest he created.
26. The green herb of the field he created.
27. The lands, and the marshes, and the swamps.
28. The cow and her young, the calf, the ewe and her young, the lamb of the fold.

29. Orchards and forests.
30. wild sheep (and) mountain rams he. . . ?
31. The lord Marduk placed a dam by the side of the sea.
32. a marsh, a channel he made.
33. [. . .] he caused to be.
34. [reeds he form]ed, trees he created.

We note here that Marduk creates a city (Babylon) even *before* he creates man, and then he creates the animals *after* creating man. The point of interest, however, is the fact that man was created by a union of Marduk with his spouse, Aruru. This should be compared with the words of Parley P. Pratt concerning the creation of mankind:

> Earth, its mineral, vegetable and animal wealth, its Paradise prepared, down comes from yonder world on high, a Son of God with his beloved spouse. And thus a colony from heaven, it may be from the sun, is transplanted on our soil. The blessings of their Father are upon them, and the first great law of heaven and earth is again repeated, "Be fruitful and multiply."[28]

One final note on creation myths concerns the breath of life, which according to one Sumerian text, was given to many by the god, Ningirsu, the chief deity of the ancient city of Lagash.[29]

Other Rituals in Sumerian Temples

We might also find the purification rituals interesting. The Sumerians, like the Hebrews but unlike the Akkadian population, had a religion with a well-developed concept of holiness (a hallmark of hierocentric religions as opposed to nonhierocentric religions, which are generally concerned almost exclusively with purity).[30] In Sumerian (as in Hebrew) religious thinking, holiness was associated with the temple and the potential presence of deity there; purity, however, was possible anywhere but was also a prerequisite for entrance to that sacred area. Therefore, purification rituals were a necessary preliminary step to approaching deity in the temple.

One such purification ritual performed by the king is described in the text known as *VAS* 17 no. 28 (=VAT 8395); it appears to deal with a ritual designed to remove an evil spell or fate that has been determined for the king. The text is damaged, and the first several lines do not contribute greatly to our understanding of what is taking place, even though references to Enki and the abzu are made. The last 17 lines, however, are more informative.[31]

16. Its body is cedar, its sides (are) *ḫašḫur*-wood.
17. Holy water, water of the abzu, in its water the *naga*-plant . . .
18. The sustenance of the gods, the branch of the holy *naga*-plant . . .
19. The branch of the holy *naga*-plant. . . . .
20. His body, the knowledge(?) of the gods . . .
21. In pure water, pure water. . . . .
22. the king of the city, son of. . . . .
23. Holy water, his head. . . . .
24. Pure [water], his body. . . . .
25. Clear water. . . . .
26. Water of purity. . . . .
27. Holy water, on his body. . . . .
28. Pure water on his body, pure. . . . . . .
29. Clear water on his body, clear. . . . .
30. The darkness, the evil of his body has been. . . . .
31. The darkness, its swine(?). . . . .
32. An incantation to render ineffective the (malevolent) fate of the king.

This text, referring as it does to the bathing ritual of a king, may indeed be related to the later *bīt rimki* rituals, which were important purification rituals involving three actors: the king, a priest, and a *mašmašu*-priest. This would seem especially likely in view of the purpose given in line 32. In any case, bathing rituals for purposes of purification are well attested in the ancient Near East, especially for kings.[32]

Another ceremony that may have taken place in Sumerian temples—in which the supplicant took the hand of the god who was thought to dwell in that particular temple—is not well understood. Whether the hand he took was that of a statue or of someone playing the role of the god is not clear. One such text is the Great Hymn to Nabu,[33] in which the supplicant asks the god Nabu to take his hand and raise him out of the mire and to exalt him so that he may gain life powers. Unfortunately, that text was written in Akkadian and is therefore significantly later than the Ur III period under discussion, but it may well preserve an earlier Sumerian ritual.

The Great Temple at Ur

A Brief History of Ur

The ancient Sumerian city of Ur (modern al-Muqqayer) is located in southern Iraq, approximately one hundred km southeast of Baghdad. The first dynasty of Ur was founded by Mesanepada. He was a contemporary of Mebaragesi, the eighth ruler of Kish (ca. 2490 B.C.). Mesanepada apparently conquered Kish from Aka, the son of Mebaragesi, for he eventually used the title *king of Kish*.

During the early days of Ur, that is, during the Early Dynastic III period (ca. 2700–2370 B.C.), some peculiar burials included the interment of great wealth as well as of numerous attendants. These burials were examined by Leonard Woolley, who excavated Ur during the 1920s and 1930s. He also excavated the ziggurat of Ur-Nammu.[34]

The city of Ur was conquered by Sargon—who had founded the first great Semitic empire in Mesopotamia around 2340 B.C.—and did not regain independence or prominence until after the fall of the Akkadian empire and the expulsion of the Gutians, who had succeeded the Sargonic dynasty. That expulsion was accomplished by Utuhegal of Uruk around 2116 B.C. Ur-Nammu, the founder of the Third Dynasty of Ur, had been a deputy of Utuhegal but broke away from him over a border dispute and founded his own dynasty in Ur around 2111 B.C. Ur-Nammu rebuilt the temple in Ur and constructed the great ziggurat that still stands there.

The most impressive ruler of the Ur III period, however, was Ur-Nammu's son, Shulgi, who reigned for half a century (2094–2045 B.C.). In fact, his very name should be of some interest to Latter-day Saints because it consists of the Sumerian words šul and gi. The word šul means something like "hero," and gi is multivalent, but in this case may mean "firm, reliable." The šul component is important, because it is also attested as the name of a king in the Book of Mormon (see Ether 1:31).

In addition, Shulgi was a remarkable ruler in other regards. He is perhaps the first musician-king (David would later have that role in Israel) and is reported to have mastered as many as eight different instruments. He also introduced a number of changes by creating a standing army, reorganizing the temple economies, creating a unified administrative system for both northern and southern Babylonia, overhauling the system of state revenues and taxation, creating an enormous bureaucratic apparatus and a system of scribal schools, reforming the writing system, introducing new accounting and recording procedures, reorganizing the system of weights and measures, and introducing the imperial calendar.[35]

Although the Ur III period lasted only a single century (ca. 2111–2003 B.C.), it is significant for two reasons. First, the influence of Ur during that time stretched from the Persian Gulf almost to the Mediterranean and was maintained by economic factors rather than by military power. Second, it is quite possible that Abraham lived in or near that city during that time.

After the city was destroyed by a combination of Elamites and Subarians in 2003 B.C., it never again recovered its former stature and eventually became absorbed in the later Semitic empires of Babylonia.

As in other Sumerian city-states (as noted above), the political organization of the city had originally consisted of a town council (ukkin) and a political leader called the "big man" (lú-gal). The religious life centered around the temple, and the chief clerical figure was the en-priestess. The main deity of Ur was the moon-god, Nanna (Semitic name: Sin). The worship of this god was carried out in the main temple in Ur, which was called the Ekishnugal. This temple was also the center point of the economic life in Ur during the early days, but that role shifted to the royal household during the later periods when the secular bureaucracy grew to keep pace with the expanding empire.

Abraham's Connection to Ur

Before the 1920s, scholars tended to locate the city of Abraham somewhere in northern Mesopotamia. Since the excavations of Woolley in the 1920s and 1930s, however, the majority opinion has swung toward accepting the Ur

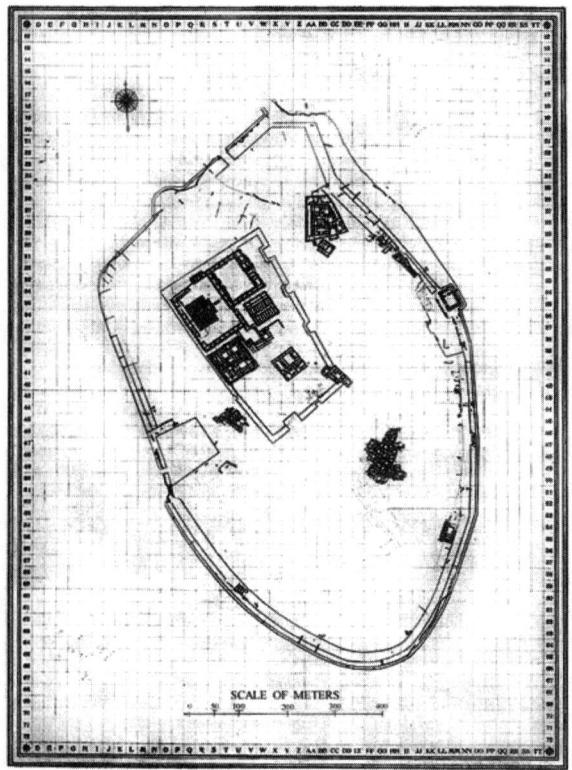

Figure 13. Layout of Ur.

excavated by him in southern Mesopotamia as the one mentioned in Genesis in connection with Abraham. During the 1950s and 1960s, an exchange appeared in the journal *Iraq* between Cyrus Gordon and H. W. F. Saggs; the former argued for a northern site for Ur and the latter responded to his arguments and established a case for accepting the southern location. That controversy continues, especially among Latter-day Saint scholars, who tend to favor the northern theory (partly influenced by Gordon). I favor the southern location for reasons too involved to discuss here. Therefore, let us recognize that the subject is not yet closed and that if the Ur excavated by Woolley was the Ur of Abraham, then Abraham must have lived there before its destruction in 2003 B.C.

Indeed, two tantalizing notes in the Book of Abraham fit in well with what we know of the southern Ur. The first is the mention of a famine in Abraham 1:30 and 2:1. In the days of the Ibbi-Sin, the last king of Ur, a terrible famine occurred. One of his officers, Ishbierra, was asked to send grain up the canal to Ur to save the city from the ripening rebellion. Ishbierra knew that if he stalled, the city, and therefore also the king, would be overthrown (from within if not from without), and he would be able to set himself up as king in a nearby city, which he did.

The other fact that surfaces in the Book of Abraham is long known from Jewish legends: Abraham's father, Terah, worshiped idols in Ur and returned to that practice in Haran (see Abraham 2:5). The fascinating feature here is that the moon-god Nanna was worshiped in two cities in Mesopotamia: Ur and Haran. It therefore seems possible that Terah might have been the one who took the idolatrous god of Ur (namely Nanna) to Haran and introduced the worship of him there.

Layout of the Ekishnugal

The Ekishnugal comprised a complex of buildings located on a surface of close to seventy thousand square meters. As was common in ancient Mesopotamia, the corners of the buildings, not the sides, faced the four cardinal directions. The main shrine of Nanna was on the west-facing corner of the complex, and the great ziggurat was just to the southeast (see fig. 14). Surrounding the ziggurat was a large courtyard called in Sumerian the kisal-maḫ or é-temen-nì-gur.[36] Northeast of that was another courtyard—

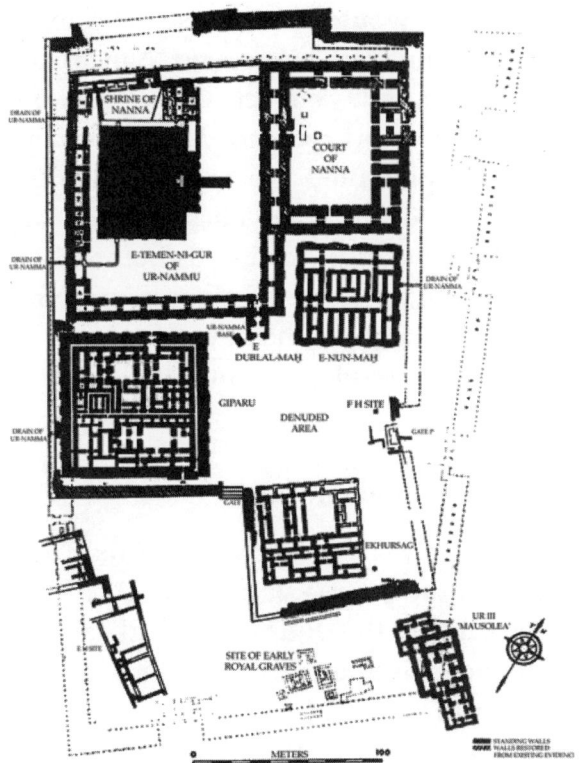

Figure 14. A floor plan of the temple of Nanna (Ekishnugal) in Ur.

the court of Nanna, or kisal-sag-an-na, which Levine and Hallo translate as "upper court."[37] The excavator, Woolley, thought the main entrance to the complex was near the eastern corner through a building called the é-dub-la-maḫ in later periods, but originally known as the dá-gal-maḫ.[38]

In order to appreciate the layout of the temple better, it is helpful to follow the footsteps of a king who visited the temple complex on an official visit to pay homage to the god, Nanna.[39] The king, Rim-Sin, first stopped at the main gate with his entourage, where he was obliged to propitiate the divine guardians of the temple. It was assumed that those lesser deities would then advise the chief inhabitants of the temple, Nanna and his consort, Ningal, of Rim-Sin's visit. After a hymn had been recited, the party then entered the temple complex and proceeded to the next stop, which was the abzu—represented as a body of water bordered by reeds.[40] Finally the entourage passed to the adytum, but they had to pass by additional gods before they could be admitted into the presence of Nanna and Ningal. Once they arrived at the adytum, however, food and drink offerings may have represented a communal meal in the presence of the gods.

Rituals in the Ekishnugal

One very informative text about rituals in the Ekishnugal is a hymn to Nanna, known as *UET* VI/1 67. This text is remarkable in that it describes Enki as the author of all purity in the temple and also mentions the washing and anointing of the statue of Nanna in the abzu room. Although the text was already treated by Charpin,[41] it has not, to my knowledge, been made available in English. I will therefore present the text here with my own translation from the Sumerian.

> Oh son of a prince! When you come out of the holy sea, you are resplendent, . . .
> 2   The "mountain" of the pure MEs,[42] the sanctuary of the abzu, the interior . . . broad, the "mountain" . . .
> The exalted "base". . .
> 4   From the "underground water" (= abzu), carrying a terrifying splendor, . . . a luster,
> You raise your head toward your happy destiny, toward your greatness and exaltation,
> 6   You march exaltedly toward the destiny that will be declared for you,

The great An[43] has lavishly provided for your sovereignty
    over the universe,

8   Enlil[44] has perfected regality for your great status as son
    of the Prince,

Enlil has manifested the exalted (status of a) deity for you.

10/11 For your exalted path from the lower sea,

Has Enki, from sea of the holy interior, placed a sweet
    earth, the sweet mother, as (your daily) destiny be-
    neath your feet.

12   Enlil has engendered you in magnificence and in the high
    priesthood.

Oh Nanna! Your crescent is called "the crescent of the sev-
    enth day."

14   Enlil has called your name for you in the universe, your
    name, your holy name!

Oh son of a prince, he has made your greatness pre-eminent
    in the universe!

16   The great assembly has granted you the office/status of
    Enlil

Enki has decreed your regality and exaltation from the
    sanctuary of Eridu.

18   From the exalted abzu, the sanctuary of Eridu, for your
    great high priesthood,

Oh king of the universe . . . for your greatness.

20   Oh Nanna, he has chosen (as your) portion, the elevation of
    your head among the Anuna-gods,

You dwell in a holy dwelling, among the pure MES of joy.

22   He has called the great gods to the great sacrifice,

They have taken (their) seats in the shrine, (their) hearts
    filled with tremendous delight.

24   He gives the great gods the drink offerings of joy.

In the place of exaltation, in the holy place, you dwell.

26   Oh Nanna! In the holy place, your holy residence, you dwell.

Enki, who purified the dwelling place for you, who
    cleansed the dwelling place for you,

28   He has sanctified heaven for you, he . . . earth for you.

He has prepared the Ekishnugal, the temple of the cedar forest, (pointing) toward heaven.

30 Your exalted residence, the holy place, he has made for you For the illumination of heaven and earth.

The patterns for your exalted šu-luḫ[45] ceremony he has prepared for you.

32 For . . . your . . . brightness(?), he has cleaned a table for you in a holy place.

. . . your evening meal, and morning (meal),

34 . . . he prepared for you.

The šu-luḫ ceremony he has sanctified for you, he has made brilliant(?) for you.

36 . . . he has made beautiful.

. . . he has called.

38 Enki, having created them in his abzu, has instituted for you the šu-luḫ ceremony,

(The god) Kusu has brought the šu-luḫ ceremony, which was created in its own temple.

40 Beside the nether sea: an oven, oxen, sheep, bread; beside the sea: that šu-luḫ ceremony.

For the temple the oil is purified, and held in readiness, and the arms, hands and feet are touched(?),

42 Toward the sacred šu-luḫ ceremony which is not to be cast aside, from the exalted lake,

From the broad, holy sea, that fate goes forth.

44 The Ekishnugal, on the sacred, exalted throne, perfected in the exalted great MEs of the universe,

When you have bathed at the exalted bank of the holy sea,

46 When you have sprinkled the mountain oil on your holy body,

Oh Nanna, (when) you have been placed on your exalted throne,

48 Girded with a fine linen garment, Oh (thou with) raised head and the shining horn, girded with a lordly headdress.

The exalted oil, the oil of regality, the oil of your great storehouse, on the holy body and sides.

50   At the shining quay, the exalted quay, his holy quay,
     Ningublaga[46] has sanctified the hands of the high priest.
52   Dara-abzu[47] of Eridu has purified those hands with oil.
     In order that you may place pure hands upon the provi-
          sions of the table of your great banquet hall,
54   Kusu sanctifies the hand—the pure hand, the shining hand.
     Dara-abzu of Eridu has purified those hands with oil.
56   The sanctuary of the abzu, being the exalted throne of Ur,
          according to the good and great destiny decreed,
     The Ekishnugal, being the good and holy dwelling place of
          Ningal, that exalted Lady,
58   The holy dwelling place where you are queen to Nanna,
          your king.
     The Ekishnugal, and the holy Enun[48] (are) the temples of
          your royalty.
60   Nanna and Ningal rejoice in the dwelling place.
     Oh Su'en,[49] the lord of the exalted wisdom of the universe,
          Your crown is an exalted crown!
62   The glory . . . of the universe . . . Ashimbabbar,[50] may he
          sanctify (his) hand!
     May it be holy like heaven, may it be brilliant(?) like the
          earth,
64   May it shine like the heart of heaven!
     The crown of the universe, the holy crown, may he ele-
          vate it!
66   Su'en, the lord of the exalted wisdom of the universe,
          perfected on the pure throne,
     Ashimbabbar, on (his) head the true crown, the exalted
          horns . . .
68   He shall raise his head!
Left edge: holy oil, purified oil, shining oil!

We thus see from this text alone that such concepts as
priesthood, communal meals with deity, sanctification
rituals involving bathing followed by anointing of the
limbs with oil, and then dressing in special temple clothing
were found.

Perhaps other rituals may be inferred from later sources, such as a *hieros gamos* (sacred marriage rite)—which may have involved the concept of Nanna descending from heaven to a bedroom located atop the ziggurat, but these are still somewhat controversial for the period under consideration.

Summary and Conclusions

The study of religious material from cuneiform sources is of great interest and importance for the history of religion in general, but also specifically to Latter-day Saints because Sumerian religion was also hierocentric (temple-centered). The material presented here will suffice to indicate that many of the practices we recognize today as integral to temple worship were indeed present in one form or another for thousands of years.

Notes

1. For example, see Stephen D. Ricks and Michael A. Carter, "Temple-Building Motifs: Mesopotamia, Ancient Israel, Ugarit, and Kirtland," as well as John M. Lundquist, "What Is a Temple? A Preliminary Typology," in *Temples of the Ancient World: Ritual and Symbolism*, ed. Donald W. Parry (Salt Lake City: Deseret Book and FARMS, 1994), 152–76, 83–117, respectively.

2. See John M. Lundquist, "The Legitimizing Role of the Temple in the Origin of the State," in *Temples of the Ancient World*, 179–235.

3. See J. Kaplan, "Mesopotamian Elements in the Middle Bronze II Culture of Palestine," *Journal of Near Eastern Studies* 30/4 (1971): 293–307.

4. Kaplan's summary in "Mesopotamian Elements," 305–6, includes the following statements:

> As was seen earlier, the pottery of group B points to an association with Ur III; and it appears plausible that this

association originated at the end of Ur III, at which period the West Semites who over the centuries had become assimilated to Mesopotamian civilization were beginning to fan out all over the Near East and also reached Palestine. Very likely the biblical tradition of Abraham's family migration from Mesopotamia to Harran and south-westward to Palestine distantly recalls this migratory movement of the West Semites. It thus emerges that the end of Ur III is the only date possible at which the first indications of Mesopotamian culture could have appeared in Palestine; and the material adduced in this article furnishes the archeological evidence to substantiate this date; i.e. *ca.* 2000 B.C.

5. See Heinrich J. Lenzen, "Mesopotamische Tempelanlagen von der Frühzeit bis zum zweiten Jahrtausend," *Zeitschrift für Assyriologie und vorderasiatische Archäologie* 51, NF 17 (1955): 21–22.

6. See F. R. Kraus, "Le rôle des temples depuis la troisième dynastie d'Ur jusqu'à la première dynastie de Babylone," *Cahiers d'histoire mondiale* 1 (1954): 521.

7. In this respect, the so-called "pyramids" of Mesoamerica are really not pyramids either, but ziggurat-like structures, because they are also stepped buildings with sanctuaries or shrines on top.

8. See Lenzen, "Mesopotamische Tempelanlagen," 26.

9. We should note here that the Book of Mormon account of this event does not mention the name of the city at all, but only refers to a "great tower" (Ether 1:33). Hence, it is possible that the name of the city "Babel" (=Babylon) in the Genesis account is a later gloss.

10. See Michael Roaf, "Palaces and Temples in Ancient Mesopotamia," in *Civilizations of the Ancient Near East*, ed. Jack M. Sasson (New York: Scribner's Sons, 1995), 1:429–31.

11. Åke W. Sjöberg and E. Bergmann, *The Collection of the*

Sumerian Temple Hymns (Locust Valley, N.Y.: Augustin, 1969), 17 (no. 1, line 1).

12. *Ur Excavations, Texts (UET)* VI/1 103:33.

13. As is customary in the field, all Akkadian words appear in italics and all Sumerian words in roman font.

14. The term is presumably Sumerian, although Eric Burrows, "Problems of the Abzu," *Orientalia* 1 (1932): 235, mentions a theory of A. T. Clay that abzu comes from Amorite ʾfs meaning "end of the earth, denoting the land on which Eridu was built."

15. See Burrows, "Problems of the Abzu," 238.

16. The line in question is line 40 of hymn no. 3, in Sjöberg and Bergmann, *Sumerian Temple Hymns,* 19: temen šu-luḫ-sikil-zu abzu-a lá-a, "Foundation, your pure laving rite spreads over the Abzu."

17. For the Sumerian transcription of the text, compare R. Borger, "Das dritte 'Haus' der Serie *bīt rimki,*" *Journal of Cuneiform Studies* 21 (1967): 1–17, or else E. Jan Wilson, *"Holiness" and "Purity" in Mesopotamia,* Alter Orient und altes Testament, vol. 237 (Neukirchen-Vluyn: Neukirchener, 1994), 19–24.

18. é du$_6$-kù ú-sikil-la rig$_7$-ga, in Sjöberg and Bergmann, *Sumerian Temple Hymns,* 17 (no. 1, line 4).

19. See *Yale Oriental Series (YOS)* I 45.

20. See J. Renger, "Untersuchungen zum Priestertum in der altbabylonischen Zeit," *Zeitschrift für Assyriologie und vorderasiatische Archäologie* 58 (1967): 131. The actual practice of the *hieros gamos* during early times is still a matter of discussion.

21. During the Isin-Larsa period, Lipit-Ištar and his son, Warad-Sin, were *sanga*-priests of Šamaš in Sippar. J. Renger, "Untersuchungen zum Priestertum der altbabylonischen Zeit: 2. Teil," *Zeitschrift für Assyriologie* 59 (1969): 119.

22. For an example of the use of this garment in a ceremony, compare *UET* VI/I 101, line 18: ᵈḫa-ià lú-šu-luḫ-sikil-la-engur-ra-ke₄ ᵗᵘᵍma₆ túg lá-lá, "Haya, the man of the pure šu-luḫ ceremony of the Engur (temple), who is clothed in the *ma*-garment" (my translation). The transliteration can also be found in Dominique

Charpin, *Le clergé d'Ur au siècle d'Hammurabi* (Geneva: Librairie Droz, 1986), 344.

On the connection between this garment and access to the MEs, see Horst Steible, "Ein Lied an den Gott Haja" (Ph.D. diss., Freiburg University, 1967), 87, where he notes that all those people who have access to the ME are permitted to wear the *ma*-garment.

23. For an example and discussion of one such silver account, see John B. Curtis and William W. Hallo, "Money and Merchants in Ur III," *Hebrew Union College Annual* 30 (1959): 103–39.

24. This was already mentioned by Stephen D. Ricks in his article, "Liturgy and Cosmogony: The Ritual Use of Creation Accounts in the Ancient Near East," in *Temples of the Ancient World,* 119.

25. As Samuel N. Kramer, "Mythology of Sumer and Akkad," in *Mythologies of the Ancient World,* ed. Samuel N. Kramer (Garden City, N.Y.: Anchor Books, 1961), 102–3, has pointed out, some of the creation material almost makes more sense in Sumerian than in Hebrew. For example, in the Sumerian accounts, one of the figures involved in the creation of man is the goddess Ninti, whose name is a wordplay because it can be translated either as "the Lady of the Rib" or "the Lady of Life."

26. The text is in Sumerian with an Akkadian translation. Because the Akkadian is somewhat less ambiguous, I will offer my translation from the Akkadian rather than from the Sumerian. The differences are negligible. I should also mention that although this is from a later period than Ur III, it nevertheless shows an important variation on the creation theme which may have had earlier roots, and because of its obvious interest to a Latter-day Saint audience, I have included it here.

27. Wolframm von Soden, *Akkadisches Handwörterbuch* (Wiesbaden: Harrassowitz, 1972), 963–64, *rāṭu(m)*, point 1b mentions this text and translates it "Rinne." This might be clarified when one accepts Alexander Heidel, *The Babylonian Genesis: The Story of the Creation* (Chicago: University of Chicago Press, 1951), 62 nn. 7–8.

28. Parley P. Pratt, *Key to Theology*, 8th ed. (Salt Lake City: Deseret Book, 1938), 54–55. I am not aware that this was ever accepted as doctrine, but it is worth noting because of the similarity to parts of the bilingual creation myth quoted; in both cases mankind is the offspring of divine parents, not only spiritually, but also physically. The obvious difference, of course, is that in the Mesopotamian version, the original parents remain divine, while in Parley Pratt's version, the original parents apparently become Adam and Eve.

29. Compare Samuel N. Kramer, *The Sacred Marriage Rite: Aspects of Faith, Myth, and Ritual in Ancient Sumer* (Bloomington: Indiana University Press, 1969), 32.

30. For a discussion of the relationship of holiness to purity among the Sumerians, see Wilson, *"Holiness" and "Purity,"* esp. pp. 40–46 and 64–65.

31. The translations of the Sumerian texts in this article are mine unless otherwise noted.

32. Kramer, *Sacred Marriage Rite*, 128, notes that baptismal rituals may have been performed by kings as early as the time of Dumuzi, especially in Eridu, the seat of the water-god Enki.

33. For a full treatment of that hymn, compare Wolfram von Soden, "Der große Hymnus an Nabû," *Zeitschrift für Assyriologie und vorderasiatische Archäologie* 61 (1971): 44–71.

34. For an interesting account of Woolley's excavations, see Leonard Woolley, *Ur of the Chaldees*, revised and updated by P. R. S. Moorey (London: Herbert, 1982).

35. For a full discussion of Shulgi's reign, see Piotr Steinkeller, "The Administrative and Economic Organization of the Ur III State: The Core and the Periphery," in *The Organization of Power: Aspects of Bureaucracy in the Ancient Near East*, ed. McGuire Gibson and Robert D. Biggs (Chicago: Oriental Institute of the University of Chicago, 1987), 19–41.

36. Baruch A. Levine and William W. Hallo, "Offerings to the Temple Gates at Ur," *Hebrew Union College Annual* 38 (1967): 47, say that the kisal-maḫ was just the court of the ziggurat, but Charpin, *Le clergé d'Ur*, 333, argues that kisal-maḫ was the term

for the whole of the two courts: the ziggurat court plus the court of Nanna.

37. Levine and Hallo, "Offerings," 47.

38. See *UET* V, 28.

39. This visit of Rim-Sin is recorded in *UET* VI/I 103, 105–6, and these texts are treated by Charpin, *Le clergé d'Ur*, 280–301.

40. Charpin, *Le clergé d'Ur*, 335, suggests that the abzu of the Ekishnugal may have been located southeast of the ziggurat on the ziggurat terrace where Woolley found a cistern of four compartments beside a well. Charpin himself compares the imagery of the abzu with that of baptismal fonts.

41. See ibid., 366–70.

42. The Sumerian word ME is often translated as "offices," but it seems that the word really refers to rituals, and should therefore probably be translated as "rituals."

43. The father of the gods.

44. A son of An (and the father of Nanna) who essentially became the chief deity in Sumer. His main city was Nippur.

45. The šu-luḫ ceremony appears to have been some sort of special hand-washing ceremony of great importance as a means of preparing to enter the presence of deity.

46. This is a son of Nanna who aids in the ceremony, and who had his own sanctuary in Ur.

47. This name, which means "stag of the abzu" is another name for Enki.

48. The Enun was the temple of the goddess Ningal, the wife of Nanna. It was located just southeast of the Court of Nanna (see fig. 14).

49. This is another name for Nanna, and the Sumerogram means "lord of knowledge."

50. Ashimbabbar is a form of Nanna as the god of the new moon.

CONTRIBUTORS

Richard O. Cowan (Ph.D., Stanford University) is Professor of Church History and Doctrine at Brigham Young University.

Richard D. Draper (Ph.D., Brigham Young University) is Associate Professor of Ancient Scripture at Brigham Young University.

John Gee (Ph.D., Yale University) is Assistant Research Professor of Egyptology at the Foundation for Ancient Research and Mormon Studies (FARMS) at Brigham Young University.

Brian M. Hauglid (Ph.D. , University of Utah) is Assistant Professor of Ancient Scripture at Brigham Young University.

Hugh W. Nibley (Ph.D., University of California, Berkeley) is Professor Emeritus of History and Religion at Brigham Young University.

Alan K. Parrish (Ed.D., University of Southern California) is Associate Professor of Ancient Scripture at Brigham Young University.

Donald W. Parry (Ph.D., University of Utah) is Associate Professor of Hebrew Language and Literature at Brigham Young University.

Stephen D. Ricks (Ph.D., University of California, Berkeley, and Graduate Theological Union) is Professor of Hebrew and Semitic Languages at Brigham Young University.

John A. Tvedtnes (M.A., University of Utah) is Associate Director of Research at FARMS.

Gaye Strathearn (Ph.D. candidate, Claremont Graduate University) is Instructor of Ancient Scripture at Brigham Young University.

Thomas R. Valletta (Ph.D., Northern Illinois University) is Manager of College Curriculum for the Church Educational System.

E. Jan Wilson (Ph.D., Hebrew Union College) is Associate Director of the Center for the Preservation of Ancient Religious Texts, Brigham Young University.

Citation Index

Sukkah
51a–51b, p. 41 n. 58

Taʾanit
26a–b, p. 94 n. 34

Ḥagigah
12b, p. 93 n. 25
14b, p. 255 n. 14
16a, p. 96 n. 39

Yevamot
32b, p. xi

Baba Bathra
4a, p. x

Sanhedrin
20b, p. x

ʿAvoda Zara
43a, p. x

Menaḥot
28b, p. x

MIDRASH

Genesis Rabbah
3:4, p. xi
39:7–9, p. 38 n. 15
43:7, pp. 38 n. 4, 39 n. 31

Exodus Rabbah
15:8, p. x
36:1, p. xi

Hadar, Leviticus
9:2, p. 93 n. 25

Numbers Rabbah
1:3, p. x
12:12, p. 93 n. 25

Pesikta de-Rav Kahana Pisqa
21:5, p. xi

Psalm
110:1, pp. 37–38 n. 2

Seder Rabba de-Bereshit
24, p. 93 n. 25

JEWISH AUTHORS AND
WORKS

Bahir
123–24, 138, p. 94 n. 34
135, p. 82
139, p. 82

Chronicles of Jerahmeel
52:7, p. 63

Josephus, *Against Apion*
2.79, p. x n. 1

Josephus, *Antiquities*
1.176, p. 38 n. 16
15.384, p. x n. 3

Josephus, *Wars*
5.2, p. 301 n. 89
6.10.1, p. 231 n. 60
6.267, p. x n. 2

Maimonides, *Dalalat*
3.45, p. 39 n. 21

Philo, *De Abrahamo*
235, p. 86

Philo, *De Opificio Mundi*
70, p. 41 n. 54

Pirqe de Rabbi Eliezer
8, p. 83
44, p. 82

Sepher Raziʾel
441, p. 89

Sepher ha-Razim
p. 65

SUBJECT INDEX

Great Mosque of Mecca, 276
  Bait Allah, 278
  as the holy center of Islam,
    278
  prayer five times a day to-
    ward, 278
  revelation while in the, 290
great tower, 329 n. 9
Greek as a prestige language,
  264 n. 89
Greek Magical Papyri, 245
Greek papyrus showing induction ritual of priests, 242
Greek, translation of documents into, 244
Greeks, adoption of Egyptian
  gods by, 244
Grieshammer, R., 242
growth, 162
guardians, 240, 246
  at the veils, passing by, 88
Gudea, 303
gudu-priest, 312
Gutians, 319

Hades, teaching the dead in, 60
Hagar, 283
ḥajj, 285
  description of the, 300 n. 65
  as a form of sacrifice, 292
  performing of, on behalf of
    deceased relatives, 290
  performing of, on behalf of
    elderly relatives, 289
hall of the Two Truths, 239
hand, taking the supplicant by
  the, 318
hands
  lifting of, to heaven, 93 n. 25
  spreading forth of, 80
  stretching out of, in prayer, 82

hands and feet, washing of, 102
Haran, 322
Haran, Menahem, 189
hard-heartedness and stiff-
  neckedness, 203
hardening of one's heart, 215,
  217–19, 220
Harris, J. Rendel, 60
Harut and Marut, 229 n. 39
Hasmonaeans, 58
head of the woman covered in
  prayer, 89
healing the sick, 186
heaven
  entering, 245
  successive ascension toward,
    237, 243, 251, 286
Heavenly Father, love of, 149
Hebrew grammar in book of
  Moses, 30
heirs of God and Christ, becoming, 137
hekhalot literature, 233, 249–51,
  272 n. 168
  earliest manuscripts of, 235
  from Egypt, 250
  themes in, 235
hell
  chains of, 215
  Christ's descent into, 60, 61,
    75 n. 16
heresy, spread of, 139
Herod's Temple, 79, 104, 107
Herodotus, 308
Hezekiah, 84
hierarchy, problem of, 27
hieros gamos, 312, 328
high priest, 89
Hippolytus, 60
al-Ḥijr, 289

FARMS Publications

Teachings of the Book of Mormon

The Geography of Book of Mormon Events: A Source Book

The Book of Mormon Text Reformatted according to Parallelistic Patterns

Eldin Ricks's Thorough Concordance of the LDS Standard Works

A Guide to Publications on the Book of Mormon: A Selected Annotated Bibliography

Book of Mormon Authorship Revisited: The Evidence for Ancient Origins

Ancient Scrolls from the Dead Sea: Photographs and Commentary on a Unique Collection of Scrolls

LDS Perspectives on the Dead Sea Scrolls

Images of Ancient America: Visualizing Book of Mormon Life

Isaiah in the Book of Mormon

King Benjamin's Speech: "That Ye May Learn Wisdom"

Mormons, Scripture, and the Ancient World: Studies in Honor of John L. Sorenson

Latter-day Christianity: Ten Basic Issues

Illuminating the Sermon at the Temple and Sermon on the Mount

Scripture Study: Tools and Suggestions

Finding Biblical Hebrew and Other Ancient Literary Forms in the Book of Mormon

Charting the Book of Mormon: Visual Aids for Personal Study and Teaching

Pressing Forward with the Book of Mormon: The FARMS Updates of the 1990s

King Benjamin's Speech Made Simple

Romans 1: Notes and Reflections

Periodicals

Insights: A Window on the Ancient World

FARMS Review of Books

Journal of Book of Mormon Studies

Reprint Series

Book of Mormon Authorship: New Light on Ancient Origins

The Doctrine and Covenants by Themes

Offenders for a Word

Copublished with Deseret Book Company

An Ancient American Setting for the Book of Mormon

Warfare in the Book of Mormon

By Study and Also by Faith: Essays in Honor of Hugh W. Nibley

The Sermon at the Temple and the Sermon on the Mount

Rediscovering the Book of Mormon

Reexploring the Book of Mormon

Of All Things! Classic Quotations from Hugh Nibley

The Allegory of the Olive Tree

Temples of the Ancient World

Expressions of Faith: Testimonies from LDS Scholars

Feasting on the Word: The Literary Testimony of the Book of Mormon

The Collected Works of Hugh Nibley

Old Testament and Related Studies

Enoch the Prophet

The World and the Prophets

Mormonism and Early Christianity

Lehi in the Desert; The World of the Jaredites; There Were Jaredites

An Approach to the Book of Mormon

Since Cumorah

The Prophetic Book of Mormon

Approaching Zion

The Ancient State

Tinkling Cymbals and Sounding Brass

Temple and Cosmos

Brother Brigham Challenges the Saints

Publications of the FARMS Center for the Preservation of Ancient Religious Texts

The Incoherence of the Philosophers

Dead Sea Scrolls Electronic Reference Library

PUBLISHED THROUGH RESEARCH PRESS
Pre-Columbian Contact with the Americas across the Oceans: An Annotated
    Bibliography
A Comprehensive Annotated Book of Mormon Bibliography
New World Figurine Project, vol. 1
Chiasmus in Antiquity (reprint)
Chiasmus Bibliography

THE FOUNDATION FOR ANCIENT RESEARCH
AND MORMON STUDIES

The Foundation for Ancient Research and Mormon Studies (FARMS) encourages and supports research and publication about the Book of Mormon: Another Testament of Jesus Christ and other ancient scriptures.

FARMS is a nonprofit, tax-exempt educational foundation affiliated with Brigham Young University. Its main research interests in the scriptures include ancient history, language, literature, culture, geography, politics, religion, and law. Although research on such subjects is of secondary importance when compared with the spiritual and eternal messages of the scriptures, solid scholarly research can supply certain kinds of useful information, even if only tentatively, concerning many significant and interesting questions about the ancient backgrounds, origins, composition, and meanings of scripture.

The work of the Foundation rests on the premise that the Book of Mormon and other scriptures were written by prophets of God. Belief in this premise—in the divinity of scripture—is a matter of faith. Religious truths require divine witness to establish the faith of the believer. While scholarly research cannot replace that witness, such studies may reinforce and encourage individual testimonies by fostering understanding and appreciation of the scriptures. It is hoped that this information will help people to "come unto Christ" (Jacob 1:7) and to understand and take more seriously these ancient witnesses of the atonement of Jesus Christ, the Son of God.

The Foundation works to make interim and final reports about its research available widely, promptly, and economically, both in scholarly and in popular formats. FARMS publishes information about the Book of Mormon and other ancient scripture in the *Insights* newsletter, books and research papers, *FARMS Review of Books, Journal of Book of Mormon Studies*, reprints of published scholarly papers, and videos and audiotapes. FARMS also supports the preparation of the Collected Works of Hugh Nibley.

To facilitate the sharing of information, FARMS sponsors lectures, seminars, symposia, firesides, and radio and television broadcasts in which research findings are communicated to working scholars and to anyone interested in faithful, reliable information about the scriptures. Through Research Press, a publishing arm of the Foundation, FARMS publishes materials addressed primarily to working scholars.

For more information about the Foundation and its activities, contact the FARMS office at
    1-800-327-6715 or (801) 373-5111. You can also visit the FARMS website at www.farmsresearch.com.

THE TEMPLE IN TIME AND ETERNITY

The Temple in Time and Eternity, edited by Donald W. Parry and Stephen D. Ricks, is the second volume in the series Temples through the Ages. The importance of the temple to the religious community of the ancient Near East and Mediterranean world can scarcely be exaggerated. The eleven articles in this volume are divided topically into three sections—"Temple and Ritual," "Temples in the Israelite Tradition," and "Temples in the Non-Israelite Tradition."

The "Temple and Ritual" section features Hugh Nibley's discussion on "Abraham's Temple Drama," which identifies elements of the creation drama that appear in the Book of Abraham and elsewhere in the ancient world. An article by Ricks discusses oaths and oath taking in the Old Testament. John A. Tvedtnes shows that baptizing for the dead was known in various parts of the Mediterranean world and in Egypt. In a second article, Tvedtnes enlightens our understanding of the form and purposes of temple prayer in ancient times.

Richard O. Cowan, in the section "Temples in the Israelite Tradition," traces the development of temples to modern times. Richard D. Draper and Parry make intriguing comparisons of temple symbolism between Genesis 2–3 and Revelation 2–3, focusing particularly on promises and blessings. Alan K. Parrish shares with us insights into modern temple worship through the eyes of John A. Widtsoe, and Thomas R. Valletta examines priesthood and temple issues by contrasting "the holy order of the Son of God and its spurious counterpart, the order of Nehor."

The concluding chapters of the book, grouped in the section "Temples in the Non-Israelite Tradition," include John Gee's discussion of getting past the gatekeeper (gleaned from various Egyptian literary corpuses), a fascinating study by Gaye Strathearn and Brian M. Hauglid of the Great Mosque and its Ka'ba in light of John Lundquist's typology of ancient Near Eastern temples, and E. Jan Wilson's enlightening treatment of the features of a Sumerian temple.

9 780934 893466   52495